People of the Drum of God—Come!

SIL International and
International Museum of Cultures
Publications in Ethnography

Publication 35

Publications in Ethnography (formerly International Museum of Cultures
Series) is a series published jointly by SIL International and the
International Museum of Cultures. The series focuses on cultural studies
of minority peoples of various parts of the world. While most volumes
are authored by members of SIL International who have done ethnologic
research in a minority language, suitable works by others will also
occasionally form part of the series.

Series Editor

Barbara Jean Moore

Volume Editors

Rhonda L. Hartell
Bonnie Brown

Production Staff

Bonnie Brown, Managing Editor
Laurie Nelson, Production Editor
Karoline Fisher, Compositor
Hazel Shorey, Graphic Artist

People of the Drum of God—Come!

Paul Neeley

A Publication of
SIL International
and
The International Museum of Cultures

© 1999 by SIL International
Library of Congress Catalog No: 98–60919
ISBN: 1–55671–013–5
ISSN: 0–0895–9897

09 08 07 06 05 04 03 02 01 00 10 9 8 7 6 5 4 3 2 1

Copies of this and other publications of SIL International may be obtained from

International Academic Bookstore
SIL International
7500 W. Camp Wisdom Rd.
Dallas, TX 75236-5699

Voice: 972-708-7404
Fax: 972-708-7433
Email: academic_books@sil.org
Internet: http://www.sil.org

Contents

Acknowledgements

The drumming described in this volume has been made available through relationships with many people in a Cameroon community. The drumming comes from the lives of my teachers in Cameroon whom I want to acknowledge: Papa Antoine, M. Innocent in Mekomba, Atemengue in Mfou-villáge, Manga Luc in Yaoundé and Chief Owoudou Marcus of Mekomba. I am honored to have worked with such creative men and want to give testimony to their wisdom and to their generosity in sharing their knowledge with the world-wide community.

For translation help in Mekomba, thanks to Larry Seguin, Dennis Punches, Peter Vuh, Kate Loft-Simpson, and especially to Jürg Stalder for encouragement when needed. For help in the translation of books and articles, thanks to Sharon Rand and Peter Knapp. Pastors Joseph Etua and Dr. François Akoa-Mongo were very helpful in checking the Ewondo-English translations and providing additional information on drum use in and out of the church setting.

To the people of Mekomba, especially President Amougou Florian and Chief Owoudou Marcus, I express my deep appreciation and gratitude for their help and hospitality. A special thanks goes to Angela, Christine, and Imman for assistance and to Monseigneur Balla Kye in Yaoundé for information on Ewondo catechists. Thanks to Manga Luc in Yaoundé for an introduction to Ewondo dance drumming.

This study was carried out in 1988 through the auspices of the Société Internationale de Linguistique (SIL) in Yaoundé. Thanks to many of my colleagues there for help in difficult times. Special thanks goes to Tim Hunter for drum transportation.

This book is an expanded revision of my 1991 thesis substitute. Thanks goes to Gloria Eyres for guidance through the interdisciplinary graduate program at the University of Texas at Arlington. I greatly appreciate the time and care put into this project by my thesis committee: chairperson, Dr. Mary Morgan (sociolinguistics), Dr. Carol McKinney (African anthropology), and Dr. Donald Burquest (linguistics). Many of this book's virtues are due to their help.

Because a single person cannot be a specialist in every field, I have depended on many colleagues who have graciously given comments in their area of expertise. These include Dr. James Redden (Ewondo linguistics), Dr. Robert Longacre (discourse analysis), Dr. Kenneth Pike (emic/etic analysis and modes), Karen Boring (ethnomusicology), and Brian Schrag (cognition). Their questions, insights, and confirmations have deepened my own understanding.

Appreciation also goes to editors Dr. Henry Bradley, Marilyn Mayers, and Rhonda Hartell for their valuable input and guidance, and to Dr. William Merrifield, series editor, for encouragement that this project was possible.

Thanks also go to Dr. James Redden for Ewondo books and cassette and to Clay Johnston, Randy Boring, and Don Smith for computer help, and to Chris Coffyn and Ken Rudy for preparing the audio tapes.

A special thanks goes to the Phonetics Institute at the University of Hamburg. Dr. Elmar Ternes, director, and Nadja Schluter located and provided a copy of Heepe's 1912–13 recordings of Ewondo drum speech. Their effort and kindness made it possible to compare drum recordings made about 75 years apart.

I am indebted to interlibrary loan personnel at four locations for tracking down many elusive references. Many thanks go the the library staff at Indiana University (Bloomington), University of Texas (Arlington), Summer Institute of Linguistics (Dallas), and Pontotoc County Library (Mississippi).

Most of all, I thank Linda: typist, editor, translator, wife, mother, and survivor of an-ant-attack-in-the-night. The project would have been truly impossible without her.

Finally, I wish to acknowledge Antoine, whose photograph appears on the cover. May Antoine's "words from the heart" motivate people to pray as much as it does people of Mekomba. Thanks be to God, "the most wise authority."

bo- t be nkul n- ton- do be- se n- to- be- gan m- bo- me- gan

Bot be nkul Ntondo bese, ntobegan, mbomegan.

Tous les gens du tam-tam de Dieu, rencontrons-nous, rassemblons-nous.
All people of the drum of God, let us meet, let us unite.

(Beginning of drummed church summons in Ewondo by Protestant catechist of Mbangu, Mbolo Elie, tape example 27.)

Introduction

This study of Ewondo drumming deals with a set of communicative/aesthetic/social transactions, specifically, a "call to church" drummed by Antoine Owono, an Ewondo catechist in Cameroon. The basis for the study is participant observation and recorded performances. Numerous disciplines, including linguistics, anthropology, cognition, and ethnomusicology, have contributed to an understanding and analysis of these performances.

"Talking drums," or speech surrogates, have been the subject of numerous previous studies. Almost sixty of these were published in Sebeok and Umiker-Sebeok's (1976) massive collection *Speech Surrogates*. Many of the previous studies, however, are lacking in several areas: (1) the exact relationship between drum strokes and speech phonology is often not explored from a linguistic viewpoint. Few previous writers deal adequately with the exact manner in which the drumming represents spoken communication; (2) many studies have collected a wide (but superficial) sampling of brief drum texts over an extensive range of topics, without examining closely the repertoire within one genre, or the repertoire of one individual; and (3) once an example is published by one author, it may appear in successive studies by other authors, though the variability of the original aurally-perceived art is often not recognized or noted. As Maxwell graphically states, "the written accounts, with an authority acquired by their immutability, almost incestually spawn second and third generations of literate renditions. Each of these reinforces the prejudiced selections and interpretation of previous literate accounts" (1983:44).

1

This book examines an individual's paradigm of multiple performances by analyzing ten different drummed speech acts in one genre, collected over a four-month period in Cameroon. It would have been fairly easy to do a standard discourse analysis of one transcribed text: charting the position of pronouns, counting repetitions, looking for flow, and marking thematic sections. The result would be an acceptable analysis of one written text that would find its way into folklore collections and be quoted in studies by other scholars. All of this literate activity would miss the point of variation and re-creation of texts in multiple performances because the focus would be on one text pinned to the page like an attractive but dead insect. In truth, the performance paradigm is constantly changing.

My interest in this topic was sparked before I went to Africa. Prior to my fieldwork in Ghana and Cameroon, I compared two recorded versions of the following drum poem.

Okwan atware asuo,	The path crosses the river,
Asuo atware okwan.	The river crosses the path.
Opanin ne hwan?	Which is the older?
Yeboo kwan no kotoo asuo no.	We made the path and found the river.
Asuo no fini tete.	The river is from long ago.[1]
	(Nketia 1958:49)

The observation of their noticeable differences caused me to wonder how many different ways a drum text could be drummed and still be understood. How exact is the correlation between speech sounds and drumstrokes? Are variations in performance acceptable? Do the performance texts change over time? Little did I guess that some change twice a week. These questions led me to suspect that there may be more phonological and discourse variability than is commonly found on the written page. My research in Cameroon has proven that these variabilities are indeed true in regard to the Ewondo speech surrogate system.

In this study of an Ewondo speech surrogate, one focus will be on the relationship between drumstrokes and speech. Phonological phenomena (including vowel elision, consonant clusters, speech rhythm, and tone) are considered.

The second focus concentrates on the specific formulaic repertoire of an individual performer in a particular genre (calling church members to gather twice a week at dawn) and on the interconnectedness of all genres through common stock phrases. Discourse and oral-formulaic theory are

---

[1]This drum poem is an excerpt from a longer drum text of the Akan people of Ghana, mentioned in numerous articles and books by Nketia and others.

the main methods of analysis. Variation within one drummer's performances and variation between performances of different drummers are
both examined.

A third focus emphasizes the variability of the original aural art and
provides a diachronic, comparative analysis showing some similarities
and contrasts between the recorded performances. This focus on creativity and variability uses insights gained from cross-cultural studies of the
improvisation/composition continuum in music and concepts from oral-
formulaic theory.

A fourth focus examines the performance paradigm as a communica-
tive/aesthetic/social transaction and how it relates to the Ewondo culture
and the local community.

In the fifth focus, equal emphasis is given to the drummer's creation
of the sound, the sound itself, and the community's understanding of that
sound.

A sixth focus includes a discussion of the sociolinguistic, anthropological, and performance contexts of the drumming.

Other factors which enhance understanding of the topic are discussed
as well, including semiotics, learning styles, cognition, performance technique, instrument manufacture and categorization, African dance
drumming, and orality and literacy.

It is hoped that by applying all of these approaches to the study of
speech surrogate drumming, the fullest etic comprehension available to
someone outside the Ewondo culture will be reached. An attempt is also
made to communicate a more emic understanding of what the catechist's
drumming means to an Ewondo person in the village of Mekomba. The
differences between these two understandings are pointed out in detail.

To summarize, moving from general to specific, this study deals with
the larger Ewondo speech surrogate system, with a particular drummer
and his repertoire in a specific genre, and with the creation and comprehension of drummed speech acts. Macro- to microlevels of analysis and
commentary on the drumming are given, from religious ritual to the
phonology of drumstrokes.

1

Speech Surrogates and Semiotics

Introduction to speech surrogates

"Talking drums" have been reported in the ethnographic literature from three regions: (1) the Circum-Caribbean; (2) Melanesia; (3) Africa, particularly West Africa and the Kongo area, but extending at least as far east as the Baganda of Uganda....Only the African drumming is clearly language-derived in the sense that an attempt is made to reproduce some aspect of an underlying linguistic text. (Ames, Gregersen, and Neugebauer 1971:25)

A SPEECH SURROGATE replicates the tone and rhythm patterns of oral speech. Many musical instruments can be used in this way such as horns, whistles, flutes, chordophones, bells, xylophones, and drums. Even non-musical objects have been used, such as sticks or tree roots (Carrington 1949b:33–39) or the anvil beaten by the Yoruba blacksmith that greets a passerby (Thieme 1969:370). Human whistle languages also serve as speech surrogates (Cowan 1948, Busnel and Classe 1976). People may even loudly shout the tones of drum syllables to carry across a short distance (Carrington 1949b:40–41).[2]

Nketia (1963) has grouped messages on Akan "talking drums" of Ghana into two broad categories: speech and signal. In the speech mode,

---

[2]Human whistle languages are different in nature from other speech surrogate languages in that they are actual modified mouth sounds (cf. Busnel and Classe 1976:107). In the remainder of this book, the term speech surrogate refers specifically to nonwhistle languages and nonsignal drumming.

5

each performed piece is intended to be understood as language. In contrast, signal drums or other instruments typically repeat short rhythmic patterns which often have a corresponding mnemonic verbal phrase, but cannot be combined to carry any extensive message.

Talking drums based on African languages and social functions have been transported outside of Africa. For instance, Santería religion and *bátà* drums acting as speech surrogates were taken by Yoruba slaves from Nigeria to Caribbean areas such as Cuba, and from there to New York City. Most other non-African talking drums found outside of Africa function primarily as signal drums (see Umiker 1974:499–503 and Carrington 1949b:109–14). Within Africa, some drums function only as true speech surrogates; many are used also as signal drums and/or dance drums. Rattray (1923:243) has coined the words TYMPANOSEMANTIC for drum signalling and TYMPANOPHONY for true drum speech.

Both writing and drumming serve as speech surrogates. Literacy provides a visual speech surrogate whereas drums are "closer to the source" as they share the acoustic channel with oral speech (Sebeok and Umiker-Sebeok 1976:xv). Linguistic features such as intonation and vowel elision can potentially be reproduced on an aurally-perceived surrogate, though the written surrogate can carry much more phonetic information (vowels and consonants). A drum language "eliminates segmental features of the spoken language, and reproduces only its suprasegmental features, whereas writing, especially the alphabet, does the reverse to a great extent" (Kawada 1986:161).

It is not uncommon for speech surrogates to have religious connections. Porter (1985) analyzed a jazz saxophone solo by John Coltrane and found it to be a "wordless recitation" (speech surrogate) of Coltrane's religious poem *A Love Supreme*.

Euba (1991:207) asserts that "the faithful" may speak through the Yoruba drum surrogate to the spirits. In Indonesia, the spirits speak through the flute surrogate to the faithful (Perlman 1991).

The act of striking wood to gather church members has a long history in the Christian church. For hundreds of years, before church bells became common, congregations were called together for meetings by striking a wooden board, known as a SEMANTRON. The Cameroon catechist's drumming has no historical ties with the semantron, of course, but it is interesting to note that the early church (circa A.D. 300–500) created an extremely simple speech surrogate (one word) by striking a piece of wood to gather the congregation (Price 1983:80).

This gathering function of a speech surrogate is not uncommon throughout much of Africa wherever the surrogate language system was already in place.

Sign systems

Drumstrokes are aurally perceived, while words are inferred from the word-surrogate sounds. How exactly do the drum sounds become recognized as words? How do any signs symbolize words, and words symbolize concepts? To answer these types of questions, a theory of signs was developed by Sebeok as a way of proceeding by inference from what is perceived through senses to the unperceived (1976:47). He describes a semiotic classification system of six types of signs (pp. 42–45). The drumstrokes, which are perceived through sound, are ICONS; they show similarity between SIGNIFIER (drum sounds) and SIGNIFIED (verbal phrases). The unperceived words act as a SIGNAL by triggering an expected action by the audience. Whereas spoken words are part of an organismal sign system "produced by the body alone," drumstrokes are part of an artifactual sign system, "produced by the body amplified" (p. 31).

Drum phrases are not iconic on the phonetic level, since no vowels and consonants are actually drummed. Instead, they are iconic on the semantic level (p. 193). The main verbal characteristics reproduced on a speech surrogate are prosodic elements of pitch and rhythm, along with intonation patterns in some cases. Drum messages "are also iconic on the positional level in that they normally follow the word order, or syntactic patterning, of the speech they represent" (Sebeok and Umiker-Sebeok 1976:xviii).

Signs can stand for other signs. Most speech surrogate systems can be considered primary or FIRST-ORDER SUBSTITUTIVE SYSTEMS: the drum signs (signifier) represent the signs (signified) of oral language, which in turn represent the original concepts (Umiker 1974:498).[3] Substitutive signalling systems may operate in two ways: through an arbitrary principle of ENCODING, where the sign bears no essential physical similarity to the feature it represents, or through a nonarbitrary principle of ABRIDGMENT, where the sign represents some partial acoustic features (such as tone and rhythm) of the base utterance (Stern 1957/1976:125). Signs of the written alphabet and acoustic Morse code, therefore, function within encoding systems, while speech surrogate signs are generally utilized within abridgment systems.

---

[3]Morse code is an example of secondary or second-order substitutive system. The dots and dashes represent the written alphabet, which is itself a first-order system. As Sapir recognized, the telegraph code is a symbol of a symbol of a symbol (Umiker 1974:498–99).

Use of surrogate signs

Vygotsky (1978:106) claims that written language has gradually become DIRECT SYMBOLISM of concepts, since the intermediate link of spoken
language may be ignored in practical use of the alphabet, i.e., fluent
reading and writing. He says that "written language is converted into a
system of signs that directly symbolize the entities and relations between
them." When people are fluent users of the written surrogate signs, these
alphabetic signs can lose at least some of their surrogate quality and
more directly represent the reality behind the word.

How much does the regular practice of Antoine's drumming rely on
the intermediate link of spoken Ewondo language? He drums words
faster than the normal rate of speech. He does not mutter the words
under his breath while performing, neither do audience members mouth
the words while interpreting the drum speech (neither do they when
interpreting oral speech). Words are in the mind without being verbalized on either end of the communication transaction. It is probable that
the drummer's mind and speech articulator (hands) do not consciously
pass through a level of oral speech. Since audience members do not
usually verbalize their interpretation (they just come or not come when
called), oral speech is bypassed on their side as well. This process is
related to that of people using the visual surrogate of the alphabet in
writing and reading. Either type of sign can be verbalized, but this is not
necessary. When people are fluent users of the aural surrogate signs, the
drumstrokes can lose at least some of their surrogate quality and more
directly represent the reality behind the sound. Through habitual use
(4,000 performances of this paradigm in Mekomba) the speech community has associated meanings with prosodic patterns of tone and time.

The drumming is built through combining formulaic phrases that are
memorized (to different degrees) by members of the speech community.
The performer and audience probably have formulaic phrases in their
mind much as readers of written discourse do with words, using the
surrogate signs on a level that is conscious but not focused on. When
asked if a drummer must think about every drumstroke, Innocent said,
"It's like when you write someone a letter, you don't think about the
alphabet." When signs are used in stereotyped formulas, a drum phrase
can be started then progress to its conclusion more or less automatically
in regards to the performer's drumming and the audience's comprehension (Ong 1977:116). This automatic progression is related to rapidly
typing or reading words—the spelling's static form is more or less automatic for people who are fluent in the signs' use.

A fluent reader or writer uses words at phrase level, giving little
attention to some words such as functors. Creativity comes primarily in

combining words or drum phrases into actual discourse, not in creating new spellings for words or new drumstroke patterns for known phrases.

Surrogate shouting of a surrogate language

On some occasions, a person may verbally express the equivalent of drum syllables. Using syllables such as *ku, ke,* and *ge,* a vocal SECOND-ORDER SUB-STITUTIVE SYSTEM represents the two pitches and durations of drumstrokes. Over long distances, the acoustic frequencies and harmonics of complex speech waves that distinguish specific vowels and consonants are diminished or even lost (cf. Umiker 1974:516), but the tone and rhythm of a shouted voice can still be heard (though not as far as the drum sound). The Ewondos term this *ekiga* 'language of tones without words' (Guillemin 1948:74).

Nkili reports, "A woman who wants to make her son return to the house from a walk, or call her neighbors, or someone who receives a drum message in the field and wants to respond in leaving, uses their voice in a way that the musical tones are like those of the *nkul*. The technique of transmission remains the same for the two phenomena" (1975/6:37).

2
Models and Comparisons

Models of analysis

The drumming event in Mekomba was not approached with any "required theoretical referent" (Seeger 1991:346) such as formalism, structuralism, or deconstructionism. An eclectic set of analytical models has been applied to the performance paradigm, with the approach that any theoretical model is useful insofar as it accurately reflects realities and refines comprehension of those realities. I have tried to let the performance paradigm determine which model sections are usefully applied, rather than the reverse.

Since this book is based on an interdisciplinary study, I have tried to make theories and terms from one discipline accessible to nonspecialists. Specialists in each field are asked to overlook simplification of theories in their own field for the sake of easily understanding theories from less familiar fields.

To avoid overgeneralizing, claims made in this book apply only to the performances which have been transcribed and analyzed here.

Despite the noticeable diversity in the Ewondo speech surrogate system as practiced by different drummers, broader conclusions and implications are suggested about the Ewondo system, other speech surrogates, language, and music when appropriate.

Rather than invent new terminology, I have freely used technical terms developed by other scholars, such as, co-occurent cluster and homophonous surrogate signs, and defined them in the context of the

11

drummed performance paradigm. This use of accepted terms facilitates comparisons between Antoine's drumming and other verbal and musical arts having related features. Few completely new analytical models are proposed in this study; the main theoretical advances are the bringing together of models already suggested in different disciplines.

Tripartite models

A three-part model for language analysis has been proposed by Pike (1971). It is helpful in applying the model utilized by Nattiez (1990) for semiological analysis of music which is related to a model suggested for the ethnography of communication by Saville-Troike (1989). Together with other models, a framework can be established in which the total communicative/aesthetic/social transaction can be discerned.

A work is constituted by the act of creation (composition) and the act of cognition (perception and interpretation) (Nattiez 1990:ix). Some analyses reduce a work to only one of its dimensions, but such reduction is misleading and cannot point to "the total musical fact," in Nattiez' term. The existence of a work is in the interaction of creative strategies, the resultant sound event, and cognitive strategies brought to bear upon the sound event (p. 70).

Nattiez, building on earlier work by Jean Molino, points out that any communication transaction has three elements: the act of creation, the act of comprehension, and the material reality of the work, i.e., physical traces such as sound waves.[4] These three elements correspond in turn to three related but distinct analyses. Analyses of compositional and comprehension strategies are explicative in nature, while analysis of sound structures is descriptive.

Communication in this model is not seen as going in one direction, from sender to receiver. Instead, the message is not received at all but reconstructed by the audience through comprehension strategies. The entire process can be diagrammed as follows:

composition process→ sound structure ← comprehension process
(creation strategies)   (sound event)   (cognition strategies)

An advantage of this model is that it highlights the necessary work of audience members; they must actively reconstruct the message and meaning, not just passively receive them. The creative act results in

---

[4]The original terms used by Nattiez are "poietic process, esthetic process, and imma-nent trace." I have decided to rename these three elements in this book because of possible confusion between those terms and "poetic and aesthetic processes" which mean something very different.

sound structures upon which people bring to bear active comprehension strategies. Although Nattiez applies this model primarily to music, it is equally relevant to verbal interaction.

Pike (1971:510–13), adopting terms used by physicists in the study of light, suggests that language can be described from three different perspectives: PARTICLE, WAVE, and FIELD. These three views, respectively, illuminate Nattiez' conception of sound structure, creative strategy, and comprehension strategy of music.

Saville-Troike (1989:3) writes that the ethnography of communication "takes language first and foremost as a socially situated cultural form, while recognizing the necessity to analyze the code itself and the cognitive process of its speakers and hearers." Put together, these analytic models specify the creative process *wave* of speakers/drummers, the comprehension process *field* of hearers, and the *particle code* (sound structure) itself and its various associations, all activated through performance in a culturally defined form within a particular social situation.

Performance models

It is relevant to note that the concept of performance has become increasingly important in models of linguistics, folklore, anthropology, and ethnomusicology.[5]

The topic of this book, however, is strikingly lacking in many concerns common to typical performance studies: the speech event is one man drumming out of the audience's sight, while the community involuntarily listens. Many of the elements which make performance such a rich model are not present here. By virtue of being a drummed speech surrogate under these circumstances, the speech act is something of an oddity when viewed through the lens of performance models: a performance which no one sees or immediately interacts with, involving only sound.

The particular isolated context is a determining factor: a drummed speech surrogate may also communicate to individuals within a physically present crowd, e.g., directing dancers (Nketia 1963). This context would fit more readily in the stereotypical models of performance

---

[5]The following list reflects a sample of scholars who utilize a performance-centered approach: in **sociolinguistics**, see Saville-Troike 1989 and Fleming 1988 for performance-centered analyses of communicative events and communication transactions, respectively; in **folklore**, see Hymes 1964, 1972, Tedlock 1977, Okpewho 1979, 1990a and b, Bauman 1976, 1977, 1986, Briggs 1988, Abrahams 1977, Fine 1980, 1984, and Ben-Amos and Goldstein 1975 for performance-centered analyses of folklore, verbal art, and oral poetry; in **anthropology**, see Turner 1986 and Schieffelin 1985 for analyses of ritual as performance; and in **ethnomusicology**, see Stone 1982, 1988, Blacking 1981a and b, Seeger 1987, Béhague 1984, Herndon and Brunyate 1976, Herndon and McLeod 1980, Locke 1990, 1992, Waterhouse 1986, and George 1990 for analyses of musical event performance.

because there is much more direct interaction between drummers, dancers, and other participants physically assembled.

This interaction and the changing relationships between art event and
society lead to an important facet of performance studies called "the
emergent quality" by Bauman (1977:38). Applied to the performance
paradigm, the "emergent quality of performance resides in the interplay
between communicative resources [drum language], individual competence [in creation and comprehension], and the goals of participants
[persuasion and a timely reminder, a 'poetic alarm clock'], within the
contexts of particular situations" (p. 38). In a social setting where people
are directly interacting, what emerges in performance will differ every
time. In the case of the drummed church summons, even the details of
resources, competence, goals, and context remain the same, and what
emerges has been nearly the same in all four thousand performances that
Antoine has drummed in Mekomba. The performance models point out
how many typical elements of performance are missing in this performance paradigm and that what remains is stable to a very large degree.

Ethnomusicology models

Ethnomusicology models were also helpful in understanding the performance paradigm. According to Rice (1987:484), we can profitably ask,

$$\text{"How do people} \begin{Bmatrix} \text{historically} \\ \text{socially} \\ \text{individually} \end{Bmatrix} \begin{Bmatrix} \text{create/construct} \\ \text{maintain} \\ \text{experience} \end{Bmatrix} \text{music?"}$$

Seeger asks the basic questions of a musical ethnography in another
helpful way: "(1) What are the principles that organize the combinations
of sounds and their arrangement in time when people make music? (2)
How are these sounds similar to or different from other musical traditions? (3) Why does a particular individual or social group perform or
listen to the sounds he/she/it does in any given context?" (1991:347).
Answers to all of these questions are integrated into this book.

Etics and unspoken emics of analysis

Kippen and others have called for informants to be involved as analysts "through all stages of the research up to and including its
conclusions" (Kippen 1989:176). This dialectic process was pursued as
far as possible in this book.

Regarding the phonological correlation between oral speech and
speech surrogate, most of the analysis and conclusions came about

through interaction between Innocent and the author, bringing etic (surface structure) and emic (deep structure) viewpoints to bear on Antoine's drummed data. The correlation was not usually analyzed in the Ewondo culture at the lowest level (matching individual drumstrokes and syllables), but would only be discussed at the higher formulaic phrase level (demonstrating explicit knowledge). It was difficult for anyone in the local speech community to verbalize and analyze the exact correlation at the lowest level because it was emically not in focus (implicit knowledge). Innocent persevered with me, however, and the phonological analysis at this level represents an emic understanding of one drummer's performances, considering that the understanding was prompted by etic questions from an analyst who tried to account for every drumstroke and syllable. The resultant analysis is my own, using comparative data and western models of analysis.

Emically, the surface structure variations were noncontrastive and ignored by the performer (Antoine), the local analyst (Innocent), and the audience. The variations exist in the aural context, but are brought to light only with tools of tape recorder and written transcriptions. People in Mekomba have literacy skills and tape recorders, but would not think of using them in a comparative study such as this one. Indeed, most of this study seemed to be irrelevant to Mekomba residents. They could understand why I might want to write down the drummed summons once; but to do it repeatedly and make comparisons was not emically relevant.

Sound event participants may or may not commonly discuss matters of interest to the analyst. It is not necessary for people to be consciously aware of how they create and comprehend performances, or choose to explain these processes verbally to produce acceptable sound. Words concerning nonverbal events are not equivalent to the events' actual sounds. We must distinguish between what people do and what they (or we) conceptualize and say they do (cf. Seeger 1969:231). Compositional and comprehension procedures can be used without being explicitly discussed by the people who practice in a particular culture.

The Ewondo situation of unspoken emic conceptions and rules of performance creation seems similar to the situation which Nattiez describes for the Inuit song genre of *katajjaq*:

> The singers draw motifs, shaped according to certain rules, from a stock furnished by memory; these rules are not (so far as I know) explicitly defined within the culture, though they can be reconstructed inductively by analysis, based on observing the singers' practices. (Nattiez 1990:88)

Nattiez (1990:194–96) writes that a "maximally complete view of the works considered" can be reached through an interaction, "a dialogue," between the indigenous discourse about art and the researcher's discourse and analysis. In this vein I have attempted to mark distinctions between emic and etic conceptions of the performance paradigm and to present them on these pages. As asserted by Geertz (1973) and summarized by Feld: "ethnographies are supposed to be what we ethnographers think about things as much as they are supposed to be accounts of what we think the locals think they are doing" (1990:253).

Writing about people's sounds

You may listen to two hours of Ewondo drumming on cassette tapes and still feel there has been very little communication. This book is a commentary about the original drumming sound, concepts, and behavior in order that a limited form of communication, out of the original context, may still take place between an Ewondo drummer and English readers of this book. This ethnography of speech surrogate drumming fits Seeger's definition of musicology as the "cross communicatory, cross disciplinary, cross cultural speech study" of music (1991:346). Concepts are communicated through writing (graphein) about sounds of a particular people (ethnos), producing an "ethno-sound-graphy."

In the original communicative/aesthetic/social transactions, a drummed speech surrogate language was used to pair meanings with aurally perceived signs to enable people to exchange thoughts. In this written communication transaction, a different system of surrogate language signs is used to pair meanings with graphic signs (the alphabet) to enable the exchange of thoughts. Both communication transactions are monologues, or one-way exchanges of thoughts with no verbal feedback expected from the audiences.

Different sign systems are used in these communication transactions. Mekomba residents must make an INTERSEMIOTIC TRANSLATION[6] as they interpret the performed verbal signs (drumstrokes) representing the spoken verbal signs (formulaic phrases). Using written musical signs to record aurally perceived performances also leads to an intersemiotic translation to help the reader.

Translation occurs not only between sign systems and between languages, but also between concepts. The local consultants speak according to culturally determined categories; the researcher translates these

---

[6]The term intersemiotic translation was earlier used by Roman Jakobson and Eugene Nida (cf. Fine 1984:205). It is applied to speech surrogate communication by Sebeok and Umiker-Sebeok (1976:xiv).

concepts according to his own culture's categories and writes them down (cf. Nattiez 1990:197).

Written knowledge of speech surrogate drumming is vastly different from the hands-on knowledge of drumming (cf. Seeger 1977:16). As Nattiez (1990:154) points out, the perceptual processes of listeners in real time should not be confused with the very different perceptual processes utilized in producing and reading this book.

Intra-paradigm comparisons

It is impossible to take one transcribed text of any drummer's perform-ance paradigm and declare, "This text is the authoritative version." And it would be pointless to analyze a particular version in minute detail as is done to literary texts, assuming that every part of the structure is communicatively and/or aesthetically significant (Barber 1984:508). In this aurally perceived drum poetry, the structural details of a single performance are not significant to the community in regard to the mean-ing or aesthetics of the message, because the choice and temporal arrangement of phrases will probably never be repeated exactly the same way in subsequent performances. This phenomenon of noncontrastive variations is well known in phonology at the phonemic level as well as in music and verbal art.

Concerning the emic insignificance of variation in performances of Yoruba *oríkì*, Barber writes that the oral art has "a constant variability which is *usually not even noticed* because to performer and audience alike it has no significance" (emphasis mine) (1984:508). This attitude is shared by the Ewondo community in Mekomba.

Therefore a paradigm of ten performances by Antoine (and a second paradigm of three by Atemengue), emically interchangable in social func-tion, communicative meaning, and aesthetic response, were recorded in performance context (along with dictated texts). This re-elicitation of one genre's performances by separate performers can be construed as a use of the comparative method (Dundes 1989:74). Analysis of all of the texts reveals the genre significance of specific discourse creation strategies (such as co-occurrent clusters) and emic categories of drummed phrases (such as phrases used only in the beginning or final stanza).

To "more fully comprehend Kuna theories and practices of the poetics of performance," Sherzer (1987:135) has worked with different performances of the same stories in differing contexts and verbal styles. To gain related understanding but at the level of an individual, this book focuses on differ-ent performances within a single paradigm drummed by one communicator in identical context and style. Some comparison is made with performances

in the same genre by a different drummer (Atemengue Marcus) in the next
village and by one drummer (Manga Luc) in Yaoundé.

Cross-cultural comparisons

Comparisons can be made between Antoine's performance paradigm and
other oral poems, songs, and oral-formulaic systems. Foley (1985:68–69)
has proposed three principles which are useful in cross-cultural comparison
of aurally perceived performances: tradition dependence, genre dependence,
and text dependence. The broad tradition under study here is speech surrogate drumming in Africa and of the Ewondo people of Cameroon in particular. This genre is that of drummed church summmons. This genre is
represented by one drummer's paradigm represented by ten recorded performances, though comparisons are made inside and outside the Ewondo
tradition.

Some features in the performance paradigm are tradition dependent
(general calling function and phonology of Ewondo drum speech), other
features are genre dependent (specific church function and certain formulas such as some doctrine), and other features are text dependent
(formulas drummed only in Mekomba).

Different communication systems have different features, though many
features have correlates elsewhere in the world. Using tripartite analysis,
features in common may be at the surface structure level or at the levels of
creative or comprehension strategies: (1) some surface features of the
Ewondo speech surrogate system occur elsewhere; for example, the features
of line-final vowel prolongation and false syllable insertion to break up
consonant clusters are found in some song systems; (2) general processes of
creation may be discovered through models of composition-in-performance
and improvisation; and (3) cognitive means of interpreting two-element
patterns can be applicable to these two-toned drumming patterns.

In these cases and all others, the details of any related features usually
vary between cultural traditions, within each tradition, and even for every
performer within a single tradition. The term COMPOSITION-IN-PERFORMANCE,
for example, must be carefully defined for the subject at hand so that
differences of usage of the term are not minimized.

Similarities in surface structure sound are interesting to note but may
not necessarily reveal similar underlying conceptions. According to Nattiez, "universals of music must now be sought in what Molino would call
'universals of strategy'...strategies of production, or strategies of perception" (1990:66–67). Chapter 12 is posited on the potential universality of
rhythmic cognition, which is untested in any Ewondo study.

Comparison with all speech and music around the world would not only
be too broad; it would be impossible. Even in the comparisons made here,

many possible grounds will be ignored, and most elements do not correlate with those of the Ewondo speech surrogate system. The dissimilarities between speech acts, and between creative systems, are often greater than any similarities, and comparisons of isolated features of sound or strategy should not be taken to imply anything more comprehensive.

Cross-cultural comparisons in this book are made primarily to demonstrate that the Ewondo talking drum manifests some features at levels of sound and strategies which are also found in other systems of speech, music, and speech surrogates. The differences as well as the similarities help to precisely define what the performance paradigm is, and equally important, what it is not.

Comparative studies are useful and are accepted in various disciplines when based on detailed knowledge and not generalized assumptions. Both emic and etic perspectives are helpful in gaining the fullest comprehension of this drummed performance paradigm as the various theories are brought to bear upon the complete sound and social event. In any ethnography of communication, "the unique event [performance] and the recurrent pattern [paradigm] must be seen both from the perspective of their native participants and from the vantage point afforded by cross-cultural knowledge and comparison" (Saville-Troike 1987:661).

Different models shed light from new angles on the performance paradigm. Different descriptions suggest different facets of the reciprocal relationships of sound and society. Terms drawn from various disciplines and carefully defined in reference to this context include drummed speech act (sociolinguistics), improvisation (ethnomusicology), aurally perceived poetry (folklore), and oral-formulaic system (oral composition), all to describe the multifaceted drumming in Cameroon.

Aurally perceived performances

Scholars have searched for an adequate term to cover all nonwritten genres of heightened verbal-based communication. Folklore, oral literature, oral art, verbal art, oral poetry, and aural literature have been suggested and rejected by various scholars (Anyidoho 1983:18–23). Goody (1987:xi) prefers the term Standardized Oral Forms. Probably all of these terms cast some light and shadow on the performances under study. In the case of drummed speech surrogates, Yankah (1985) has made a convincing case for AURAL over ORAL literature.

Yankah found significant differences between oral praise and drummed praise for the same Akan chief in Ghana. He noted different lengths in rhythmic groups, different repetition patterns, and different imagery. In fact, he writes "the content and style of literary genres transmitted on drum seem to be motivated apart from their oral literary counterparts" (p. 137).

The term LITERATURE implies written texts in essentially constant form, which in this case exist only when the collector writes them as texts to share with other people not present. Some texts, including Antoine's performance paradigm, are used in essentially fluid form. They become constant only when taken out of the performance context and placed in a book. To the performers and original audiences, the drumming is not literature or a body of discourses. Literature and texts are etic ways of describing the perform-ances.[7] Perhaps AURALLY PERCEIVED PERFORMANCES would catch the current emphasis on performance studies, while including speech surrogates and other nonverbal forms in the category.

As Vansina writes, "The concept 'text' implies a stable something that exists independently of all those who interpret it. It is a written item" (1985:66). Scholars transmit frozen texts. As pointed out by Finnegan, however, "What is transmitted locally is more a storehouse of known formulas and themes and the performer's skill and experience in using these in a particular performance" (1988:169). The Ewondo speech sur-rogate system is not "a body of literature made up of texts," but it is rather a paradigmatic and syntagmatic system of creative communica-tion, whose existence is completely dependent upon performers and audiences. The performances are aurally perceived, then vanish: the structure as well as the sound.

Though a performance of drum language remains at some level in the minds of performer and audience, it is only in actual performance that it becomes realized as more than a thought. What is really in the mind is the stock of formulaic phrases agreed upon by the speech community for this social, religious, aesthetic, and communicative purpose. Each re-creation of Antoine's drum poem appears in its exact form only once, and is not repeated later on the drum or in the memory of performer and audience.

In some cultures an oral poem can have a static form. It may be precomposed, rehearsed, and exactly memorized before performance, as in some Pacific Islands examples (Finnegan 1988:91–109). In other cases, including this Ewondo speech surrogate summons, there is no single poem which is repeated inviolate. Analysts conditioned by literacy, how-ever, may constrict the flow of aurally perceived plural performances into a single TEXTCENTRIC purpose (cf. Maxwell 1983:xix). The evanescent tradition in time becomes an object bound in space for leisured reflection whether on paper or cassette.

---

[7]On the question "must literature be written?" see Finnegan 1988:61–77. For further discussion of the term "oral literature" see Bauman 1986:1.

The original drumming is community based, sending a message with a response intended. This book will most likely be used by solitary scholars with no response required. The original communication in context is "human verbal symbolic interaction of a performing kind" (Ben-Amos and Goldstein 1975:3). This printed book out of context does not lend itself to interaction or performance. The subsequent differences in understanding should not be minimized.

Each performance of Antoine's drummed discourse is about two-and-a-half to three minutes long. It is short enough to be easily memorized in a static form if that was what he wanted. The fact that it is not memorized indicates that attention should be given to the generative process of performance as much as to any individual product or text recorded.

A performance drummed is a manifestation of *parole,* while the speech surrogate system as a whole exists in an abstract manner as *langue.* Any language is a "virtual system of available options not yet in use," while a specific text or performance is an "actual system in which options have been taken from their repertoires and utilized in a particular structure" (Beaugrande and Dressler 1981:35). Options from the large number of Ewondo speech surrogate phrases *(langue)* are selected through rapid compositional choice, creating an evanescent manifestation of *parole* as the drumstrokes' sound fades away.

3
Performance-Based Texts

Overview of Ewondo phonology

Ewondo, alternately Yaoundé, Jaunde, and Yaunde, is spoken by approximately 577,700 people in the area northeast and southwest of Yaoundé, and is included the in Yaunde-Fang group of the Northwest Bantu language family of southern Cameroon.

Various linguists have analyzed different dialects of Ewondo and reached different conclusions (see Redden 1979, Angenot 1971, Essono n.d.). Depending on analysis and dialect, Ewondo has twenty or twenty-three consonants and six, seven, or eight vowels. Redden's framework will be used primarily because it is the most recent. Phonological elements most relevant to the study of Ewondo drum language will be summarized here.

Ewondo is a terraced-tone language with three tone phonemes: high, mid, and low (Redden 1979:6). The mid tone is actually a downstepped high tone. The language also has grammatical tones that mark tense (p. 10).

Many vowel elisions and contractions occur in everyday speech and affect the tones of the vowels. This study will demonstrate how the drum speech replicates vowel elisions.

The syllable types in Ewondo are V, VC, CV, CCV, and CCVC. Redden (p. 6) gives the following rules: CC are homorganic nasals plus stops, not prenasalized stop phonemes. Nasals separate from the stops and become part of the preceding syllable if preceded by a vowel. Consonant clusters in borrowed words are divided by the insertion of vowels.

Ewondo is an affixal language. Most word stems occur with prefixes and many occur with suffixes as well. "Most stems cannot be said to belong to a word class, i.e., to be a noun, verb, etc., unless they occur with prefixes and/or suffixes" (Redden 1979:15). There are eleven noun classes marked by prefixes (p. 34). "Ewondo has no true adjectives, but nouns do serve as modifiers of other nouns in a similar way to the use of brick in the noun phrase a brick house" (p. 15). Ewondo is a SVO language (p. 153). The grammar of the drummed speech surrogate is that of oral speech for the most part (with the exception that a few words may be repeated several times for emphasis), and is not dealt with in any depth in this book.

The Ewondo phonemes in (1) and (2) are taken from Redden (1979:5–6).

(1)   Consonant phonemes

		labials	alveolars		palatals	velars	labio-velars
stops	vl.		t	ts		k	kp
	vd.	b	d	dz		g	gb
fricatives	vl.	f	s				
	vd.	v	z				
nasals		m	n		ny	ŋ	
lateral			l				
semivowels		w			y		

(2)   Vowel phonemes

	front	central	back
high	i		u
mid	e	ə	o
low	ɛ	a	ɔ

Methodology

Learning and analysis

Learning the speech surrogate phrases as an outsider was a multistep process with several steps going on with different transcriptions at the same time.

1. I recorded Antoine's performances at dawn on cassette.
2. I transcribed the drum patterns in musical form, playing the cassette at one-third normal speed.
3. I isolated aural lines and phrases using Antoine's pauses as a guide.
4. I practiced the separate phrases on a drum and performed them for Antoine. It was found that listening to a recording of his own perform- ance, even the same day, presented difficulties in comprehension to Antoine, and we worked mostly from my live copy of his performances.
5. With the assistance of Innocent, I wrote down the verbal meaning of each phrase.
6. I matched the drumstrokes with the syllables with Innocent's help.
7. I played the drum and spoke the syllables. Antoine evaluated and corrected my spoken and drummed performance of the phrases, which were based on my transcription of his original performances. (Drumming enabled me to understand the complete performance, but understanding of the composition-in-performance process came later.)
8. I connected drumstrokes with specific syllables because after spend- ing some time with this process, I could see by the drum pattern transcriptions that Antoine was remarkably consistent as to how he drummed each phrase.
9. My transcriptions and interpretations of all recorded performances were checked with Antoine from start to finish as well as phrase by phrase.

My method of tonal-rhythmic-structural analysis paralleled that advo- cated by Yeston for the analysis of Western musical rhythm. In the first stage, the sound's transcription was "seen as a long, complex, and uninter- preted summation of all its attacks, durations, and rests" (1976:37). Yeston calls this the GROSS RHYTHMIC STRUCTURE. The first two transcriptions that I compared demonstrated that the gross rhythmic structure of the perform- ances was different, implying that the verbal phrases were also different.

The second stage of analysis was to discover RHYTHMIC SUBPATTERNS of the piece, "configurations of duration and contour that may be isolated within the whole resultant pattern" (p. 37). These subpatterns were subsequently identified as formulaic verbal phrases.

The third stage was to discover ways in which rhythmic subpatterns may interact. For instance, several patterns may combine into one line, and several lines may combine in varying combinations to form a stanza. This interaction of rhythmic subpatterns is based on the verbal discourse structure of each performance.

Hierarchical units were discovered during analysis and later compared with other oral, drummed, and written poetries. Etic terms such as FOR-MULA, LINE, and STANZA were found to be applicable to the paradigm of Ewondo drum poems when narrowly defined to fit the paratactic aural structure. These performance components are not emically discussed or named within the Ewondo culture, but are still demonstrably the con-stituent parts of the performance paradigm.

Transcription key

The drum pattern transcription was both descriptive and prescriptive, in that I wrote down what Antoine played and based my own perform-ance on it. This was one reason I chose the Western notation symbols of ♪ (short duration) and ♩ (long duration). Almost any agreed-upon symbol would have worked. I found that in general, Antoine's rhythms were highly regular and could be adequately represented by symbols of short and long durations and high and low tones. The tones never changed; the rhythm was occasionally irregular, and I marked the places where the rhythm did not keep to the usual steady pulse. The musical notes indi-cated relative duration and pitch, and no time division into measures or metrical stress patterns is implied.

(3) ♩   ♪ ♩ ♪ ♩

         ♩   ♪ ♩

mi zu wo- go do- a- te- ne
you come hear doctrine

The top two musical lines in the transcriptions represent the rhythm and tone of the drumstrokes. The next lines of words are the oral back-translation in which Antoine and Innocent connected the drumstrokes with the oral phrases. The upper text line marks vowel elision, as in /wu-lu˜a/ where /˜/ indicates that the following vowel is elided into the preceding vowel. This elision is marked with one drumstroke above the first vowel.

This transcription line also indicates how the drum, in general, will not permit two consonants side by side. This happens in two ways, according to Innocent's idiosyncratic verbal translation of drumstrokes: (1) consonant clusters are broken up, as in /be-ke-ri-se-te-ne/ for the borrowed word *bekristen,* and (2) the drum will usually insert a vowel between the consonants if the final consonant of a word is followed by an initial consonant of the next word. For example, *mvog tara* will become /mvo-go tara/. It must be noted that this manner of orally translating the speech surrogate into speech is Innocent's conception of what the drum says and how he verbalizes it in phonemes. To some extent these transition vowels are spoken in normal speech, though not as consistently as when spoken on the drum.

mvo-go tara could have been written */mvog-o tara/ which keeps the written form of the original word. However, it was decided that the written surrogate format of /mvo-go tara/ accurately reflects the emphasis that the added drumstroke marks the final consonant of the first word. When the final consonant of a word is followed by an initial vowel of the next word, one drumstroke per syllable will usually suffice; for example, /mot a-be/ is correct, not */mo-tə a-be/. Homorganic nasal consonant clusters are divided according to Redden's rule (1979:6); the rules already given for the oral translation of drumstrokes often may not apply to homorganic nasals.

The middle verbal line of the transcriptions is the way a word is written (in Innocent's orthography) if it varies from the way the drum would reproduce it. A word on the middle line indicates the drum has given it extra strokes, as seen on the top line. If a word does not appear on the middle line, the drumstrokes equal the number of spoken syllables.

The bottom line of the transcriptions is a fairly literal English translation of the Ewondo.[8] After fieldwork, the translations were checked with two Cameroonian pastors working in the United States, one speaking Bulu and one speaking Beti and both having knowledge of drum language. Brackets indicate implied information.

Oral discourse has been divided on the written page by scholars in various manners using pauses (breath groups), syntactic units (clauses), phonological phrasing (intonation), and rhetorical units (marked by adverbial particles). In this book, the main criteria for discourse division transcribed on the page is the formulaic phrase unit, with other relevant criteria indicated on the page as well. An indented line marks continuation of the previous formula.

All punctuation has been added by me to these written texts. A vertical line | indicates the aural pauses within Antoine's performances at least

---

[8]I have retained the spellings and translations suggested by Innocent in Mekomba for the most part. Those he gave me (through French) were occasionally in minor conflict with the ones given by Etua and Akoa-Mongo (direct to English), partly related to dialect differences.

equal to the duration of a long drumstroke ♩. Occasionally, he used shorter pauses, which I have marked in the transcriptions with apostrophes ' (like a breath mark in a musical score).

In a few cases, Innocent and I could not find any syllable to match a drumstroke or vice versa. These cases are marked with a question mark in the transcriptions. Some verbal syllables receive more than one drumstroke. This is indicated with hyphens and vertical alignment in (4).

(4)   ♩   ♩   ♪   ♪   ♪
           ♪   ♪   ♪
        n-da-   o-yo a –   –

Each performance transcription ends with a sequence of drumstrokes without a verbal meaning, acting as an ending marker. This is discussed at the end of chapter 6.

Signs and the semiotics of transcription

A true performance-based text should adequately represent not only the text (the verbal elements), but also such elements as the style of delivery (including tempo, mood, dynamics, intonation, kinesics, use of artifacts) and audience reaction and participation (see Finnegan 1986:74).

All of these elements are important and usually carry significant semantic weight in performances. Unfortunately, some ethnographers rely on written texts dictated out of context, the limitations of which Tedlock has pointed out:

> The sound of such texts is limited to phonetic considerations which represent little more than a systematic adaptation of the Latin alphabet (adorned by diacritics), and they are set forth in gray masses of printed prose. (1977:508)

All of the nonalphabetic features may be missing. This omission may also mean that the written text is distorted, especially as regards the emic viewpoint of the local culture.[9] The primary performance cannot be fully captured and recorded by any means; the secondary reality, the only one available to us if we were not present, is the fixed object on the page (or film or cassette).

---

[9]For comments on oral language transcription see O'Connell and O'Connell (1991). They mention the selectivity and bias of all transcription and point out that the assumptions of the transcriber after repeated playbacks may not be in any way the same assumptions of the original participants who often have only one chance to hear the sounds.

The sound of drumstrokes is obviously missing from the printed page. Additionally, three important features heard in performance cannot be easily replicated in transcription. One feature missing on these pages is the vital sense of rhythm, propelling the words at a rapid clip. In these transcriptions, the spacing of rhythmic notes is subservient to the spacing of syllables below. The syllables, of one to four letters each, determine the spacing in this interlinear format. In the actual performances, the syllables (drumstrokes) come in a crisp short/long spacing format, which would be represented better visually as two shorts equal one long (♪ ♪ equals ♩). The initial phrase of performance 9 is given as an example in (5), with rhythmic spacing adjusted to reflect more accurately what is heard (not what is seen out of the performance context). One dot equals one pulse.

(5)   . . . .

   ♩   ♪ ♪ ♩   ♪   ♪ ♪ ♩   ♩   ♪

   ♩   ♩ ♪ ♪ ♩   ♪   ♩

This transcription has the advantage of visually clarifying the rhythm and demonstrating that it is an aesthetically pleasing musical phrase. The disadvantage is that it is difficult to accurately align the verbal syllables below because they are not short or long—the number of letters in the syllable has no relation to the actual performed rhythms notated above, e.g., /a/ equals long ♩ while /mvog/ equals short ♪.

The difficulty of a performance-based text comes about because the transcriptions are simultaneously showing two visual speech surrogates, one rhythmic and one phonetic. The original performances consist of one aurally perceived speech, with phonetic features only implied. These transcriptions are visual surrogates of a surrogate perceived through another channel.[10]

Drum language is sometimes thought to be similar to Morse code. Though both are language surrogates, an important difference is that Morse code uses the alphabet of written language as its base; the sequence of transmission in different media is visual→aural→visual. In drum language, on the other hand, features of the base spoken language such as vowel elision and long-distance intonation may be carried over

---

[10]Cf. Ong 1977:93. The alphabetic symbols represent sounds originally composed of consonants and vowels—"verbal" symbols. The note symbols represent sounds originally composed of pitches and durations—"musical" symbols. The latter sounds are perceived, the former sounds are signified. See Arom 1976:118–21 for another system of drum language transcription using different symbols.

in the surrogate language. Transmission of drum language is entirely done in the aural medium (except out of context as in this study).

The musical note transcriptions utilize second-order surrogate signs: notated signs standing for drummed signs standing for speech signs (Sebeok and Umiker-Sebeok 1976:xv). Antoine and Innocent provided verbal translations of the drummed signs, which means that their spoken words were actually second-order surrogate signs. The printed verbal phrases in these transcriptions stand for those verbal signs and are, therefore, themselves third-order surrogate signs.

The aesthetic musicalness of the drumming is severely muted in this transcription limitation because it is difficult to visually align all of the surrogate signs of the surrogate sound.[11]

A second performance element that is not visually foregrounded in these transcriptions is the aural line length, separated by pauses. Visually, the eye takes in each phrase at leisure, then drops to the line below. Each phrase is printed on one line for purposes of analysis. In the actual performances, however, up to six phrases may come tumbling on the heels of one another before a pause. It can be difficult to comprehend and digest one phrase before the others crowd it out of the aural moment. The difficulty in transcribing this rhythmic performance element could be partially overcome by printing on paper six times the normal width.

A third performance feature which changes radically in transcription is the perception of the sound event in time.

> The first and most obvious impact of analytic notation is to transfer the musical structure out of the uni-directional continuum of experienced (Bergsonian) time (in which the musical dialectic takes place) into the spatialized perfectly reversible (Newtonian) time of the printed page. In sound, the musical experience begins at the beginning and must be taken in the (irreversible) order and at the rate at which it comes to the listener... In the score, however, the whole span of the music appears to exist in a timeless, spatialized, present. We may peruse its content at any rate and in any order. (Shepherd et al. 1977:141)

With writing, "a sentence can have a synchronic character as well as a diachronic character" (Goody 1987:186). The sound structures can be examined simultaneously rather than only successively. The atemporal dimension of transcription permits the fleeting moment in real-time performance to be "captured for direct verbal dissection in the musical

---

[11]"Since performance is an aesthetic mode of communication, the ideal text would allow the reader to perceive the performance not simply as a communicative process, but as an asthetic mode of communication" (Fine 1984:87).

mortuary" (Shepherd et al. 1977:144). Through tape recording, what was a direct aural transaction can be delayed, repeated, and rechecked at liberty. Through transcription, time can be halted and "examined from the outside" (p. 23) as individual drumstrokes are studied, and even analyzed as separate from their maker. Such details as I wanted necessitated recordings and studying the score, as comparative analysis could not be done during a performance or even as it was heard later on cassette.

People in Mekomba cannot see any reason for this type of detailed examination, though they possess the tape recorders and literacy skills necessary. The sound is a call to action, not a subject for study. In context, the sound of the drum is ephemeral, goes by quickly, does not hang in the air to be compared with next week's performances. In the interactive context, it does not matter.

Out of context, analysis must be developed from the score, but I have tried (as much as possible through written words) to keep attention focused on the sound as experienced by repeatedly reminding readers of the aurally-perceived performances.

All three of these performance elements missing in the transcriptions— regular rapid rhythm, variable aural line length, and nonreversible time perception—may be recovered by listening to the cassettes (that are available from the author). Readers are urged to become hearers also so that they may better appreciate both the drumming artistry and the difficulty of quick comprehension.

Three performance transcriptions are presented in appendix 1 as examples of the high variability of the recorded performance paradigm. (Seven other transcriptions of Antoine's performances are in a separate book available from the author.) Together, performances 1, 2, and 5 show the structural diversity and similarity that are typical of Antoine's performance paradigm. The performances are numbered according to the order in which they were originally recorded in Mekomba.

4
Ethnography of a Speech Surrogate Performance Paradigm

This book is an ETHNOGRAPHY because it consists of writing about sound and society. SPEECH SURROGATE is appropriate because the language heard is pure prosody, the musical elements of speech: pitch, loudness, and rhythm. Cues for meaning are provided through semiotic signs combined in formulaic patterns of sound. A PERFORMANCE PARADIGM is involved because the study is primarily based on a set of ten recorded-in-context performances by one drummer. This set is a small sample of about 4,000 performances which are in paradigmatic relationship and which are interchangeable in the eyes and ears of the community. It is a paradigm of twice-weekly performances, of component phrases and ways of combining phrases into drummed discourse, as well as regularized ways of interaction between participants and regularized meaning developed through regularized context. We will look first at performance paradigms, then at an ethnography of communication before looking at a particular speech community.

Performance paradigm as relationships, signs, processes, and products

Each performance in the paradigm is composed of relationships between drumstrokes, words, and people. Though overlapping, these relationships can be analyzed as six broad types: (a) between words

(grammar); (b) between words and drumstrokes (phonology); (c) between drumstrokes (musical performance); (d) between drumstrokes and
people (aesthetic transaction); (e) between words and people (communicative transaction); and (f) among the people of Mekomba village (social
transaction).

In the regular combination and interaction of these relationships is
found the identity of the performance paradigm as a whole and of each
performance text. Each single performance in the paradigm is literally an
ensemble of various voices, being composed of some common stock
phrases that are generations old, some phrases used by a number of
Ewondo catechists, and some phrases peculiar to this village and this
catechist.

In my approach to the speech surrogate performance paradigm, the
drumstrokes are iconic signs of a FIRST-ORDER SUBSTITUTIVE SYSTEM (Sebeok
and Umiker-Sebeok 1976:xv): the drummed signs stand for verbal signs
in the Ewondo oral communication system. The drumstrokes, meaningless in isolation, become communicatively significant through several
processes: the drummer's hand movements, phonological adjustment
from speech to speech surrogate, discourse composition-in-performance,
and audience comprehension. Each performance is a mix of signs and
processes which will lead to a specific action being taken by community
members.

A focus of this book is on the performance paradigm as product and
process. What is created, memorized, and transmitted is not only a set of
individual drum phrases, but a way of selecting and joining phrases into
coherent and cohesive discourse. The creative process can hardly be
separated from the finished product, for each performance is at once an
aural manifestation of the tradition and the tradition itself. Processes,
product, relationships, and signs are roughly the same every time, while
the details of each vary every time.

The details of the performance paradigm can be studied as a series of
choices, "as a document of decision, selection, and combination"
(Beaugrande anad Kessler 1981:35). The communicative/aesthetic/social
transaction is always roughly the same: performance context, function,
meaning, participants, goals, creative process, audience comprehension,
and drum patterns. All variable details, however, require decisions. The
drumming catechist makes most structural decisions, but the individual
members of the congregation must make the most important choice:
whether to respond to the drumming. This choice is the basis for all of
Antoine's decisions made while drumming, though most of his choices in
performance have little actual influence on behavioral choices of the
hearers.

Antoine's performance paradigm is a set of rapid decisions actualized in fleeting aural form as a set of rapid drumstrokes requiring rapid comprehension. Much oral communication is unpredictable because it has an emergent structure: one cannot always predict which choices will be made until the choice is verbalized.

This emergent structure is true also in the drummed performance paradigm; no one, not even Antoine, knows beforehand precisely which phrases will be chosen from those possible or how they will be fitted together into lines and stanzas. Within paradigmatic formulaic phrases, choices of one or another option must be made. Even some syntagmatic formulas have variant surface structure drum patterns, though some choices here are conditioned by the immediate textual context.

Regarding Western musical composers, Meyer suggests that their compositional choices "can be understood and explained only in light of the intentions generated by goals—goals that are implicit in the constraints of the style, and are largely set by the ideology of the culture" (1989:36). The goal of each performance is identical, and so is the catechist's intention. Therefore, once the choice of genre is made according to temporal context (Tuesday and Friday dawn), the choice, order, and arrangement of particular drum phrases (within the genre's parameters) do not matter a great deal to performer or audience; nor do these particular choices affect the intended response of church attendance. In this paratactic discourse structure, the choices made within the performance paradigm make little difference in regards to communication of general meaning, aesthetics, or social interaction. Choices at discourse line level, however, have a major impact on the efficiency of verbal comprehension by the audience.

The main choices are already made by the community: out of all resources available, this drummer should perform this genre in this community on this occasion for this purpose, which has happened twice a week for forty years. Within this framework, other choices have little significant impact on message content, form, or function. This is why all four thousand performances may be grouped as one paradigm with substitutable parts. The exact choice of phrases and their arrangement into aural lines and stanzas is made by the drummer, but these choices are not especially noted or seen as important even by him. "It's all the same every time," Antoine kept reminding me.

Where Antoine apparently has chosen not to make a choice is in the final stanza, where the content and arrangement of phrases is always the same. This stanza contains the discourse peak and is marked by being the one section that is always internally predictable. Its placement at the paratactic discourse end is arbitrary, however, because the penultimate stanza can contain a number of possible phrases. At some point Antoine must consciously decide "it's time to finish drumming" and begin the final stanza.

Even within this stanza, pauses are variable from performance to performance, thus creating differing aural lines where the differences are significant
only as they affect ease of comprehension.

Saville-Troike states that "communicative competence includes knowing the alternatives and the rules for appropriate choice from among
them. Accounting for the system for such decision-making is part of the
task of describing communication within any group" (1987:663). In this
performance paradigm, the basic communicative decisions were apparently made decades ago. The twice-weekly decisions regarding details of
discourse composition-in-performance are not based on participant interaction because no one is directly present in front of the catechist's house.
The discourse decisions of exact form and content are made rather on the
basis of the drummer's memory, force of habit in using co-occurrent
clusters, and internal aesthetic sense.

Each Ewondo catechist working in the genre of drummed church
summons has a typical set of discourse choices which can be contrasted
with choices of other speech surrogate drummers. By comparison of
typical drummed decisions, an individual style of each drummer can be
defined by his choice of common phrases and common ways of interlocking them in performance. Each speech surrogate drummer makes choices
within a rather severe set of verbal, musical, and situational restraints to
replicate the general pattern of the communicative/aesthetic/social
transaction agreed upon by the local speech community. The stylistic
choices are left up to each drummer.

Within a drummer's idiosyncratic style in a given genre, most choices
have little significance in regard to meaning, artistic form, or social
function of the message, though choices may have significance in regard
to comprehension; one series of performance choices is emically considered equivalent to any other series of choices.

The result is a series of choices made twice a week which require great
expertise to flow smoothly. There is not a single memorized text, but a
set of quick decisions which lead to separate but equal, equivalent but
nonidentical, performances that are re-created through constant choice.

An ethnography of communication

An ethnography of communication examines the way communication
is patterned and organized within a speech community, or particular
context within that community (Saville-Troike 1989:16).

This book addresses many concerns that are common to ethnographies
of communication: traditional verbal art, communicative competence,
the relationship between orality and literacy, ritual and formal speech,

determination of line length, definition of speech community, emic and etic conceptions, the relationship between text and context, transcription, real-time discourse production and comprehension, and cultural patterning of speech behavior.[12]

Analysis of a communicative event must mention the components that pertain to the speech act under study. There are fifteen components (based on the works of Saville-Troike, Hymes, Biber, and Friedrich) that provide a framework for the analysis of the drummed speech acts:

1. The GENRE is a hortatory discourse, a church summons.
2. The TOPIC is a reminder that now is the time for church members to gather.
3. The FUNCTION is a wake-up call and persuasive discourse.
4. The SETTING for message production is in front of the catechist's house, centered in the village, at dawn on Tuesdays and Fridays. The setting for message reception is everyone's house within a radius of several kilometers.
5. The EMOTIONAL KEY of the discourse ranges from sarcasm to authoritative commands to imploring action to provoking thoughts about death and the afterlife.
6. The PARTICIPANTS include Antoine, the catechist, as the only performer, with everyone else in auditory range as the audience. Participants share frames of time and aural space and represent a fairly homogenous group in regard to social class, ethnicity, and farming occupation.
7. The SPEECH FORM is a paratactic poem made up of formulaic phrases.
8. The MESSAGE CONTENT is made up of historical references, proverbs, and motivations to action.
9. The SEQUENCE of communicative acts is that Antoine drums, then people come (or do not come) to church.
10. The RULES FOR INTERACTION are that Antoine plays and should not be interrupted.
11. The NORMS OF INTERPRETATION include some knowledge of the surrogate language system and sociocultural presuppositions.
12. The RELATIONS AMONG PARTICIPANTS include social role relations: church leader addresses the congregation included within the community; personal relations: people live together in a small community and frequently interact in various contexts; shared knowledge: general meaning of this drummed speech act is known by all through regular context; and specific knowledge: verbal interpretation of drum patterns is not shared by all participants.

---

[12]Many of these topics are mentioned in Sherzer's summary on the ethnography of speaking (1992:420).

13. The RELATION OF PARTICIPANTS TO THE TEXT is that each text is produced through a form of composition-in-performance, i.e., it is not memorized as a static whole by the drummer. Participants both produce and comprehend the drum language in real time, and the audience has no opportunity to interact with the text or performer at this moment.

14. The SOCIAL EVALUATION of the communicative event refers to the participant's attitudes toward the event itself and the message content which are valued by the community as a whole.

15. The CHANNEL is a wooden slit drum (idiophone) serving as a speech surrogate, wholly in the aurally perceived communication mode.

Speech community and communication competence

The concept of speech community is central to the ethnography of communication. Many definitions have been proposed, based on shared language and language attitudes (Saville-Troike 1989:16).

Dialect can be defined as a variety of a language according to user and location. In this study, dialect applies not only to the drummer, but to the local speech community as well.

COMMUNICATIVE COMPETENCE is a term connecting language choice and use, social context, and communicative intent and comprehension. It represents the complexities of the socially and culturally determined norms for appropriate production and interpretation of speech (Saville-Troike 1992:273). Communicative competence has five major components (based on Canale 1983 and Saville-Troike 1989:24): linguistic knowledge, sociolinguistic interaction skills, discourse organization capability, shared cultural knowledge and values, and strategic competence which may compensate for breakdowns in the other areas. Each speech community defines its own norms of communicative competence, including expected outcomes, acceptable linguistic variations, register choice, nonverbal communication, and the use of silence.

Canale (1983) distinguishes between communicative competence (abstract systems of knowledge and skill) and actual communication (use of such knowledge and skill under real-life conditions such as memory restraints, fatigue, background noise, and distractions). Each actual communicative act may have different limitations in its creation and comprehension.

There are different competency levels and types of competency within the speech community of Mekomba.[13] Everyone in Mekomba can report on Antoine's drummed speech acts and interpret the meaning of the

---

[13]For sociocultural variables connected to communicative competence, see Munby 1977.

drum within the society. Fewer people can explain or verbally interpret all of the drum phrases, though a number comprehend and can interpret portions. Although no one can repeat a lengthy performance exactly, a handful of drummers can repeat phrases that have been in the common stock for decades.

It must be noted that since every performance is emically the same in meaning, function, and form, it is repeatable. By making recordings and comparative charts, however, an outsider finds that the performance is etically not exactly repeatable (as most oral speech acts cannot be repeated exactly).

Only shared RECEPTIVE COMPETENCE, not productive competence, is necessary for successful communication (Saville-Troike 1989:23). Communication can take place in Mekomba even if only a handful of residents can produce actual drummed speech acts as long as other residents have the knowledge and skill to interpret. Because language is a social institution, the passive communicative competency of the audience is as important as the active competency of the performer in maintaining viable communication.[14]

When competency dimensions such as interpretable and repeatable are brought to bear on a lengthy discourse, the speech community becomes very tiny. One catechist cannot fully interpret and repeat the drummed discourse of the neighboring catechists sharing the same genre. My study with two other church drummers in other locations revealed that they usually understood only the portions of another's performance that were part of the common stock of Ewondo speech surrogate phrases.

A particular speech community

This study attempts to bring a balanced view between community tradition and individual talent. As Bauman says, "one of the most notable features of the new literary perspective in folklore is the departure from an emphasis on folklore as collective, traditional, anonymous literature....Recent studies have examined the unique artistic product of individually named artists" (1977b:128) Since the mid-twentieth century, Westerners have been interested not only in African cultural products, but are also increasingly interested in the individuals who create them. Credit must be given for individuals' creativity while recognizing the shaping of art by the social milieu. It is not proper "to expropriate the traditions as *objets d'art* or as documents for scholarship" without attending to the people who share

---

[14]See Herndon and McLeod 1980:185–92 for further sociolinguistic views of competence applied to ethnomusicology. See Stone 1982:24 for Hymes' communication theory applied in an African music context.

and create these traditions (Hymes 1975:69–70). In connection with this point, a brief introduction to the locale and to the men who shared equally in this work is necessary.

The village of Mekomba

Mekomba, where the research was carried out, was established in 1916. The name literally means 'an enviable place' because other people were envious of the location with its nearby water supply. The father of the town's current chief and president was one of the town's founders. Mekomba is thirty kilometers south of Yaoundé in the district of Mfou (Province du Centre).

People of three main lineages currently inhabit Mekomba. The best-known lineage founder is Owondzuli who lived over a hundred years ago. He used the name Owono; later, his mother's name of Ndzuli was added to distinguish him from other men sharing the Owono name. His children founded numerous Ewondo villages in the Mfou district. These villages include a total of more than ten thousand people. His descendants live along the route from Mfou to Mekomba.

The descendants of another lineage founder, Mba Nnembe, were numerous before the time of Owondzuli, and the descendants of both men intermarried through the years. A third lineage founder, Eboa, is more recent and is not mentioned in Antoine's drummed discourse. The school that divides the two main lineages is referred to on the drum as *ya suga mvog Mba Nmembe* 'at the end of the lineage of Mba Nmembe'. One main road passes through the village with lineages laid out in this rough pattern:

school		Antoine's house	
←———————			———————→
lineage of Mba Nnembe	lineage of Owondzuli	Innocent's house	lineage of Eboa

Neither Antoine nor Innocent claim Mekomba as their native village; both are "strangers" even after years of residence.

There are roughly twenty *nkul* 'log drums' in Mekomba, with others in nearby areas. The town population is about four hundred people. Ten to fifteen of these people are men who are recognized as having ability on the *nkul* as a dance drum. A handful of older men are recognized as having extensive ability on the *nkul* as a speech surrogate drum; several others have limited ability.

The drummers

Several drummers participated in this study to varying degrees. The drumming of Antoine Owono holds a predominant place, though Atemengue Marcus and Manga Luc also contributed. Appendices 1 and 2 are transcribed performances by Antoine Owono and Atemengue Marcus.

An equally vital part in this study was played by Nkoa Mbida Innocent, who helped to gather and translate the data and assisted with language analysis. Antoine, as performer, and I, as researcher, would not have connected in any meaningful way without Innocent acting as a bridge for words, thoughts, and hearts. I want to give him credit for "enlightening my eyes."

Antoine Owono. Antoine Owono was born around 1910, "before the Germans came in World War One." His father taught him to play the drum language, and he played "traditional messages," later using his skills in the service of the church. He has served as a Catholic catechist for more than six decades. From 1932 to 1950, he was assigned to various Ewondo villages. He came to Mekomba around 1950 as their fifth catechist. He and Innocent are distant cousins, and both are farmers. He has one wife and two adult daughters.

Nkoa Mbida Innocent. Nkoa Mbida Innocent was born in the village of Endoum (seven kilometers from Mekomba) in 1934. His father, a Catholic catechist who died in 1947, drummed the call for Christians to gather. Innocent was not very interested in learning the drum talk as a child. He has a primary school education and taught at primary school (including French) for two years.

In 1960 Innocent began seeing spiritual visions. When God told him in a vision to become a Protestant, he became a Protestant catechist for a small Presbyterian church at Meven. The church there already paid someone else to drum the call each Sunday.

Innocent was then catechist at Mfou Presbyterian Church from 1961 to 1965. At that time also, someone else was drumming the call on Sunday mornings.

He has since lived in various Ewondo towns and has a broad view of the use of talking drums in Ewondo churches. He knows some drum speech and is familiar with verb tenses, grammar, syllables, tones, and similar linguistic concepts.

Fluent in French and an expressive communicator, Innocent was a charming, kind host who went out of his way many times to be helpful. More than an interpreter, he helped me hear how the drum spoke consonants and extra vowels (realized in my transcriptions), wrote some texts and notes, and helped with linguistic data and personal contacts.

Atemengue Marcus. Atemengue Marcus has been the Roman Catholic catechist in Mfou-villáge for about fifteen years. He was born in 1926 and is the sixth catechist for Mfou-villáge, all of whom have been drummers. He speaks some French. Atemengue started drumming when he was about ten years old and was taught by his maternal uncle.

Mfou-villáge is located about halfway between Mfou (the market town) and Mekomba (residence of Antoine). The population is about two hundred people with roughly ninety registered Roman Catholics. Atemengue states that everyone knows that he is calling the church together because of the context, but he estimates that only about ten people (five percent) understand the actual words.

Atemengue drums his church summons about 6 a.m. on Tuesdays and Fridays, slightly later than Antoine who drums at first light. Atemengue usually drums while standing up, bent over at the waist, also a typical farming position. He occasionally sits on the ground with legs extended straight and the drum resting on top of his ankles. This position is also used by some dance drummers.

Manga Luc. Manga Luc learned drum language as a teenager in the village of Ekolmekak. During my fieldwork, he was temporarily residing in Yaoundé while helping to establish a Catholic church. He was one of the church's chief musicians, making and playing the *balafon* 'xylophone', *nkul* 'slit drum', and *mbei* 'tall membranophone drum'. He said that the "calling of Christians" is not drummed at his Yaoundé church, but everyone waits for the proper hour. He learned this church summons in the Catholic church in his home village. I recorded one performance of his drummed church summons in his house. Though he gave me three verbal phrases, I was completely unable to make any correlations between his drumstrokes and his words. I attribute this to the fact that Innocent was not with me in Yaoundé to act as a go-between. If Innocent had not worked with me in Mekomba and Mfou-villáge, the results in those places would likely have been equally disappointing.

The drummers' styles

A style description may be either taxonomic, based on distinctive features of the artist's work, or generative, based on characteristic processes in the artist's activity (Wollheim 1978:9). Both types of style descriptions can prove to be helpful in a comparison of performance paradigms by Antoine, Atemengue, and Manga Luc.

Distinctive features in this aurally-perceived context relate to different formulaic phrases, including stall patterns, nonverbal beginning and ending patterns, and textual phrases. The styles of Antoine, Atemengue, and Manga can be distinguished by the different material they work with, though some material is also shared.

Antoine's repertoire in this genre includes about a hundred formulaic phrases. In Atemengue's recorded paradigm, some phrases appear only once, and it is difficult to estimate the total number of phrases he may use in this genre. Manga wrote down for me the three phrases in (6) which he said represent his entire drummed performance.

(6) *bekristen bese, bese bese*   Christians all, all all,
     be zu kogelan ai zamba   they [should] come pray to God,
     bela bela, bebae bebae   three by three, two by two.

The ways in which the three drummers assemble the material in performance are similar yet still distinguishable. Generative processes of representing words as drumstrokes are assumed to be generally the same for any Ewondo drummer, though the exact phonological fit can differ. For example, to sound the word *bekristen* 'Christians', Antoine uses six drumstrokes, Atemengue uses five or six, and Manga uses only three, depending on how the consonant clusters are separated.

Generative processes of composition in performance are again distinguished. Manga's performance uses almost no pauses; it is one very long aural line. Antoine and Atemengue frequently utilize stops and starts, providing the sense of peristaltic movement. Co-occurrent clusters are used in lengthy performances by Antoine and Atemengue, who also use the stall pattern with a similar function as a place to think ahead. Atemengue's discourses, however, tend to be choppier than Antoine's, with shorter clusters and heavy use of his two typical stall patterns. Repetition of large units is part of Antoine's generative process, but repetition is much less prevalent in the way Atemengue builds his drummed discourses. Perhaps Manga does not use any stall pattern or co-occurrent clusters when building his discourse, but this could not be verified because I could never match his phrases with his drumstrokes.

The generative styles of the two neighboring catechists can be categorized as variants within one generative process, while the style of Manga in Yaoundé is very different.

Even if no underlying words are recognized, the distinctive sound patterns of the three church drummers are sufficiently different so that each can be recognized by their respective speech community. The mix of common stock phrases, community tradition, and an individual artist's style makes each performance something very familiar yet very fresh—something simultaneously known and unknown.

Comparisons between Antoine and Atemengue. Atemengue says, "I play what I think" in contrast to Antoine who says he "plays from the heart." The difference could be tied to the different levels of awareness expressed by each catechist. Atemengue acknowledges there can be different opening phrases and various reorderings of phrases throughout the summons. In contrast, Antoine preferred to say that "it's the same every time," focusing on the purpose and genre-level of the communicative act. Probably both are aware that the summons does change and does not change at different levels with every performance, but each drummer expressed one of these truths to me as the question-asking analyst.[15]

The function, general meaning, and even some phrases of each drumming catechist's church summons are identical. There are, however, some major differences between the discourses.

One difference (striking to an outsider) is that Antoine's drum poem has several possible beginnings and a single stable ending, while the discourse structure drummed by Atemengue is the reverse. All four texts I recorded by him start with the same metaphor of "children of the most wise authority" but have different endings. There is less sense of an obvious discourse peak consistently appearing in Atemengue's performance paradigm.

A second difference is the length of the drumming and internal repetition. Antoine usually plays for two-and-a-half to three minutes, while Atemengue plays less than half that time. Atemengue uses almost no repetition of phrases within a given performance except two stall patterns (to which he assigns verbal texts), while Antoine can easily repeat a block of twenty or more phrases within a performance.

A third major difference involves their use of stall patterns. Atemengue uses some at the beginning, middle, and towards the end of his discourses that are not used by Antoine. The drummers share one common stall pattern. To Atemengue, however, it represents the words *a doten a doten* 'to doctrine to doctrine'. Antoine explained that for him, the pattern was the nonmeaningful syllables of *ku ku ku ku lu ku ku ku* and used by him "only for repose. But if Atemengue explains it as *a doten* it is not false." Atemengue did recite this phrase repeatedly in dictation, while Antoine did not because he assigned it no verbal meaning. One

---

[15]Much would have been learned by bringing the two catechists together and recording their interaction on this subject. Unfortunately, it was not possible because of their farming schedules and other responsibilities. Innocent and I worked with each catechist separately and played recordings of the other and reported what the other said.

drum pattern has different underlying conceptions: one meaning-based, one not.

The fourth difference concerns variant verbal interpretations for one drum pattern. Besides the stall pattern, alternate words were given in a few other cases. The three low drumstrokes connecting 'sons' and 'daughters' was given as *aladag* 'addition' by Antoine and *afulan* 'mixture' by Atemengue. In Antoine's final stanza, the phrase *bine ma kokoa a mo* '[words of doctrine] are not in my hands' was interpreted by Atemengue as *bintu ma kokoa a mo* 'become absent from my hands'.

I played Antoine's performance 4 for Atemengue phrase-by-phrase, asking for a verbal interpretation. He quickly understood about two-thirds of Antoine's drum phrases and recognized more with a little prompting. He seemed familiar with the majority of Antoine's phrase repetoire, even phrases he himself did not use. Upon hearing a recording of Atemengue's drummed summons, Antoine did not recognize many phrases that he himself did not use.

Though residing only a few kilometers apart, the two drumming catechists have idiosyncratic ways of drumming and of verbally interpreting the drum patterns. Each one is oriented towards a local speech community of a few hundred people and will probably be only partially understood anywhere else.

The history of drumming in Cameroon

Whereas Protestant missionaries came to Cameroon in 1844, the first Catholic missionaries did not arrive from Germany until 1890 (Aka 1988:16). In the beginning, the Mvolia center in Yaoundé used a church bell to gather church members. Later, when trained catechists were sent out to various villages, they told the missionaries that slit drums could be used to gather people for various purposes. The village churches could not afford large bells, so often each church commissioned a drum to be made. When a drum was carved for a church, the drum would remain in the village when the catechist moved. Antoine's drum, however, was made by his father, and he has kept it and used it in the various villages where he served as catechist.

In the early years, there was no formal catechist school. A catechist was chosen by fellow Christians in his village because of his faithful attendance at church, not on the basis of knowing drumtalk. Usually, any drumming catechist learned speech surrogate drumming prior to becoming a catechist. If a catechist did not drum himself, he would search for a Christian in his area who "knew the drum."

The *nkul* drum has been used in connection with Ewondo churches of most denominations for decades. It can be heard on a 1950s recording of "Psalm 106" (Phillipson 1964). Drum phrases used to call people to Protestant church services include the ones in (7)

(7) *Den ane mose sondo,*   Today is Sunday,
     mos bot bese   the day all people
     a bitetea bise bi' akane Zamba. and creation worship God.
     Ve'e oyo!   Wake up!
                                    (Etua 1993)

In many Catholic and Protestant churches in the Ewondo area, an ensemble of several *nkul* and other drums is commonly played to accompany church songs.

Studies of slit drums

Geary (1989) has provided a well-documented study of immense carved slit drums in western Cameroon. Many of these large instruments were used as emblems of chiefs and secret societies and were intricately carved with anthropomorphic and zoomorphic designs. Sadly, a number of these drums have broken down and are preserved only in old photographs. Other studies of Cameroonian slit drums include Betz (1898), Dugast (1955), Meinhof (1894), and Schneider (1952, 1967). In an early book on German colonial rule, one map (Meyer 1909:490) is given showing the areas of Cameroon where "talking drums" were used.

A number of studies and brief mentions by various authors have dealt with slit drums, their messages and use within Ewondo culture. A brief contribution (Anonymous 1911) to *Atlantic Monthly* dealt with the call-drum of the Bulu/Ewondo people. Nekes (1912) described talking drums in the Yaunde/Ewondo and Duala language groups of South Cameroon. Heepe (1920) also wrote on Yaunde talking drums and helped arrange early recordings. An early collection of Yaunde texts included a few pages of an ethnic speaker describing the drumtalk (Atangana and Messi 1919:303–6). These early studies included lists of short verbal examples but no rhythmic patterns.

Guillemin (1948) wrote an article specifically on "The Calling Drum of the Ewondo." This article contains a fairly confused explanation of neumes, intensity, weak and strong tones, and rhythm. The collection of single-sentence phrases is again without rhythm markings. Heinitz (1940–41) and Hermann (1943) gave brief examples of Ewondo drum language. Good (1942) provided an informative article (with photographs) on Bulu/Ewondo speech surrogate drumming. Marfurt

(1957:27–31) provided a few examples of drum talk and his commentary. Stoll (1955) and Tsala (1955) also mention the subject.

Two decades passed before a landmark book was published by a Cameroonian (Nkili 1975/76). *Le nkul des mvele: essai d'analyse semiotique* provides a study of the *nkul* drum in society and texts for various occasions, as well as some notes on structural and literary analysis, but with no mention of rhythm markings.

Another Cameroonian scholar, Abega (1987), focused attention on Ewondo/Beti *esana,* a genre of oral literature and customs used at funerals. One, two, or three drums in an ensemble announce deaths, give invitations to funerals, and perform as speech surrogates at funerals. The drums may act as different "voices," for example, that of the deceased and that of the lineage. A drum may insult and mock the dead person and make accusations of sorcery (Abega 1987:318). Again, texts are without rhythm markings. Most of the book deals with the anthropological and cultural data within the *esana.*

An earlier study (Ngumu 1975/76) of Ewondo musical instruments, primarily the balaphone, does give a brief rhythmic transcription of an ensemble drumming a single-phrase *esani.* It also briefly mentions speech tones reproduced on the drum.

Certainly no previous single study of the Ewondo *nkul* has mentioned all the pertinent factors of the drum language and context. No author has dealt adequately with the linguistic structure; some barely mention tone. With regards to rhythm notation and analysis, exactly one phrase has been handled adequately (Ngumu 1975/76:23). The earlier text collections were entirely of short, single phrases (Nekes 1976, Heepe 1920). The longer texts published in the two more recent books (Abega 1987, Nkili 1975/76) are usually one or two pages at most. And as is common, authors record phrases and texts and publish them without determining if there are alternate renderings, thereby giving a false impression about the fixity or fluidity of the drum patterns in performance.

These previous studies opened the door to knowledge of the Ewondo speech surrogate system but only scratched the surface of some elements and completely ignored others. In the last few decades, theoretical advances have been made in fields as diverse as discourse analysis, oral-formulaic theory, semiotics, and musical improvisation. Recent models in these and other fields are pertinent to an in-depth interdisciplinary study of part of the Ewondo speech surrogate system.

5

The Ewondo *nkul*

Classification

Different cultures have diverse ways of classifying musical instruments. The most common western classification system is the 1914 Sachs-Hornbostel system (translated in Baines and Wachsmann 1961). It categorizes instruments according to what is vibrating: air column, stretched string, stretched membrane, or the non-stretched instrument itself. According to this classification, the Ewondo *nkul* is considered an idiophone, or "self-sounding" instrument. Instruments of this type are often referred to as SLIT GONGS, emphasizing that they are without a vibrating drumhead, but are rather instruments of which the body itself vibrates. Slit identifies the type of sound hole cut into the vibrating material (wood). This type of instrument is classified as a "struck idiophone individual percussion tube," or number 111.231 in the Sachs-Hornbostel system.

This system is to some extent adequate to deal with the question of what is vibrating when we hear this instrument. Hood (1971:123–96) has pointed out other questions that should be asked about musical instruments. He proposed a "symbolic taxonomy" that can include such information as physical description, techniques of performance, musical function, decoration, and socio-cultural considerations. He devised a system of symbols, ORGANOGRAMS, that can succinctly include information in a visual form and lend themselves to quick, easy comparison.

49

An organogram for the *nkul* would be diagramed as in (8).[16]

(8) Organogram of *nkul*

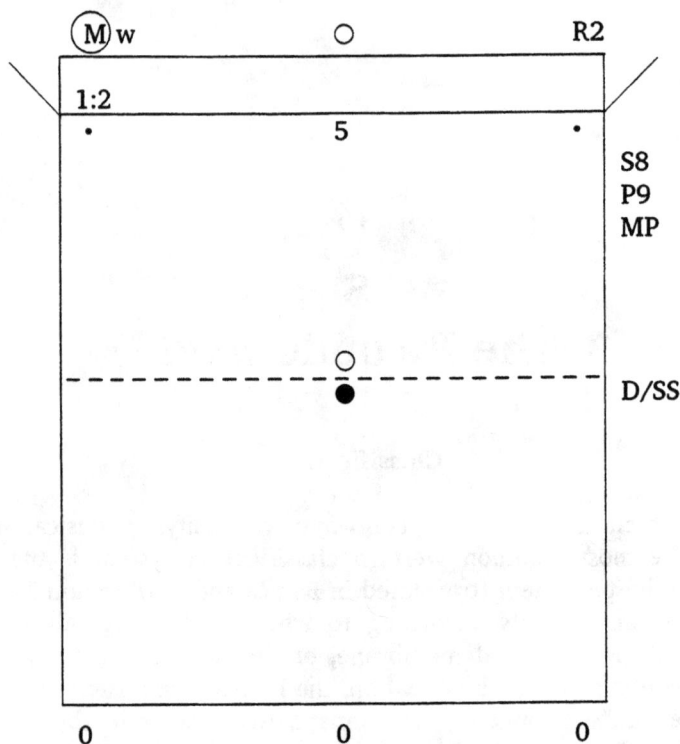

Symbol	Location	Explanation
□	center	The square indicates that the instrument is an idiophone.
⊟	top	The internal shape of the instrument is cylindrical.
⅄	top left and right	The instrument is struck with two sticks in performance.

---

[16]I have not used all of Hood's information symbols and have added one of my own (D/SS). The explanation chart for the organogram was based on Monts' chart for the *kleng*, a similar instrument of Liberia (Monts 1980:113–15). The numbers in S8 and P9 are my personal evaluations based on observation.

Symbol	Location	Explanation
[• •]	top left and right	One stick is held in each hand.
[1:2]	top left	The instrument has one longitudinal slit with two tongues.
5	top center	The instrument is made of wood.
(M)w	top left	The instrument is played primarily by M (men) and by fewer w (women).
[○]	top center	The instrument is an individual percussion tube.
R2	top right	The instrument is tuned to two R (relative) pitches.
[▪▪▪▪]	center	The instrument is played in a horizontal position in front of the performer.
[○ ●]	center	The instrument may have two players (at dances), one optional, seated on logs.
▆	bottom	The instrument has direct contact with the ground.
000	bottom	The instrument has no artistic motifs, techniques, or finishes applied.
S8	right side	The S (society) regards the value of the instrument at 8 out of 10.
P9	right side	The P (performer) regards the value of the instrument at 9 out of 10.
MP	right side	The M (maker) is the P (performer) in some cases.
D/SS	right side	The instrument is used in D (dance) and as a S (speech) S (surrogate).

These Western instrument classification systems are valuable, but there is much to be gained as well from the emic indigenous classification vocabulary (Kartomi 1990). The Ewondo do not group the *nkul* with other idiophones such as bells, based on material of vibration, but group it with drums (membranophones), based on method of performance. The three main Ewondo drums are the *nkul* (various sizes), the tall cylindrical membranophone *mbae,* and the short cylindrical membranophone *ngom.* Both membranophone drums are played with the hands, while the *nkul* drum is struck with sticks. In this book, the more emic category of slit drum will be applied to the *nkul,* though it is recognized that western literature often uses the term slit gong.

Manufacture

There are no drum makers resident in Mekomba. I commissioned one large *nkul* to be made by Atemengue, the catechist, drummer, and drum maker of the neighboring village, and purchased a small *nkul* already made by Betianga. Atemengue said that all three types of Ewondo drums are commonly made from any of three kinds of woods: *ebae (Cordia platythyrsa), esil* or *mbel (padouk: Pterocarpus soyauxii),* or *evouvous. abang (iroko: Chlorophora excelsa)* is also mentioned by Guillemin (1948:71).[17] Atemengue said the different types of wood produced no noticeable differences in sound. Often a tree is chopped down with an axe and left to dry. Atemengue made several drums from a tree felled when someone cleared his farmland by burning. One sixty-foot tree may make five to fifteen drums, depending on the presence of holes in the wood and sizes of drums designed. Small drums are roughly 28–32 inches long and 4–7 inches in diameter. Large drums to carry sound through the forest to far villages can be twice as large or more (Marfurt 1957:30).

The drum maker may take several weeks to carve a *nkul,* working on it after farming hours; two to three weeks is a common time frame. Much rough work is done where the tree lies in the forest. When it weighs less, it is carried to town and completed. The artisan uses a large chisel *(obak)* and a scraper *(funenga)* (Guillemin 1948:69–70).

The drum is designed to produce two different pitches. The low-pitch side of the drum is carved thinner than the high-pitch side. A five centimeter wide slit is cut into the top of the drum, and the hollowing-out work with chisel and scraper is done through this slit known as *anyu nkul* 'mouth of the drum'.

---

[17]Good (1942:70), describing the manufacture of Bulu *nkul,* lists the typical three trees as *mbel (Pterocarpus osun),* *ebae* (probably *Pentaclethra macrophylla),* and *olom* or *ololom.*

(9)   Diagram of the Ewondo *nkul* (based on Abega 1987:17ff.)

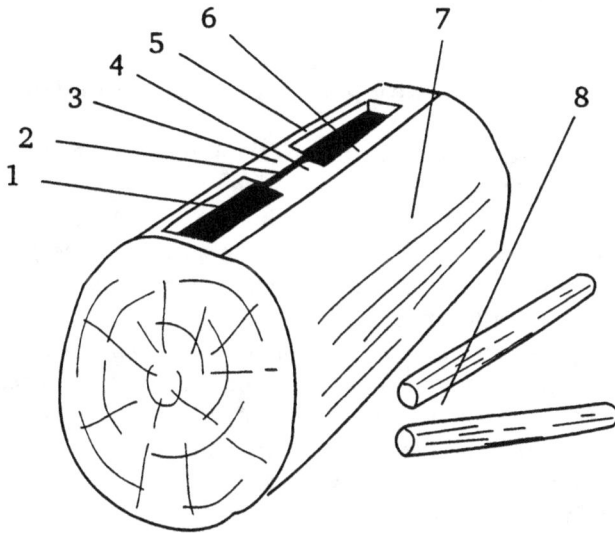

1. soundhole between two lips
2. soundhole restricted through two tongues
3. high-pitched tongue
4. low-pitched tongue
5. high-pitched lip
6. low-pitched lip
7. body of drum
8. sticks of drum

Each side of the slit is called a lip as in the illustration in (9). The higher-pitched lip is *eya anyu ya yob* 'lip of the mouth that is high' (like the sky); the lower-pitched lip is *eya anyu ya si* 'lip of the mouth that is low' (like the ground). In the middle of each lip is a tongue, which is about five to ten centimeters wide and a few millimeters apart (almost touching). The high-pitched tongue is *otad nkul ya yob;* the low-pitched tongue is *otad nkul ya si.*[18] The lips on Antoine's drum were broken off, which is not uncommon for very old drums. His drum is well over a hundred years old by his reckoning, as it first belonged to his father.

The body of the drum is *nkuk nkul* 'trunk of the drum' and the two drumsticks are *mimba mi nkul* 'sticks of drum' (see Abega 1987:17ff. and Nkili 1975/76:29ff.). Each drumstick is about a foot long and is made of

---

[18]In 1942, Good reported that on Bulu drums, the tongues (or "crier") are different sizes; that of the "man" is nearly twice as broad as the "tongue of the woman." I did not see this feature on Ewondo drums forty-six years later.

soft, lightweight wood. Good (1942:70–71) gives three sources for Bulu drumstick material.

Performance practice, gender, and taboos

The drummer usually sits low to the ground, on a log or a stool. The drum rests on the ground, with the high-pitched lip toward the drummer. Sometimes the drum is propped with a block at the bottom so it will not roll. Alternate playing positions include sitting on the ground with the drum on top of the legs extended straight or standing up and bending over at the waist to drum (a common farming position as well).

Although a large number of women understand drum messages (receptive communicative competence), only a few might occasionally play (productive competence) the *nkul* for speech surrogate purposes, but never in the musical mode at dances. The wife of Mekomba's president and all her sisters know how to drum messages, while the president himself does not. Nkili reports that

> Numerous and diverse are the legends about the woman and the *nkul*. Some people think that she who beats the *nkul* with the ability of a man excells in sorcery and will be sterile as a consequence. Others affirm that a menstruating woman defiles everything, so she must throw a twig of wood into the *nkul* before she sits down so as not to disturb its resonance. The oldest of the group do not approve this prohibition. The *nkul* has never been the sole property of the male. Examples of the mothers of families who played the *nkul* abound in the history of the Mvele. (1975/76:33)

Taboos for male performers have also been reported. Bulu drummers of *nkul* were told "a good drummer must not eat chicken wings; give them to someone else. The flapping of a chicken's wings does not sound far" (Good 1942:74), meaning that eating chicken wings would decrease the carrying power of the drummer's sound.

nkul origin myth

The Cameroonian folklorist Belinga (1965:159) has recorded an origin myth for the *nkul*. In the story of *Mesi me Kodo Endon* in (10), the chimpanzee called Ekondene Mba prepares to send a message to his brothers:

(10)   He rose all smiles before the calling drum,
        and took two ivory sticks;
        he struck one side, he struck the other, and said,
        "this side is not alone;
        perhaps is it the only one to be struck?...

        O *nkul*, give me the word,
        I give you the sticks.

        O chimpanzees of the Bulu area,
        O chimpanzees of the areas of the world.
        The chimpanzee that is called Ekondene Mba wants you,
        here tomorrow morning, on time.
        A message presses me deep within myself,
        it is this message that I must say to you..."
                    (Nkili 1975/76:32–33)

Expressions using *nkul*

The name of the *nkul* reportedly comes from the word *kua* 'to cry out' (cf. Nkili 1975/76:29). Three Ewondo verbs in (11) are commonly used to describe its speech surrogate function:

(11)   *nkul wa kobo* 'drum it speaks'. This verb implies nonsemantic sounds such as *ku ku ku* or *ken ken ken*—used as a signal drum.

        nkul wa dzo 'drum it says'. This verb implies semantic sounds that replicate words—used as a speech surrogate.

        nkul wa lon 'drum it calls'. This verb is used when the drum is calling a person or group of people, often by name.

All three aspects of drum communication are found in Antoine's performance paradigm. The stall pattern and final coda are nonsemantic drum patterns. The body of each performance is surrogate language. Three direct address phrases are used to identify lineages and the village by name. One phrase in (12), drummed by Antoine in performances 8, 9, and 10, is reflexive commentary on the act of calling.

(12)   *man etug nkul a lono lono lono lono lono lono*
        ve mi bo asi otutu dza
        A small, old, broken drum calls and calls [a long time] but you
        are on the bed in your little old village.

An entire drum discourse of any genre may be termed *foe nkul,* and
the term *nkobo nkul* is used for 'drum speech'.

People called by drum names

The drum is used to gather people for diverse situations. One purpose
is to call individual men, women, or children. Many people have a drum
name or *nkul edan,* often bestowed by their father. If a person hears this
name drummed at the beginning of a drum message, he knows the
message is intended for him. Some examples of drum appellations may
be heard on audio cassettes.

The drum name of Atemengue Marcus of Mfou-villáge partially means
'I see you [spiritually] when you're doing good, I see you when you're
bad' (tape example 23). The drum name of Manga Luc of Yaoundé means
'Jealousy is not good to have among brothers' (tape example 24). This
drum name was also used by his uncles. The drum name given to me by
Antoine[19] means 'sword hanging at hip, husband of daughter [son-in-
law] of Mbida Mengue' (tape example 25), the first part referring to an
authority figure. The phrase is part of an entire drum message concerning
the coming of a European. This same descriptive drum phrase is used for
God, the "highest authority figure," by Atemengue, the drumming catechist in the neighboring village.

The drum name of René of Mekomba partially means 'I walk along
thinking of death' because his father died before René knew him (tape
example 26). The drum name of Mekomba's chief, Owoudou Marcus, has
three parts (tape example 30). The first phrase is *a nga bia-lī˜e-tam a nga
bia-lī˜e-tam Owondou* 'he is born alone, he is born alone, Owoudou'. The
chief was an only child of his mother. 'He is born alone' is part of a larger
common stock phrase, 'a man walks alone, he is born alone' (Heepe
1920/1976:327). These two phrases were demonstrated from a 1913
tape recording. The second part of the chief's name, *man mbon o bege bisie*
'the little rafter carries the raffia thatch [roof]', implies 'the rafter-father
carries the thatch-roof-son'. The last phrase in the chief's drum name *a*

---

[19]This drum name is not peculiar to me alone by any means. Guillemin (1948:83) notes
that these two phrases make up the drum name "of the whites" when prefaced with the
phrase *mfari nnam angfari nnam* 'thief of the country has stolen the country'. Other drum
names used for Europeans are given by Heepe (1920/1976:321).

nga ke sob anyie mvog Owondzuli, means, 'he has gone to stay [build a house] at the edge of the lineage of Owondzuli' (referring to Owoudou's grandfather).

Drum names take very diverse forms. Guillemin (1948:79–83) groups drum names into twelve categories, relating to things such as wealth, war, gossip, beauty, and friendship.

In some cases several people have the same *nkul edan;* when this happens they are distinguished by an additional drum name *metilan* relating to their family or home region, such as *mon kal awono* 'son of sister of Awono' (p. 74).

A series of distinguishing drum names is the norm for a person and is localized to particular villages and drummers. Owoudou told me that he could not call Innocent on the drum even if he had a proverbial drum name because he did not know the name of Innocent's father or other relatives.

Besides individuals, clans may also have drum names. The Ewondo clan of Mvog Atangana-Abala use the drum name *ngul ene nye a makong* 'power to them with their lances' (Marfurt 1957:29). Heepe (1920/1976:321–23) gives over a dozen drum names for related "tribes and kin groups."

nkul with various speech genres

According to Nkili, "the *nkul* participates in all the [Ewondo] genres of oral literature, for it accompanies song, epic recitations exalting the exploits of clan ancestors, story, and initiation prayer" (1975/76:34).

During a typical week in Mekomba, *nkul* drummed as a speech surrogate might be heard five times or so. Antoine played at least twice a week to call an occasional afternoon meeting and to call people to morning doctrine classes. Death announcements would be heard, or an order for men to assemble for communal labor might be drummed by the chief. During one fierce storm the chief's son played a message telling the wind to stop.

The drum was also previously used at wrestling matches. In the morning the drum would announce the wrestling match with phrases such as *ebongo bayi ku asi* 'the boys who have courage to fall down on the ground' (Heepe 1976:329). People would come from distant villages because a match would involve different tribes from many villages. When they were gathered, one drum would coach the wrestlers from the sidelines (cf. Good 1942:74) while another drum could play musical rhythms. The drum name of the person who is winning would be broadcast by the 'drum for wrestling' *nkul mesin* (Etua 1993 personal communication).

nkul awu is the drum that announces the death of a person from village to village (tape example 42). The theme of death is also commonly used in an individual's drum name: *akar ke awulu angawu y'okoba* 'even though he goes walking now he is headed toward death' was the drum name of catechist Pierre Mebe (Marfurt 1957:29). The drum name of one man was 'you'll die of witchcraft at midnight' (Good 1942:73). Another drum name is *bot bese bene mvog bekon* 'all people are of the tribe of the dead' (Guillemin 1948:82).

The drum is commonly used to call for food or drink, using common stock phrases after the drum names of message sender and recipient. Good (1942:72) gives the message *za'a w'awulu avo, avo, m'awo o zae te ngele* 'come walk quickly, quickly, I feel hunger not small'. Owoudou Marcus of Mekomba taught me several similar phrases in (13).

(13)   *ma lon mon womo amougou jean na*
        I am calling my son Amougou Jean so that...

        a zu me ve meyok kin dza kod ma abui
        He brings to me some palm wine because I am thirsty.

        zag me ve bidi ma wog zie
        Come to give me food, I have hunger.

Another related message was given by Atemengue of Mfou-villáge (tape example 28).

(14)   *a man mininga*
        To a young girl

        za ma ve dzom ma di e
        Bring me something to eat.

        makar wog zie abum
        I am very hungry.

        me nteleya abog maye dzile za dzom
        I am about to kill what doesn't belong to me.

        za ma ve dzom ma di
        Bring me something to eat.

        avol mbi, avol mbi, avol mbi
        Run quickly, run quickly.

The *nkul abok* 'drum of dancers' is sometimes used to direct dancers, giving advice to "stand up, sit down, come out, turn his back so, or stoop forward" (Good 1942:74).[20] *nkul abok* is also used to call people to a festival (Atangana and Messi 1919:305). When people dance *elak*, they beat *nkul elak* (Akoa-Mongo 1993).

Examples of nearly twenty genres are given by Nkili (1975/76:41–100) for the Mvele *nkul*. A few of them will be mentioned here, based on elaboration by Akoa-Mongo (1993).

nkul bisie 'drum of work' is used to call people for communal labor, such as building roads and schools and clearing the bush. *nkul bisie* is also used to mark starting and stopping times of such communal labor, including a noon break.

If someone in the village needs some voluntary help from other people for a personal job, they can call for workers with *nkul ekamba*. The host will provide food, drink, and music in return for assistance.

When there are disputes between two people or families, *nkul adzo* 'drum of quarrel' can be beaten to call people from neighboring villages to assist in the judgment of the problem. A public tribunal will take at least a day to deal with such cases. Penalties, fines, reconciliation, or prohibitions are possible outcomes of the judgment.

If a dangerous animal has been sighted nearby or trapped, *nkul akon* 'drum of spear' will gather people to get their spears to kill the animal. This genre may also be drummed when there is any other danger against the whole group; for instance, it can be used when calling people to prepare for war with another tribe.

If someone is assassinated, or if an enemy tribe attacks, *nkul bita* 'drum of war' is beaten so that warriors can become ready for battle.

nkul mengan 'drum of triumph' is beaten by people in victory, over either a dangerous animal in the hunt or another tribe in war.

During the colonial period, administrators would sometimes send soldiers into villages to arrest people for forced labor at plantations or in building railroads, bridges, administrative houses, and so forth. So that people could be warned and run away, *nkul ebi* 'drum of arrest' would speak to let area villages know that the soldiers were coming to conscript people.

At the funeral of an old and respected person, *nkul esana* 'drum of funeral' will be drummed. Adults holding spears and youth holding *adjom* (a wild plant) will dance in the compound where the deceased is laid out (cf. Abega 1987).

These are some of the genres of Ewondo *foe nkul* 'drum discourse'. Genres are differentiated by social function. Numerous other examples of drum names and diverse types of messages may be found in Atangana

---

[20]It is not uncommon for membranophone dance drums to speak instructions or give comments to dancers, as among the Akan (Nketia 1963) and Yoruba (Euba 1991).

and Messi (1919:303–6), Good (1942), Guillemin (1948), Heepe (1920), and Nkili (1975/76).

Use of *nkul* with drum music

The same drum is used as a musical instrument for village dance events such as funerals and for market town events such as church services. It is rarely played alone when serving a musical function; the most common ensemble is three *nkul* of graded sizes and one tall membranophone *mbae* played by men or boys (tape example 36). Women often play rattles and concussion sticks. The short membranophone *ngom* may also be added.

When played at a dance, two players may face each other across the drum. One plays the lips of the drum, while the other plays a regulative rhythm on the left and right edges of the drum top. This high-pitched sound of solid wood (to either side of the resonance chamber) is not used when the drum is speaking and acoustically distinguishes the separate functions of the drum.

Some musical drum patterns include those used in the contexts of funerals, a Presbyterian church service, and a traditional religious healing service. A number of these musical drum patterns have been transcribed in appendices 1 and 2 and can be heard on tape examples 32–37 and 43.

There is an emic distinction between function of the speaking drum and that of the dance drum, though the instrument is the same. In speech function, the *nkul* is always played solo. Used at a dance, several *nkul* function in a mixed percussion ensemble.

Dance drummers are not necessarily speech drummers and vice versa. Speech drummers tend to be older men; dance drummers (and dancers) tend to be younger. In Mekomba it was not common to find a man who was highly regarded as both; drummers tend to specialize in one function of the *nkul*, though there is some overlap of drumming knowledge. Mekomba has roughly fifteen men who know something of dance drumming, and less who have much ability to make the drum talk. Younger men are more likely to participate in all-night dances; older men may have more need to call a family member or pass a death announcement from village to village. Antoine said he had drummed for dances when he was younger.

At an all-night funeral in Mekomba I observed that the oldest drummer in the ensemble would perform drum speech, then immediately the other ensemble drummers would begin dance rhythms. These functions of the *nkul* would go back and forth, but people always stopped dancing when it was a solo drum speaking. At dawn during this funeral, the chief put his drum on one side of the funeral compound and played a conversation with another *nkul* among the dance drummers on the other side

of the compound. Also at this time, a drum from another village re-
sponded to the Mekomba chief's drum.[21]

With the exception of the drum speaking to dancers, surrogate speech
and dance rhythms seem to be two separate spheres for one instrument,
though they can be switched at any moment by the same performer if
necessary. Drum music and drum language can be "intermingled on
social occasions" as among the Akan (Nketia 1963:28), but for the most
part performers and audience make a clear distinction by function and
sound where one stops and the other begins.

---

[21]See Abega 1987 for examples of *esana* texts drummed at funerals. An Ewondo funeral
drum text is heard on tape example 33.

6
Oral and Drummed Ewondo Language

Spoken syllables and drumstrokes

A four-note pattern began a church summons as drummed by Manga Luc in Yaoundé. I played this pattern for Innocent in Mekomba who interpreted it as *bot bese* 'all people', which is the way the phrase is drummed by Antoine. Upon hearing Innocent's interpretation, Manga said, "Yes, it could be *bot bese*, but it is the way I play *bekristen* ['Christians']. When Antoine uses six drumstrokes to play *bekristen* it is too long."

Antoine understood very little of Manga's recorded church summons and vice versa, in spite of the fact that they had some verbal phrases in common. There are several reasons for this lack of understanding, one of which is that the phonological system which each drummer uses on the speech surrogate drum seems to differ slightly from that of every other drummer.

The relation between words and drum patterns is arbitrary to some extent. Some observations will be given in this chapter which hold true for Antoine's idiolect, but not necessarily for other Ewondo drummers. A wide study would need to be undertaken to determine the variety of each drummer's phonology across the Ewondo area.

There is often a one-to-one correlation between syllables and drum-strokes, especially the syllables that follow a V, CV, VC, or CVC pattern.[22]

(15)

    ♩
    ♩

    a   a   to

       ♩ ♪
   ♩   ♩

   en- go- ko- mo   engokomo   type of tree

       ♩
   ♩

   be- kon   bekon   dead

In the case of syllable patterns which contain consonant clusters, the correlation between syllables and drumstrokes becomes more variable. The only consonant clusters in Ewondo consist of a homorganic nasal plus a stop. The nasal does not commonly get a separate drumstroke in words such as *nkul* or *ngogo,* but there are five words given in (16) in which the nasal is separated from the stop.

(16) ♪ ♪

    m-ba   Mba   proper name

    ♪ ♪ ♪

    m-bo- lo   mbolo   what

     ♪
      ♩

    n- tu   ntu   old

        ♪
   ♩ ♪   ♩

   n- ton-do-be   Ntondobe   God

---

[22]The two notes in (15) are a doubled drum stroke.

♪

♩

n- da   nda   house

In borrowed words, all consonant clusters are broken up on the drum as in (17); even when consonant clusters are contiguous across word boundaries as in (18), they are often separated and played with two drumstrokes.

(17)   ♪

♩ ♪ ♩ ♪ ♪

be- ke- ri- se- te- ne   bekristen   Christians

(18) ♪   ♩

♩ ♪

mvo-go ta-ra   mvog tara   lineage

♪ ♪ ♪   ♪ ♪ ♩ ♪

♪   ♩

bi-bu-gi n-ne- mə wa ko- bo bibug nnem wa kobo   everything
                                                  the heart
                                                  speaks

Syllable addition and vowel insertion

In oral speech as well as in drum speech, the insertion of transition vowels between adjoining consonants is common. If a word-final consonant precedes a word-initial consonant in the next word, an extra spoken syllable or drumstroke is often heard. In Innocent's vocal rendering of the drum patterns, a transition vowel is usually inserted between the two consonants.[23] This insertion means that the word-final consonant (with the added vowel) is changed into a separate syllable, requiring a separate drumstroke.[24] It must be remembered that this added syllable really concerns the

---

[23]This transition vowel is technically called an EPENTHETIC or ANAPTYCTIC vowel.

[24]An alternative interpretation is that the added vowel alone is the new syllable. It is more likely, however, that the drumstrokes represent the consonants already existing in the words, and that the transition vowels are added to these consonants though drummers do not think in terms of vowels and consonants. The interpretaion that spoken transition vowels are often replicated in drum speech was a key to understanding Antoine's percussion pattern. When Antoine drums bekristen, doten or lom mot, each consonant gets a separate drumstroke.

phonology of the surrogate vocalizing of the surrogate drumstrokes of the
original words and is Innocent's subjective interpretation.[25]

Rhythms are created in terms of formulaic phrases and not in terms of
single words. Sometimes a word is drummed with two rhythms, depending on whether the next word-initial phoneme is a vowel in (19) or
consonant in (20).

(19)

mvog o-wo-ndzu-li   mvog Owondzuli   lineage of Owondzuli

(20)

mvo-go ta-ra   mvog tara ngogo   lineage of my father

Antoine's dialect of the Ewondo speech surrogate system will not permit
two consonants side by side, either within the word (except for some nasals)
or contiguous consonants across word boundaries. Vowel insertion is commonly used to separate consonants. Transition vowels are found in other
examples of speech surrogate drumming (Wilson 1965:213) and Native
American songs (Hinton 1986:15 and Seeger 1987:45–46).

In some instances of Ewondo drumming, a word may keep its form
whether followed by a pause or by another textual phrase. In line-final
position, no added drumstroke is needed to bring separation from the next
consonant because there is no consonant immediately following. But the
word-final consonant gets a drumstroke anyway because of its formulaic
form that stays fairly constant in any context as shown in (21).[26]

(21)

do-a- te-ne| doten   doctrine

lo-mo mo-tə| lom mot   person

---

[25]This is a study on two levels: how the drum imitates speech, and how speech imitates
the drum. The first level is shared to a certain extent by all Ewondo drummers; the second
level represents Innocent's idiolect of verbal interpretation.

[26]Throughout the book examples are occasionally followed by bars indicating the end
of aural lines with | indicating long pauses and ¦ indicating shorter pauses.

The same words may be followed by a text phrase with word-initial consonant. In (22) as we would expect, the final consonant of *doten* is played on the drum. *doten* is actually pronounced [dwaten] or [do-a-ten] in slow speech. A vowel glide of spoken language is not reflected in the orthography but is heard in the speech surrogate form.

(22)

do-a-te-ne be-ke-ri-se-te-ne doten bekristen doctrine Christians

Each verbal phrase is represented by a formulaic tonal-rhythmic pattern which is consistent for the most part. The consistency is very helpful for comprehension. When the drum phrase is used in different contexts, its surface structure form is maintained to a large extent. When variant forms occur, they are usually heard in line-final position.

In a few cases, an extra syllable and its representative drumstroke are inserted between a word-final consonant and a word-initial vowel as in (23).

(23)

mo-tə an-dzi-ki   mot andziki   person did not send

a-bo-go a – ye   abog aye   when he will

Sometimes an extra syllable may be added in the middle of a word, or at the end, for no apparent linguistic reason as in (24) and (25).

(24)

mi-nin-ga ba-re-ə fe-ge ma dzo ˜a-ya
minga bar fe ma dzo aya
What else will you say to me? (lit., You will say to me what else?)

(25)

kpe-kpa-a-ga   kpekpaa   toothbrush

ma-gə me-ne   ma mene   for me

In Yoruba *dundun* drumming, an identical phenomenon is found that Euba (1991:45) terms "false syllables." In Antoine's drumming, these "false syllables" occur much more rarely and almost always in predictable places in some stereotyped formulas. They are not increased or decreased according to performance context but seem to be a consistent surface structure feature of certain formulas.

Vowel addition

In several instances, the drum adds an extra stroke for no apparent linguistic purpose. I hypothesize that this insertion is to add more length to the tonal-rhythmic phrase. Many short phrases would sound identical; longer phrases can have more diversity and be more memorable. In Innocent's verbal translation of the drumstrokes, he decided that occasionally there were extra vowels. Drummed Ewondo words that always include extra drumstokes (representing added vowels) are given in (26).

(26)

bi-ne-ə ma   bine ma   (not easily glossed)

zu-ə ma   zu ma   come

zu-ə bo   zu bo   come do

ba-re-ə fe-ge   bar fe   (not easily glossed)

wo- a dzam   wo dzam   you something

du-ə- ban   duban   baptism

For other words, vowel addition is found in certain formulas but not in others. In (27), *mi* is lengthened to *mi-a* according to which words follow.

(27)

mi- a zu mi- a wu- lu...
you come, you walk...

mi zu wo-go do- a-te-ne
you come hear doctrine

The use of false syllables on the drum, verbally interpreted as both extra consonants and vowels, does help create a lengthier surface structure for some formulas, and provides another cue for formula recognition. Manga told me, "When you speak you have many sounds, but the drum has only two sounds, so you do more on the drum to represent the words."

According to Nekes, "The Yaunde [Ewondo] reproduce a long syllable as they do two successive short ones, by two strokes; the renditions are distinguished by tempo" (1912:76). The second drumstroke is apparently related to the false syllables.

Vowel elision

Vowel elision will often occur between words when the second vowel is not a complete word itself, but rather an initial vowel with a following syllable. If the second vowel is a complete word (a or e), it will not be elided as in (28).

(28)

wu- lu-gu⁓a-vo-lo du-lu a me- kol e-
    (elision)   (no elision)
wulugu avol dulu   a mekol e
walk with quickness in the feet

ma-gə me- ne a-   za⁓e- bu- gu
    (no elision)   (elision)
ma mene a za ebugu
What concern is it to me? (lit., for me it is what concern?)

Every vowel that could be elided is not elided, hence vowel elision is optional. The important condition for comprehension is that the tonal and rhythmic formula has little or no change when repeated within a performance, or from performance to performance. In (29), there are two vowels that coalesce and two vowels that do not. This tonal-rhythmic pattern is kept constant in performances.

(29)   ♪ ♪   ♪   ♪
       ♩ _____ __♩
       a- ko- do a- si⁻a- dzal
       (no elision) (elision)
       akodo asi adzal
       He leaves the bed in his village.

In one Ewondo elision, *a* appears between two *l*s, but does not receive a drum stroke. In fast speech, this vowel is not heard; it is the same on the drum.

(30)   ♩   ♪
                 ♩
       nkul⁻a lo- no   nkul a lono   drum it calls

Tonal patterns

It is recognized by at least some Ewondo drummers that their language is tonal even if they cannot specify linguistically exactly what the tones are. Manga said, "Speaking Ewondo is like when you are singing, there are many notes... There are several notes of the mouth that go up and down." One probably needs to be consciously aware of speech tones in order to be a good speech surrogate drummer.[27]

In general, the high and low tones of the *nkul* follow spoken speech tones. Doubled drumstrokes and mid tone present more difficult data to interpret.

A doubled drumstroke is used in fourteen words of the recorded performance paradigm by Antoine to represent differing spoken tonal patterns. Example (31) gives sample comparisons between doubled drumstrokes and the spoken words represented where ⌐ is high, ⌐ is low, ∨ is low-high, ∧ is high-low, and ⊢ is mid.

---

[27]In some speech surrogate systems using membranophones, the tones of speech are distinguished on the drum by the relative intensity of drumstrokes (cf. Rouget 1964:17).

(31)   DRUMMED   SPOKEN

♩ ♪

♩   ♩   ٧

a   mvo- go   a

♩

♩   ♩   ٧   L

bo na   bo na

♩ ♪

♩   ♪   ٧   Γ

e- yie-   e- yie

         ♩

      ♩ ♪ ♩   L Λ L L

lu͂e- wu- wu- lu   e- wu- wu- lu

♩

♩   ♩   Γ   ⊦

man- yon   man- yon

♩

♩   Γ L

ndzo   n- dzo

♩   ♩

♩ ♩ ♩ ♩   Γ L Γ L

o nga/ a nga   o nga/ a nga

♩

♩   ?   ♩   L L Γ
                       ve-
ve- be-gan[28]   be-gan

♩   ♪

♩   ♪   L Γ Γ L

za͂e- bu- gu   za e- bu- gu

---

[28]Note that in *ve-be-gan* the second syllable receives no separate drumstroke. I was given no explanation for this phenomenon.

> ♩ ♩
> ♩ ♩   L L Γ
> ko-koa   ko-ko a

> ♩
> ♩   L
> kat   kat

In a phrase taught by Atemengue, a doubled drumstroke was also used to indicate coalescence of vowels with differing tones, shown in (32).

(32)   DRUMMED   SPOKEN

>   ♩   ♩   ♩
> ♩ ♩ ♩   L L L Γ Γ   Γ
> ma ye ke˜a ma- kid   ma ye ke a ma- kid
> I will go to market.

Tone perturbation is common in Ewondo speech but seems less so on the drum. For example, (33) gives one phrase as drummed and one as spoken.

(33)   DRUMMED   SPOKEN

>   ♪ ♩ ♩♩ ♩   ♪. ♪   ♪
> ♩♩ ♪♪   ♪   ♪♪ ♪ ♪
> a-ke di a- ke a n-da-   a- ke di a- kan- da[29]
> Now it goes in the house.

The last three words and their tones were coalesced in speech but not on the speech surrogate (two spoken syllables versus five drumstrokes). It is more common for the drum to lengthen phrases than to shorten them, though vowel elision produces some of the latter.

The phenomenon of tone perturbation was explained by Innocent as follows: "One syllable can influence another syllable's tone by going up or descending to search for it. When going fast, one syllable's tone can go up with a stick, knock down the 'fruit' [tone], and make it fall."

A tonal glide may be represented on the Ewondo *nkul* by either a doubled drumstroke or by two drumstrokes which come so rapidly as to be almost simultaneous. Some evidence that it may be represented either

---

[29]These are rhythmic markings for the vocal phrase to make specific what has coalesced.

way on the drum is shown in (34) from performance 2, where the word
bo 'do' is played in differing ways.

(34)

... *bo do- a- te- ne* | ... *bo- na* |
     do doctrine   do this

Ngumu (1975/76:22) believes the doubled drumstroke represents the
mid tone of spoken Ewondo.[30] Though this belief is written by an
Ewondo author, the statement is mentioned in passing within an article
on Ewondo music and no linguistic evidence is presented for the conclusion. The doubled drumstroke does reportedly represent a spoken mid
tone in some Nigerian drum speech (Armstrong 1955/1976:871).

Another question needs to be resolved: how is a three-tone language
replicated on a two-tone drum? According to Nekes (1912:77), the spoken Yaunde/Ewondo mid tone is converted to the high tone on the drum.
This conclusion agrees with Guillemin (1948:71), who reports "the middle tone assimilates to the high tone." A spoken mid tone is actually a
lowered or downstepped high tone (Redden 1979:10–11), so it is appropriate that it is played on the higher lip of the drum.[31] In (35), however,
a spoken mid tone is drummed as a low tone.

(35)

wo o- ka- tə man- yon |
You tell it in turn to your brother.

Various African speech surrogate systems have different solutions for
a three-toned language represented on a two-tone drum and for how a
spoken mid tone is represented on the drum. There are also diverse
linguistic features represented by the doubled drumstroke throughout
Africa.

---

[30]This view is also shared by Marfurt (1957:30), though with no linguistic evidence.
The evidence I have presented shows that the doubled drumstroke can represent more than
one linguistic feature, but mid tone is not one of them according to how I hear the words
spoken on tape.

[31]Downstep in tone can occur on variable pitch hourglass drums such as those used by
the Dagbamba of Ghana. See Kropp Dakubu and Read (1985:26–27) for an example, which
is explained as a lowering of musical key in the sense of western music.

Summary of phonological differences

There are differences between spoken, drummed, and written Ewondo as exhibited in Antoine's drumming.

1. False syllables are common on the drum, more so than the transition vowels used in speech.
2. Syllables may be extensively modified on the drum in terms of pitch, duration, and quantity, so that one spoken syllable may receive as many as four drumstrokes.
3. Intonation and tempo changes mark proper phrasing in speech but are much less important on the drum. The primary cue for proper scansion (poetic division) of drum phrases is the pause.
4. The free rhythm of speech is regularized into two durations on the drum.
5. Features of downstep and mid tone are not possible on the two-tone slit drum.
6. The drum and speech often exhibit vowel elision, while writing does not.
7. The drum and speech often break up contiguous consonants by the insertion of a transition vowel, while writing does not.

Ambiguities and variations

Meaning-bearing elements

Spoken Ewondo has thirty-three phonological elements that combine to mark differences in meaning: twenty consonants, seven vowels, three tones, and three juncture phonemes (Redden 1979:5). Together, these phonemes can create hundreds of syllables, which create thousands of words. All carry semantic weight, or meaning.

Drummed Ewondo reduces the meaning-bearing elements to five drumstrokes that can be short or long, high or low drumstrokes, and discourse markers including pauses (silence) and the stall pattern. Only four drummed syllables are possible (not syllable types, but actual syllables): high/short, high/long, low/short, low/long.

In spoken language, the actualization of phonemes changes considerably in varying speech contexts, between speakers, and between dialects. On a log drum, every high-pitched drumstroke is acoustically the same, though the exact pitch varies from drum to drum. The problem of phonological variance in speech is not relevant here (though there is variance in duration values on the drum).

Prosodic devices which may carry meaning are missing for the most part in Antoine's drumming. The performances do not have pitch contours (except in line-final position) or stresses that orally might indicate punctuation. They do not have "the accelerations and retardations of the speaking voice" that help mark scansion and proper phrasing (Tedlock 1983:7).

Most of Antoine's drumming is so regular that it sounds like a machine. The starts and stops found in speech are present, but not necessarily where they would fall when spoken.

The drum speech does not have varieties of accents or volume changes. In speech, many shades of meaning are carried by all of these suprasegmental features. In writing or drumming the same words, most of these features are lost.

In Ewondo speech surrogate drumming we have the paradoxical situation where the meaning-bearing elements of communication are severely reduced to the handful of prosodic features of pitch, duration, and pause, while all other prosodic elements such as stress and intonation are almost entirely missing.

Homophonous surrogate signs

It is not uncommon for different words to be represented with an identical or similar tone and rhythm pattern. Semiotically, this phenomenon is known as "homophonous surrogate signs from non-homophonous lexical items of base language" (Sebeok 1976:xvi). The key to differentiating between the possible verbal words is found in the preceding and following discourse contexts; the words must make grammatical sense in the proper sentence order (cf. Nketia 1971a:730). In (36) and (37), homophonous surrogate signs of identical and similar tone and rhythm are given.

(36)   Identical tone and rhythm

   a.

be- ke- ri- se- te- ne

... -a ke mi- a wu- lu

   b.

a mi- na- mə mi- nam

...-*ri-se-te-ne a-ke* ...

c.

zu wa-wu-lu...

...*o-wo-ndzu-li*...

d.

a mvo-go ta-ra...

...*ndzoḛe-len-de-ya-*...

(37)   Similar tone and rhythm with one note difference

a.

a bo-nə be bi-nin-ga-

...*-ke di a-ke a n-da*

b.

mvo-go ta-ra ngo-go

...*-te n-ton-do-be o-*...

Several ambiguous phrases may be combined into one aural line. The
example in (38) is taken from performance 5. Two lines, separated only
by the stall pattern, are almost identical. Out of the first eighteen drumstrokes, only three are different between the two sets of formulas.

(38)

ndzoe˜e-len- de-ya- hm mot a- be fe ke o-yo-a - mi zu wo-go...
The day has already dawned. No one must sleep any longer.
You come hear [doctrine].

[stall pattern]

a mvo- go ta-ra ngo- go mot a- be fe bo-bi- bug-i be ko-ni |
to descendants of my father, no one, he must no longer |
play tricks

The discourse context before and after these eighteen notes provides
clues for the correct interpretation. The first line above is a semantic
continuation of the previous line 'morning', whereas the second line only
occurs after a stall pattern. In addition, the two lines have distinctive
endings, which means that retrospective patterning may be used by
audience members to determine the proper verbal interpretation.

Discourse context to disambiguate

The reduction of phonetic and prosodic meaning-bearing elements in
drum speech means that each drumstroke must carry a tremendous
amount of semantic weight. Meaning emerges to the audience, however,
not one drumstroke at a time, but in a phrase in context with other
phrases. Phonemic, morphemic, and word levels may or may not have
precise relationships with drumstrokes; meaning is carried at the level of
formulaic phrase. "Man without writing thinks in terms of sound groups
and not in words, and the two do not necessarily coincide" (Lord
1960:25).

One drumstroke (or spoken syllable) is meaningless in isolation. Two
high drumstrokes can make up an aural line: ki-di 'dawn'. When heard in
the opening stanza after a certain phrase and preceeding another, these two
drumstrokes are adequate to carry semantic weight. Their duration may be
short or long. Even the length determinant of meaning is not necessary: only
two high tones in the right place are necessary for proper meaning to be
deduced.

The immediate context is very important: two high tones appear side
by side more than fifty times elsewhere in performance 2. Knowing the
context makes the audience aware that all of those occurrences of two

high tones are not *ki-di* 'dawn' which comes only in a place defined grammatically in the opening stanza.

The key to comprehension of drum speech is recognizable, memorable tonal-rhythmic units in discourse context. A unit that meets that criterion can be as little as two high notes: *ki-di,* in a highly restricted environment. In most other cases, a longer unit (up to seven notes without using context) is required for the competent audience to disambiguate tonal-rhythmic phrases.

Discourse context is important for differentiating elements at each hierarchical level: drumstrokes in pitch and speed, similar tonal-rhythmic units at the phrase level, and so on. This phenomenon is true for every level of oral speech as well: "perception of a phoneme depends as much on the context of utterance as on the acoustical properties of the message" (Sloboda 1977:117).

A process of RETROSPECTIVE PATTERNING appears at every level of understanding Antoine's discourses. At the smallest level, we gradually perceive which verbal phrase is represented by a tone and rhythm pattern as the rhythm progresses—the first two notes are usually not enough. At the largest level, we come to understand line length, stanza separation, and similar discourse features only as the performance takes place.

Variations in formulas

Occasionally, one verbal phrase will be represented by a phonological variation of the more common tonal-rhythmic surface structure. In (39) and (40), context determines which tonal-rhythmic unit the performer chooses. The first pair in (39) is in conditioned variation according to which phrase follows. The second pair in (40) is in conditioned variation according to which phrase precedes.

(39)   Conditioned by following phrase

be- ke- ri- se- te- ne be- se ya...
Christians, all of...

be- ke- ri- se- te- ne a- ke di a- ke a n- da
Christians, now it goes in the church.

(40)   Conditioned by preceding phrase

♩ ♪ ♩ ♪ ♩ |
♪ ♪ ♩♩ ♩ |

ve mi bo- a- si o- tu-tu dza |
but you are in bed in your poor little village

        ♪   ♩ |
♪ ♩ ♩ ♪ ♩ ♩ ♩ |

to- bo to- bo˜o- tu- tu- tu- tu-dza |
sit and sit in your poor little village

When variations do occur in a formula's surface structure, they happen most frequently in line-final position. This is true of semantic variations (word substitution) and phonological variations (final-vowel prolongation for aesthetics or intonation and other variations).

In (41), the final word has a substitution. The tonal-rhythmic unit remains identical. Antoine said that when he plays it the first time in a performance, he thinks of *koni* 'tricks'; if he repeats the phrase, he thinks of *fongo* 'too small'. The spoken words share the same tone.

(41)   ♩   ♪ ♪ ♪♩   ♩ |
♪ ♩ ♩ ♪ ♪   ♩ |

mot a- be fe bo- bi- bu- gi be ko- ni |
                          fon-go |
no one, he should no longer do things of tricks/ |
                            things too small |

In (42), a final set of words may have a substitution. This is not conditioned by context but is in free variation.[32]

(42) ♩   ♩ |
♩ ♪ ♩ ♩ ♪ ♩ ♪ ♩ |

o nga zu wa-wu-lu˜a zen e- se |
you come, you walk along the road

♩   ♪ ♪   ♩ |
♩ ♪ ♩ ♩ ♪ ♩   ♩ ♪   ♩ |

o nga zu wa-wu-lu ngo-no-lo nnam o-se |
you come, you walk in the countryside

---

[32]Notice that each pair in (39)–(42) shares a semantic deep structure, and the parts of each pair are functionally equivalent within the drummed discourse paradigm.

In several words occuring before a pause, the final vowel may be pro-
longed on the drum. In the four phrases in (43), this vowel prolongation is
apparently for aesthetic effect; Antoine said it was "for amusement." The
last tone rises, providing a final flourish without semantic meaning.

(43)

a-ke di a- ke a n-da- now it goes in the house

wo- go do- a- te- ne-   hear doctrine

o- fo- foe na – –   whisper that

mo- tə te dzo na– – –   no one should say this

When asked about other examples of line-final vowel prolongation,
Innocent stated that they reflect distance intonation of verbal speech,
"used for calling someone far away." In these cases, the vowel prolongation ends with a falling tone.

(44)

zu- lu me- ti- ne – –   promises/appointment

man n- tu e- yie-   small old cloth

In (45), the meaning changes slightly with the final optional flourish
from 'the doctrine' to 'this doctrine'.

(45)

wo- go do- a- te- ne te – –   hear this doctrine

Optional vowel prologation is found in Antoine's drummed performances, usually in line-final position before a pause.

Line-final prolongation is the extent of intonation replicated in Antoine's drumming. In speech, intonation is used "to guide the listener in
breaking up the message into a correct linguistic usage" (Cohen
1986:531). Verbal intonation uses cues of timing and pitch to focus
attention on specific words or syntactic structures. The general lack of
intonation in Antoine's drummed speech increases the audience's difficulty in separating lines into constituent phrases and in separating
phrases into constituent words. There are practically no phonetic or
prosodic cues given to break up the message—only silence, the stall
pattern, and the semantic sense of the signified words.

7

Speech Surrogate Formulas

Oral-formulaic theory

The initial conception of oral-formulaic theory was proposed by Parry in the 1920s to deal with poetry of classical Homer and modern Yugoslav bards. The theory was carried on by his disciple, Lord, and increasingly by other scholars through following decades. Foley (1985) in his bibliography lists more than 1,800 entries dealing with the topic, and a regular journal is also devoted to it. Most of this scholarly work is beyond the scope of the present study. Readers wanting a brief review of oral-formulaic theory are referred to Foley (1985:11–34) for a summary and to Foley (1988) for application to oral African data. Suffice it to say that the theory has been debated and modified a great deal over the last seven decades. Emphasis in this study will be on how oral-formulaic theory applies to Ewondo speech surrogate drumming and on how it gives insight into the creation of Antoine's discourse paradigm.

Parry and Lord proposed that much oral poetry is created by combining formulas together in lines and stanzas. Their original definition of a FORMULA is "a group of words which is regularly employed under the same metrical conditions to express a given essential idea" (Parry 1930:80). It will be shown that this definition comes close to fitting Ewondo speech surrogate drumming with one important change: that of rhythmical rather than metrical conditions.

METER can be defined as regular poetic stress. It implies a steady pulse and is present in much poetry and song around the world.[33]

A definition of RHYTHM is not so easily agreed upon and has been described in contradictory terms (Eskelin 1971:2). Eskelin states that in music, the "difference between rhythm and meter may be the difference between merely recurrent patterns and regularly recurrent patterns" (p. 120).

This difference is crucial to understanding my modification of Parry's original definition of the oral formula. Ewondo speech surrogate drumming is not metric nor does it have a regular accent organization, though when the same drum is used at a dance, the sound patterns then fit the regular meter of the song.[34]

Ewondo speech surrogate drumming is rhythmic, made up of recurrent, temporal patterns in sound. Antoine's poetic discourses have no regular meter at all, but are rhythmic in nature, as opposed to much oral literature to which oral-formulaic theory has been applied. Antoine's summonses have no single metrical idea, but are composed of about a hundred tonal-rhythmical (nonmetrical) sound patterns with underlying verbal text. My definition of formula, revised from Parry's original to fit this Ewondo context, is "a word or group of words iconically represented by drumstrokes which are regularly employed in the same tonal-rhythmical pattern to express a given idea." Each verbal formula is manifested by the performer and perceived by the audience as a drummed pattern of sound, though the conception and interpretation are based on spoken sound patterns. Everyone in the area of Mekomba village hears the instrumental sounds, but only a handful understand the verbal formulas.

Restrictions in drummed formulas

In the original conception of oral-formulaic theory, a basic restriction in creating and using a formula is that it fit the meter of the poetic line that is sung (Lord 1960:31–32). In Ewondo speech surrogate (nonmetrical) drumming, this restriction is not applicable; rather, a main restriction in the use of a formula is that it must be agreed upon (standardized) and socially maintained (known) by at least some members of the speech community (i.e., it cannot be made up on the spot at the drummer's whim). All meaning would be incomprehensible if the

---

[33]Meters used in Ewondo dance drumming include 12/8 and 18/8.

[34]For differences between metric poetic rhythm and musical metered rhythm with notated examples, see Brown 1948:15–30. Antoine's drumming exhibits little contrast between accented and unaccented beats; this contrast is common in much music with a metric organization. Woodson (1983) did find that *atumpan* drum speech of Ghana does use accented and unaccented drumstrokes.

tonal-rhythm patterns changed dramatically with every performance, or if only the drummer knew the signified words.

A second restriction involves "the principle of contextual elimination which enables the listener to determine which of a possible set of interpretations is the most probable" (Nketia 1971a:730). Context here refers not only to the immediate aural context of drum patterns but also to the performance context. When Mekomba residents hear drumming at dawn on Tuesdays and Fridays, they can probably eliminate verbal interpretations such as 'wife, bring food to my farm'. Hearers also relate the drumming to the village's social structure and know that the church leader is assembling the church congregation. All nonrelevant verbal texts can be eliminated from the audience's choice of interpretations. The matter then becomes one of recognizing which of Antoine's hundred or so phrases is being drummed at the moment. Although the organization of lines and phrases cannot be fully predicted, Antoine's use of co-occurrent clusters in discourse creation aids the process of contextual elimination.

Types of formulas

Three different formula types have been distinguished in oral-formulaic theory. According to Vīķis-Freibergs (1984:331), exact repetition of a string of words is a SYNTAGMATIC FORMULA: each occurrence has identical surface structure coming from a single deep structure.

A PARADIGMATIC FORMULA can be defined "as a set of syntactically identical phrases in which one or several members of the string can be substituted for in a paradigmatic manner" (p. 331). Some elements have contrastive significance, of both sound and specific meaning, in a particular position in the formula. The surface structure has some controlled variation generated from one basic deep structure with one general meaning.

Paradigmatic formulas are found in other Ewondo speech surrogate genres as well. For example, a short drum call like 'wife/sister, bring food/palm wine' has substitutable parts.

The third semantically-based formula type may have two completely different surface structures, but they must be generated out of one deep structure pattern based on semantic categories.   ·

This tripartite division of formula types is closely related to Kiparsky's taxonomy of formulas as "bound," "flexible," and "free" (Rosenberg 1978:2–3).[35]

---

[35]A similar tripartite division is made by Pawley (1992:23) in the context of everyday speech: formulaic expression (syntagmatic), formulaic construction (paradigmatic), and semantic formula (based on a single deep structure).

Formulaic patterns of long and short syllables. Short and long
syllable combinations form the basis for much poetry around the world.
Jones (1964) has undertaken a study of African poetical scansion and
meter. He concludes that the scansion of African song lyrics is not accen-
tual with regularly recurring pulses. Rather, it is more similar to the
classic Greek and Roman scansion of long and short syllables. African
poetical scansion "has, as its base, the *mora*—the unit time of the length
of spoken short syllables...the organization may be additive, consisting
of groups of unequal numbers of *morae* linked together to produce an
acceptable rhythmic phrase" (p. 13). This analysis seems true of Antoine's drumming. However, Antoine does not then use one phrase "as
the metrical basis of the poem, being repeated right through it" (p. 13).
Each drummed phrase is rhythmically coherent by itself with short and
long syllables linked in an additive (irregular) pattern, and his aural
poems have no single metrical basis.

This practice of creating memorable patterns of short and long syllables is found not only in speech surrogate drumming, but also in much
African dance drumming and oral poetry or song (Nketia 1971b:746). In
Antoine's poems, each line's short and long syllable pattern holds true
only for that line, though it remains consistent when the line's rhythmic
pattern is repeated. This is one of the main differences between Antoine's
drummed rhythmic formulas and metric formulas used in song.

Rhythmic remembrance. The mnemonic benefit of rhythm is well
known. Rubin says that "rhythm can be seen as a way to allow easier
rehearsal of verbal codes, or as a way of setting up reference points on
which words can be placed. In fact, learning a rhythm and words is often
easier than learning just the words" (1981:175).

Rhythm can aid in recall of verbal patterns, but only if the exact syllables
of the surface structure are recalled, and not a paraphrase derived from the
deep structure. "Where rhythm is present there are forces acting to preserve
the exact form as well as the meaning" (p. 177). In contrast, the exact
wording of the surface structure is quickly lost in much speech, and only the
meaning (deep structure) remains in long-term memory. When Antoine
verbally dictated a text to me out of performance context, the surface
structure of some of the phrases was changed because the drum rhythm was
not present to keep the exact formulaic form intact (tape examples 16 and
17).

One reason there seems to have been fairly stable transmission of
formulaic phrases over a long time is that the drumming is done by
specialists (cf. Nettl 1981:144). Every Ewondo speaker has in mind grammatical phrases involving speech tone and rhythm. What the drummers
alone have is the skill to shape this verbal material through a musical

medium into memorable and memorized sound patterns, and to very quickly arrange and give coherence to these sound patterns under real-time performance constraints. The drummer knows hundreds of formulas and has special ability to transfer speech acts successfully from the mouth to the hands (cf. Rosenberg 1975:97).

Formulas of Antoine's performance paradigm. Most of Antoine's drummed formulas are encoded at the drummed surface levels, producing identical repetitions. They are BOUND or syntagmatic formulas. This static surface structure is necessary in a speech surrogate medium with limited vocabulary, patterns, and context. All surface structure variants make it harder to decode the drumstrokes back into verbal text. The communication is encoded at the tonal-rhythmic pattern level (drumstrokes) in the memory of performer and speech community. One set of words is played with one drum pattern for the most part.

Some of Antoine's formulas are in a FLEXIBLE or paradigmatic relationship. Substituting of one- to four-word units may occur within the formula.

In the pair of Antoine's formulas in paradigmatic relationship in (46), the final words are in free variation, that is, not conditioned by context.

(46)

on-ga zu wa- wu-lu͞a zen e- se |
you come, you walk along the road |

on- ga zu wa- wu- lu ŋgo- no- lo nnam o- se |
you come, you walk in the countryside |

In another paradigmatic relationship, an initial phrase is completed by one of four second phrases to become a complete sentence. A third modifying phrase may be optionally added to one of the second phrases as in (47).

(47)   Initial phrase   Completing phrases   Optional modifying
                                                   phrase

       mot abe fe   *tobo a tobo tobo*   *otutu dza*
       no one, he   sit and sit and sit   in his little
       should no longer   old village

                            ke oyoa
                            sleep

                            bo bibug be koni
                            do things of tricks

                            bo bibug be fongo
                            do things too small
                            [insignificant]

Another paradigmatic formula appears in the text corpus once with a
substitution. The more common version in (48) usually introduces the
final stanza.

(48)

mo-tə te bo na
no one should do this

In the penultimate stanza of performance 2 shown in (49), however, the
common formula is drummed followed by the paradigmatic substitution.

(49)

mo-tə te bo-na
no one should do this

mo-tə te dzo na - - -
no one should say this

The direct address phrases using names of lineage founders and the
village name make up another formulaic paradigm. Two identifying
vocative phrases can each be completed by two out of three possible
locatives in (50).

(50)

Christians, all   ⟨   ↗ of Mekomba
                          ↘ at the end of the descendants of
                                 ↗ Mba Nnembe
To sons and daughters ⟨
                                 ↘ of the tree of the lineage of
                                    Owono, the son of Ndzuli

'To sons and daughters' is never completed by 'of Mekomba' because the village cannot have descendants, only the lineage founders. 'All the Christians' is never connected with Owondzuli's lineage for reasons I did not discover.

Other than these examples (and a few others) of formulas in paradigmatic relationship, Antoine's formulaic phrases are syntagmatic: they are drummed the same way within a performance and in all performances.

A formulaic phrase is defined lexico-structurally by repetition as the smallest tonal-rhythmic-verbal pattern that occurs with little or no variation and that can have various boundaries, or be put into various immediate contexts. Hence, phrase in the definition of formula does not necessarily correlate with phrase in the grammatical perspective.

Formulaic units and discourse construction. A formulaic phrase may be as short as one word: *bekristen* 'Christians' or *doten* 'doctrine'. These words may each appear in various contexts in conjunction with various other formulas. The Ewondo term *ebug nkul* 'drum word' is related to my use of formulaic phrase. The borders of *ebug nkul* are not determined by pause or grammar, but by main ideas or main words. Etua (1993, p. c.) gives the following example: A spoken sentence could say, "There is a wrestling match tonight at Ngulmekong." The drum, using three *bibug nkul* 'drum words' with repetition, would say 'wrestling, wrestling, tonight, Ngulmekong'. *ebug nkul* can be more than one word, such as 'black dog'.

In some cases a formula may be a much larger unit than a single phrase. The lines in (51) appear only as a unit with no variation, and are variously bounded at either end.

(51)   *a mvog tara ngogo / mot a kat wo dzam / wo okat manyon*
        To descendants of my father, someone tells you something, you
        in turn tell your brother.

        ku ku ku ku lu ku ku ku
        [stall pattern]

        bibug nnem wa kobo anyu te fali bise
        Everything the heart speaks, the mouth cannot say all.

'To descendants of my father' is a separate self-contained formula; it can appear in several other contexts though it is obligatory in the initial slot in this unit. Similarly, the stall pattern *(ku ku ku ku lu ku ku ku)* is a self-contained formula, but is obligatory between the two parts of the proverb-type unit in (51). All five clauses (plus two pauses) appear as a formulaic unit: a cluster of phrases, lines, pauses, and stanza marker.

An extended formulaic phrase may have several clauses that only appear together as with each clause separated by a pause in (52) from performance 4. In performance 7, these clauses are drummed together without pause as one line.

(52)   *nge mina bombo asi*   If you lie in bed,
       ma mebombo asi   I will lie in bed.
       ma mene a za ebugu   For me it is what concern?

A formulaic phrase may be used in one or more co-occurrent clusters. In (53), 'walking aimlessly' fills a middle slot of two clusters.

(53)   *mia ke mia wulu*   You go, you walk
       ewuwulu ewuwulu   walking aimlessly
       mi tame zu bo doten   you should come do doctrine.

       abog a ye wog doten   When he will hear doctrine
       a nga ke a wulu   [instead] he walks
       ewuwulu ewuwulu   walking aimlessly
       a minam minam   from place to place.

The surface structure and meaning of the formula *ewuwulu ewuwulu* 'walking aimlessly' remain the same in both contexts. The deep structure meaning of both formulaic units is closely related; the first is a direct address, while the second uses a third-person pronoun. 'Walking to doctrine' is in opposition to 'walking aimlessly'.

Formulaic phrases and formulaic units are the basic building blocks of Antoine's discourses. The manner in which they are put together illustrates an important feature of a formulaic speech surrogate system: lack of linkages between units.

The absence of linking items is noted in Antoine's discourse paradigm, making it very easy for the units of phrase, line, and stanza to be rearranged in every performance within a paratactic structure. Even within a single performance, repetitions are often not identical.

The discourse level structure (what is heard) is affected by the method of discourse composition (how it is made). Antoine's discourse is a real-time paratactic combination of formulas, affecting the choice of materials and their use.

In speech surrogates, a reordering of surface structure patterns seems to be common, made possible by the use of formulaic, consistent phrases as building blocks. One perceived surface structure drum pattern represents one concept in the semantic deep structure for the most part. In contrast, most speech (whether formulaic performance or conversation) provides various possible surface structures for one underlying concept. In the poetry of Yugoslav bards, where oral formulaic theory was developed, "the formula means the essential idea" (Lord 1960:65). Even with the formulas of Latvian folksongs, for example, "there is a veritable riot of expressions for the same basic idea" (Vīķis-Freibergs 1984:335–36). This multitude of manifestations is not feasible in a speech surrogate medium, where texts are encoded and learned at the surface structure level by the community as well as the performers. Though Antoine's repertoire contains a few formulas with multiple meanings, they are rare. Where they do occur, the drummed sound pattern does mean "the essential idea."

In some spoken or sung formulaic systems, the performer has liberty to construct formulas from interchangeable word patterns in paradigmatic relationship. The Ewondo speech surrogate system, however, consists entirely of preestablished formulas which must be well-worn if communication is to take place. Antoine's composition process is a matter of stringing together formulas in a paratactic manner.

In this paratactic poem, phrases and co-occurrent clusters are like building blocks, which can be stacked up in various orders without connectives as long as semantic and syntactic prerequisites are met. Three complete cohesive stanzas are given in (54) through (56). The shortest stanza (54) is from performance 3. The lengthier stanza in (55) from performance 10 has four direct address phrases, three imperative commands, and closes with a declarative statement. These eight phrases are drummed with only one slight hesitation in the middle; all of this information must be grasped within a few seconds. The stanza in (56) from performance 5 is shortened to two direct address phrases, two imperative commands, and the same closing declarative statement.

(54) *doten* Doctrine,
 bekristen Christians,
 ake di a ke a nda now it goes in the house [church].

(55) *bekristen bese* Christians, all
 ya suga mvog mba nnembe at the end of the lineage of Mba Nnembe,

 mvog tara ngogo descendants of my father,
 kodogan asi [all of you] leave the bed.
 ekokodo ekokodo ekokodo Leave [forever, carelessly, all at once].

mi zu wog doten	You come hear doctrine,
bekristen	Christians,
ake di a ke a nda	now it goes in the house [church].

(56) *a bon be fam aladag*   To children-males in addition
      a bon be bininga   to children-females
      ya suga mvog mba nnembe at the end of the lineage of Mba
                                 Nnembe,
      kodogan asi   [all of you] leave the bed.
      mi zu wog doten   You come hear doctrine,
      ake di a ke a nda   now it goes in the house [church].

Each of the stanzas in (54)–(56) is cohesive in itself, but a comparison of them reveals the shifting cohesiveness of building blocks that are frequently stacked in different ways. The only such blocks common to all three stanzas are 'doctrine' and 'now it goes in the house [church]'.

Speech surrogate formulas are inherently less in number than possible formulas in epic song, due to the (non-narrative) type of message and the limited medium. In this study, Antoine's total number of formulas recorded is about one hundred, with roughly eighty drummed in any given performance.

Ewondo common stock drum phrases. A number of scholars have published collections of Ewondo, Beti, and Mvele drum phrases. Some of them are found in Antoine's performances, showing that a portion of his discourse is known by other drummers (not only catechists); his individual discourses have long historical roots in the larger Ewondo speech surrogate system. The phrases in (57)–(64) are quoted in four other sources that have partial or complete correlations with phrases in Antoine's discourses. Some authors used Ewondo, others used only French or English; here all have been given English glosses. Original spellings are kept.

(57) a. *Kodan a si, kodan a si,*   Leave the bed, leave the bed,
         A mvog tada, ngog,   to descendants of my father.

      b. *A ke di a ke bekon*   Now he goes into the dead.

      c. *Mi a nga bara fe ma yen*   What else will you tell me?

      d. *bela bela bebe bebe*   three by three, two by two

      e. *A bɔngɔ be mvog Okɔm*   to children of the lineage of
                                        Okɔm.

      (Abega 1987:356–78)

(58)   The promise we promissed [sic] is fulfilled to-day (a Sunday
        morning call, Anonymous 1911:141).

(59)   If you are sleeping, wake up. The morning things (the cock, the
        partridge) have finished speaking...Come give me my
        toothbrush, I'm going to brush my teeth.

(60)   Your friends are already gathered at my house, in my dirty little
        village.

(61)   He has gone beyond the end (boundary between the living and
        the dead).

(62)   Christians and catechumens, come all of you, toil at doctrine. No
        one has sent you (each one has come freely). Come keep your
        promise (to go to doctrine). The words of the doctrine are truth.
        Do not treat the doctrine as a joke.

(63)   *Bibuk nnem wakobo; anyu toe fala bisoe.*
        Everything the heart speaks, the mouth cannot say all.
        (Guillemin 1948)

(64)   *Mot te dzo na.*   No one should say this.

        Mine wulugu avol mbil.   You walk quickly.

        Onga ke a kumnion.   You come to communion.
        (Nkili 1975/76)

Each of these phrases correlates with a phrase in Antoine's repertoire,
or is exactly the same. As Antoine re-creates each performance, he draws
on the common stock of Ewondo speech surrogate drum phrases. Examples (58), (62), and the last line of (64) are peculiar to church leaders,
while most are also used in other contexts.

A phrase may have an almost identical acoustic shape (surface structure) in various contexts, but the implications of the phrase may be very
different. A command to "wake up!" carries different connotations
whether drummed to the community in early morning or addressed to
the deceased at a funeral.

Being defined as ritual speech, these common stock phrases are "continually subject to the historical processes of recontextualization...[They are]
negotiable in significance and application to present conditions" (Du Bois
1992:336). At least some common stock phrases are apparently polysemous
according to context: 'to descendents of my father' can refer to several

'fathers' including lineage founders and God. 'Sword-hanging-at-hip' is used to refer to various authority figures, including colonial administrators and God.

The common stock formulas existing within the Ewondo speech surrogate system manifest the three qualities of what Friedrich (1986) terms "poetic indeterminacy": the formulas may be drummed in an indefinite number of contexts. They have continuous ambiguity of meaning and speak beyond the immediate situation. Oral language is altered to fit within the constraints of a specialized poetic tradition.

The cultural identity of the Ewondo people (cf. Ngumu 1985) is expressed in their common property of the *nkul* and in numerous common stock phrases heard on the drum. The history of the Ewondo speech surrogate drum in a church context goes back at least to 1911 (Anonymous 1911) in Cameroon and in a nonchurch context goes back to time immemorial. Through use of formulas passed down for generations, Antoine and other *nkul* drummers, both previous and present, create this art with collective action.

In addition, the personal identity of each speech surrogate drummer is expressed in what he does with the common stock phrases, and with his own phrases developed for the immediate speech community. Antoine's discourse paradigm is partly idiolect and partly community property.

The drummed poems are brought to life through an individual's creative act *(parole)* and socially stereotyped phrases *(langue)*. The building material of common stock formulas is supra-individual, while other formulas and the arrangement of them all are connected with specific speech communities and drummers.

All formulas in the tradition are not known to all the performers. Those known by all represent "the most common and most useful ideas" (Lord 1960:49). No two drummers have identical repertoires of formulas or use them in the same way.

Phrases which are now in the common stock probably had individual origins and their own life stories including transmission and adaptation within the Ewondo speech community (cf. Nettl 1983:111).

The process by which phrases are created, codified, and transmitted through time and space affects the "finished product," i.e., the fleeting performance. "With oral poetry we are dealing with a particular and distinctive process in which oral learning, oral composition, and oral transmission almost merge; they seem to be different facets of the same process" (Lord 1960:5). What is transmitted is a set of bones and joints, a group of phrases and potential ways of joining them in performance. Common stock phrases may appear in various genre's skeletons. They must be known by the community phrase by phrase, and not only embedded in one discourse genre.

There is a limited number of drum phrases in current use, but the full repertoire is slowly changed to meet new community needs. Phrases commonly used at any given time are in a closed corpus, but the phrase corpus is modified when necessary. This holds true for the entire Ewondo speech surrogate system as well as for each component performance paradigm.

Each single performance is synchronic, while "tradition is nothing if not diachronic" (Foley 1981c:124). The entire paradigm, including drum phrases, meaning, context, function, and strategies of creation and comprehension, has roots in the past from which the present identity grows.

Common stock phrases exist in potential use until aurally manifested in a particular performance. The drum phrases themselves are not potential, for they have had a lengthy existence in a community's memory. It is their use in a given performance that is potential.

Surface structure and deep structure of drum language formulas

Linguistically, surface structure is the actual utterance (or drum pattern). Deep structure reflects the underlying fundamental semantic and logical relationships between words and meanings (here, in the context of performance).

In most speech, one deep structure concept can be heard with various surface structures, i.e., one thought can be reworded several ways. In the context of drummed speech surrogates, the surface structure is often permitted little variance. Many variants would lead to incomprehension of communication.

The deep structure is the semantic base of the signified verbal text. The signified surface structure of words is encoded in formulaic tonal-rhythmic patterns on the drum as perceived surface structure. The perceived surface structure system (phonology of drumstrokes) shapes the sound of the signified surface structure. The signified surface structure (words) provides material to be audibly shaped on the drum. The semantic deep structure of the Ewondo language provides meaning relationships between the words.

Speech rhythm and drum rhythm

It is asserted that rhythm is the organizing principle of ordinary speech and language in general (Scollon 1981:335). When African musical patterns are produced on instruments, the patterns are often connected with speech, either nonsemantic mnemonic syllables or semantic phrases. Harps, flutes, drums, and bells play musical patterns that correlate to short verbal patterns. Often these patterns are not combined in the sense of a true speech surrogate; rather, the verbal patterns are pedagogical or aesthetic in nature, meant for teaching or enjoyment.

Kubik writes that several factors make this verbal-instrumental relationship common and effective, including relationships of tone, timbre, and phrasing. "Syllabic or syllabic-verbal patterns generally deputize for musical phrases in African cultures—and the reverse" (1984:324).

Musical rhythm and speech rhythm can interact in two different ways. In some musical systems, a small set of metrical, melodic formulas "preceded and shaped the composition of the [song] texts" (Cable 1975:11). These melodic formulas filtered out the verbal patterns that were unacceptable in the melodic/text song fusion. In Old English poetry, the deep structure contains "a set of rhythmical predispositions [meter] from which the lexical reality of the verbal formula takes its shape" (Foley 1981a:273). The rhythm pattern of the meter predetermines the verbal formula. Suprasegmental features shape the words.

In a nonmetric speech surrogate system, the opposite process takes place: the verbal formula predetermines the tonal-rhythmic pattern. Speech tone and speech rhythm lead to drum tone and drum rhythm; spoken words shape the suprasegmental drumstrokes.

In speech, "rhythm functions mainly to organize the information bearing elements of the utterance into a coherent package, thus permitting speech communication to proceed efficiently" (Allen 1975:84). In a speech surrogate system, rhythm is itself an "information bearing element of the utterance." A series of tones drummed in a haphazard rhythm will not carry verbal, semantic weight. In cognition studies of Western tonal music, rhythm was found to be just as important an organizing principle as tonality, and the two systems are mutually interactive (Sloboda 1985:188).

In some African languages, speech rhythm could be said to be phonemic; that is, it determines the meaning of contrastive pairs with identical tonal patterns and phonemes (Agawu 1987:406).

In the Ewondo speech surrogate system, speech rhythm is modified to match a fairly regular pulse to create long and short durations in the temporal ordering of drumstrokes. The surface structure of the signified verbal phrase leads to the perceived surface structure of the drum pattern. The latter is related to the rhythm of the oral phrase, but noticeably distinct. The drummer's musical aesthetics control and shape the verbal material in sound-patterning (cf. Canale 1983:19). Formulas are established and remembered not only as verbal phrases, but as phrases whose tonal-rhythmic patterns have been adjusted to be striking in terms of "pure sound."

For examples outside of Antoine's performance paradigm, note the drum patterns played by Benoit in (65).

(65)

9/8 za dzam- ə di- za dzam- ə a dze-
What is this, for what reason?

9/8 n- kia ngon   a- dze- meg a dze
The mother-in-law dances so well!

These drummed phrases are easily recognizable as sound patterns throughout Benoit's lengthy performance. Based on speech, they are "structured configurations of pure duration and contour" (Yeston 1976:36) that create coherent musical patterns.

Comparison of spoken and drummed phrases

Some writers claim that drum languages "exclusively use language melody and language rhythm" (said by Heepe [1920/1976:332] about Ewondo). Data from Antoine's performances demonstrates that the tonal/rhythmic contours of speech and speech surrogate are related but can hardly be claimed to be identical.

Examples (66)–(71) give sample phrases from the recorded performance paradigm, comparing tonal-rhythmic patterns drummed by Antoine with corresponding tonal-rhythmic patterns spoken by Innocent with standard vowel elision.

(66)   DRUMMED   SPOKEN

o ko- do a-si   o ko- do a- si
you leave the bed

(67)

♪ ♪   ♩ ♩
  ♪

ko- do- gan a- si
[all of you] leave the bed

3
♪ ♪ ♪ ♩

ko- dan a- si

(68) ♩   ♪ ♩ ♪ ♩
      ♩   ♪ ♩

mi zu wo- go do- a- te- ne
you come hear doctrine

♩   ♪   ♪♪
    ♩   ♩

mi zu wog- o do- ten

(69)   ♪ ♩ ♩ ♩ ♩
♩ ♩   ♪♪   ♪

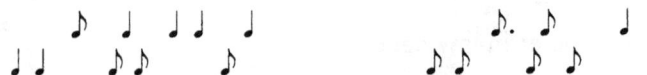

a- ke di a- ke a n- da-
now it goes in the house [church]

♪. ♪   ♩
♪ ♪   ♪ ♪

a- ke di a- kan- da

(70)   ♩ ♩
♪ ♩ ♪ ♩   ♩

wo o- ka- tə man- yon
you tell it in turn to your brother

♩ ♪ ♩ (mid)
♩ ♪♪

wo o- kat- ə man- yon

(71)
♩ ♩ ♩   ♪   ♩♩
    ♩   ♩ ♪

ki- di ndzoˉe- len- de- ya- hm
morning—the day has already dawned

♪ ♩ ♪   3
         ♪   ♩
♩ ♪ ♪ ♪

ki- di n- dzo e- len- de- ya hm

Five of the six spoken phrases have different tones as well as different rhythm patterns when drummed. False syllables may be added as in (68), short duration becomes long (in all examples) and vice versa as in (70), or tones may be elaborated as in (69). The drummed patterns generally follow the rough tonal contours of speech, while the rhythm is much more stylized in the drummed phrases, becoming a regular duple pulse. Speech patterns with a triplet feel, such as (66), (67), and (71), are changed on the drum into duple patterns. The aural aesthetics of the drummer modify word sounds into musical sounds, and the resultant sound-patterning becomes codified and memorable.

In the Akan speech surrogate language of Ghana, a short drumstroke can represent three syllable types: V, CV, or syllabic nasal (Nketia 1971a:715). It seems that the Ewondo drum language system has no such clear-cut correlations between drumstroke duration and syllable type. The choice of long or short drumstroke seems to be based more on creating a memorable drum rhythm than on slavishly imitating the rhythm of speech.

This is an area in which metrical phonology could perhaps shed some light, but it is beyond the scope of this study (see Jackendoff and Lerdahl 1982 for metric phonology rules connected with music).

Rhythmic patterns across verbal formula boundaries

It is not uncommon for a perceived surface structure pattern to cross boundaries of two verbal formulas. In (72) from Antoine's final stanza, two formulas are played without pause. The end of the first formula has a four-note pattern which is identical to the start of the second formula. When hearing these formulas front-to-back, this four-note pattern is highlighted through repetition of sound patterning.

(72)

a- ke di a- ke a n- da   mi- nin- ga ba- re-ə fe- ge ma dʒo˜a- ya
Now it goes in the   You will say to me what else
house [church].   [excuses]?

In (73), the first formula ends with three long notes. The second formula begins with two long notes. When the phrases are contiguous without pause, a striking pattern of five long notes in a row is created which crosses the boundaries of the oral formulas:

(73)

be- ke- ri- se- te- ne a- ke di a- ke a n- da-
Christians,   now it goes in the house [church].

When either of these examples (and others) is heard, the focus of attention is drawn to the repeated sound pattern in the middle which crosses formula boundaries. The mind is caught by the perceived surface structure and moves away from the signified verbal formula.

Universals of rhythmic speech

Rhythmic universals of speech "act from within phonology rather than as external constraints on performance" (Allen 1975:83). These same universals are found in Antoine's drum speech. Allen has described three rhythmic universals of ordinary speech:

1. Simple rhythms will be made of accent alternation and succession. Antoine's rhythms are made of alternating and succeeding short and long drumstrokes.
2. The role of succession of syllables should be less than one second. Counting short and long drumstrokes together, a section of performance 3 was timed at an average of about eight drumstokes per second, for an approximate metronome marking of ♩=300.
3. The variability in speech rhythm should conform to the variability of other skilled motor acts, a range of three to eleven percent. The speed and steadiness of Antoine's drum rhythms have some slight variability (see performance 2 for an example).

Homophonous surrogate signs and meaning-based drum patterns

Occasionally, one speech surrogate phrase may be given two verbal interpretations, i.e., one perceived surface structure drum pattern represents two verbal deep structures. In technical terms, two identical drum patterns are "homophonous surrogate signs for non-homophonous lexical items of the base language" (Sebeok and Umiker-Sebeok 1976:xvi). One Ewondo example is given by Marfurt (1957:29): the drum patterns are identical for *teble tebe* 'death, irreversible' and *zamba enya abele* 'it is God who holds him' (the second phrase presumably has two vowel elisions to give five drumstrokes for each phrase).

I found several examples of homophonous surrogate signs in Antoine's discourse paradigm. In (74), a different motion verb is meant depending on the immediate discourse context. Another change is the duration of the final two drumstrokes of the phrase.

(74) a.
mi- a zu mi- a wu- lu
you come, you walk (three by three)

b.
mi- a zu mi- a wu- lu
you come, you walk (honorable people)

c.
mi- a ke mi- a wu- lu
you go, you walk (aimlessly)

The signified verbal text changes according to which co-occurrent cluster the phrase appears in. The perceived surface structure pattern of the phrase also changes slightly, but at phrase end, not where the words change. The three conditioned variants of the formulaic phrase stayed consistent in each of the contexts above in every performance recorded. The meaning and sound pattern of the drummed phrase change from one co-occurrent cluster to another, but they remain stable within a particular cluster.

In speech surrogate drumming in general, when a single drum pattern has two different verbal interpretations, sometimes discourse or performance context will make one clearly correct. Other times, the basic meaning will be the same for both generated from one deep structure. In Antoine's repertoire, no whole drum pattern gets two completely divergent verbal interpretations; rather, related words may be used in paradigmatic relationship within the formula, or receive different interpretations.

Interpretive ambiguity of verbal phrases was found in comparing drum patterns between two neighboring catechists. The differences in (75)–(77) were found when playing a cassette of Antoine's drumming for Atemengue and asking for verbal interpretations.

(75) ♩   ♩   ♩
        ♪   ♩ ♪ ♪ ♩
     a mi- nin- ga zu du- e- ban when you came for baptism
     (Antoine)

        a mi- nin- ga zu ti- li- ban   when you came to be registered
     (Antoine)

        a mi- nin- ga zu ti- i- ndi   when you promised
     (Atemengue)

(76) ♩ ♪ ♪ ♩ ♪   ♪ ♪ ♩   ♩ ♪
     ♩   ♩ ♪ ♪ ♩   ♪   ♪
     a bo-ne be fam a- la- dag a bo-ne be bi- nin- ga- (Antoine)
     a bo-ne be fam a- fu- lan a bo-ne be bi- nin- ga- (Atemengue)
     to children-males added to children-females
     to children-males mixed with children-females

(77)

bi-bu-gi bi do-a-te-ne bi-ne- ə ma ko-koa a mo (Antoine)
bi-bu-gi bi do-a-te-ne bi-ntu- ə ma ko-koa a mo (Atemengue)
words of doctrine, they are not in my hands
words of doctrine became absent from my hands

We see that in some cases, a single drum pattern can have two or three verbal interpretations, but that they are all related in meaning (generated from one deep structure). The semiotic connection is somewhat direct between sound pattern on the drum (perceived surface structure) and meaning (deep structure), and purposefully not tied to a single set of words (signified surface structure). A multiplicity of verbal interpretations does not necessarily hinder use of a formula, but can even enhance it as the related meanings take on broader implications.

Meanings are created within the Ewondo gestalt. Meanings are expressed in words, and words expressed in drumstrokes, to achieve a particular social end. We see that the speech communities of Mekomba and Mfou-villáge use identical drum patterns to represent differing verbal phrases. In all of the examples in this section except (60), however, the verbal phrases share one semantic deep structure, and the basic meaning is not affected by assigning variant verbal texts to one drum pattern.

The Ewondo speech surrogate system utilizes meaning-based drum patterns: in some cases, a particular tonal-rhythmic configuration represents a general deep structure concept more than it represents a single oral phrase.

In the Dagbamba speech surrogate context, phrases are learned first as musical patterns, secondly as verbal phrases (Locke 1990:108). In the Ewondo context, where the speech surrogate function is uncommon in musical settings, drum patterns are learned as verbal phrases first.

Fixity versus fluidity of performance creativity

Besides the differences between metric and rhythmic frameworks for formulas, perhaps the major differences are connected with the surface structure fixity or fluidity of formulas. Formulas change according to the need of the performer, situation, and community.

The formulaic technique of speech surrogate drummers was developed to serve the community. The stability of a speech surrogate formula also comes from its utility, but in this case in mass media communication where fixed surface structure is paramount.[36] Bound formulas do not mean bound artists. The tight restrictions of haiku poetry and bonsai tree shaping of Japan do not lead to lesser art, but to greater appreciation for the beauty constrained within the form.

In Ewondo drum poetry, the skillful new creation takes place at the higher discourse levels. Formulas are fairly fixed in form and memorized by the speech community, and new phrases are infrequent.

An artist in a speech surrogate medium does not mechanically juxtapose common stock phrases in fixed units. Rather, he channels his personal creativity within the culture's communication code. In some societies, there may be no expectations for an aurally perceived artist to be original or different from other performers. The main expectation may not be for creativity but for technical skill in performance, a sound event that meets the community's needs and standards.

There are two different ways to be creative or original. "The first involves the invention of new rules... The second sort of originality...[involves] discerning new strategies for realizing the rules" (Meyer 1989:31). In some contexts the former may be expected and appreciated; it is more common for new compositional strategies to be developed that stay within the existing system.

Each of Antoine's performances manifests a new strategy (aural discourse structure) for realizing the rules (use of stereotyped drum patterns) to meet the community's needs (regular church summons) with high standards (technical skill in performance). The tradition of formulas (potential set of drum patterns) is sustained and changed twice a week, as some phrases are used, some omitted, and all are heard in a rapid and fleeting paratactic structure.

Niangoran-Bouah states that the speech surrogate drummer "is merely a technician. He is not an artist, he is not inventing, he is not improvising" (1981:4). I disagree with this statement and feel Antoine can hardly be called "merely a technician." Within the constraints inherent in the system, Antoine does demonstrate creativity through personal artistry, invention within tradition, and performance improvisation at discourse levels.

Formula in the Ewondo speech surrogate context

Parry's original concept of formula included an abstract syntactic or metrical frame which could be filled by words in paradigmatic relationship. It has been shown that none of the speech surrogate formulas in

---

[36]In the Ewondo speech surrogate context, the drummed formula is the offspring of the marriage of thought and pragmatics: how to speak to many people at one time through a hollow log mass medium.

Antoine's repertoire have a limiting syntactic or metrical frame. Most of the formulas are syntagmatic in nature, realized as nonvariable surface structure drum patterns.

There are differences in formula among African speech surrogate systems. In the Ewondo speech surrogate system, the basic unit is the formulaic phrase whose tradition-dependent characteristics are:[37]

1. a tonal-rhythmic pattern iconically representing a word or group of words, usually operating at the phrase level, or a nonverbal phrase (for example, stall pattern or closing stanza marker);
2. regularly employed in the same tonal-rhythmical pattern (one basic surface structure, with possible variations for a few phrases);
3. expresses a given idea (one concept in deep structure has one surface structure realization, though some formulas may be widely used in various contexts with differing implications);
4. combined into variable lines, co-occurrent clusters, stanzas, and formulaic units in performance;
5. socially created and maintained (by the speech community as much as by the performer);
6. may belong to a shared common stock of formulas with static surface form passed down through generations;
7. may be location-sensitive (recognized by members of only one village);
8. the verbal phrase provides the raw material which is modified to fit the tones and durations used on the drum (i.e., mid tone is lost and temporal spacing of drumstrokes is fairly regular). Musical aesthetics of sound patterning shape the words into memorable contours of time and tone on the drum;
9. most formulas are syntagmatic both inter- and intra-textually, with a few paradigmatic formulas (having parts which can be substituted); and
10. a tonal-rhythmic pattern may have more than one acceptable verbal interpretation which are often location-sensitive.

Having listed these characteristics does not mean we have reached an emic viewpoint of what a formula is. Rosenberg makes an important point:

> With a fixed text in front of us we can define formulas as precisely or as liberally as we choose, but the singers are not thinking in terms of formulas and systems. One of the problems in defining these terms comes about because they are the scholar's attempts to

---

[37] I am extrapolating knowledge from a few drummers to be broadly applicable within the entire Ewondo speech surrogate system.

impose a logical precision, a rationale, and a method where no such logical, rational method exists in the field—the singer's mind. (1975:98)

Composition in performance necessitates thinking on the move using whatever will work to accomplish the communicative, aesthetic, and social goals. Within an aurally perceived performance, the discourse arrangement is quickly heard then fades. The logical, rational method comes from the heart, Antoine would say, and as soon as one phrase is begun on the drum he must have another prepared. Each formula is a tool ready for potential use; the performance is the thing.

A formula is required in a particular discourse context when what can be said (content), how it is said (form), when and where it is said (context), who says it (performer), and why it is said (function) are to some extent rigidly set by social convention within the speech community (cf. Pawley 1992:22).

In everyday conversation, the English greeting, *Hello, how are you?*, generally meets the above standards for a formulaic expression. All speech is formulaic to a lesser or greater extent (Rosenberg 1975:100), and written texts may be just as formulaic as those orally composed (Fry 1981:173, Friedrich 1986:23). Due to the peculiarities in mass media function, sociolinguistic setting, and surface structure encoding within speech surrogate systems, however, these systems are among the most formulaic types of communication possible. Okpewho states that "the formulary device is simply a case of memory pressed into a pattern of convenience..." (1977:190). In speech surrogate systems of pure prosody, the formula is more than convenient, it is a necessity.

The totality of Antoine's what, how, when, where, who, and why are set by social convention in which the drummer is personally expressive primarily by choosing and reordering the formulaic phrases in his repertoire.

Arrangement of standardized, shared formulas during performance is the main way that an African drummer in speech mode is personally expressive.

Some formulas are limited to certain situations. A few are used only in a single community—those relating to lineage, founders, and the village's name. Perhaps, in his sixty years of drumming, Antoine has created some formulas to express something new that had no pre-established drum formula.

The intent of much speech surrogate communication is not to be personally expressive but to serve the community by broadcasting news, offering praise or insults, and summoning as needed. A speech surrogate system, including the formulas that make up each performance, is "a social institution: a culturally standardized recipe for binding utterance context, function, [content, performer], and form" (Pawley 1992:23).

Formulas are pervasive in ordinary language, both spoken and written. Formulas are constitutive of speech surrogate language.

8
Discourse Analysis of the Performance Paradigm

Comparative discourse analysis

Very little discourse analysis has been done on speech surrogate performance texts (cf. Kropp Dakubu 1971 and Arom 1976). One sort of analysis can be done of a single, supposedly representative text pulled out of the corpus. Another sort is advocated by Peacock in his studies of Javanese drama:

> Rather than searching for a single story "representative" of the type I wished to analyze, I confronted all the available variants and tried to construct a model which accounted for all of them. That model was composed of a set of components, all of which were manifested in the variant tales, though differently colored in each...The approach has the advantage of forcing the analyst to come to grips with the variations in a corpus instead of allowing him to vaguely survey the corpus, pick a case, and present it as "representative" of the not-yet analyzed corpus. The approach also leads us to treat the variants as parts of a system in flux, each variant being defined not as an independent type but according to the ways it contrasts with other variants. (1971:165–66)

Such an analytic approach suits a study of Antoine's performances in the paradigm. Each one is not to be analyzed as an independent type, but

107

as it contrasts with other performances. Each performance is composed of a set of components. The broad discourse features are manifested in each performance, but the total corpus of roughly one hundred textual phrases is not heard each time.

Simply listing recurrent features is not sufficient for analysis. A collection of formulas based solely on counting their appearances would be a decontextualized fiction, though helpful to an etic analysis. Structuralist method advocates that separate parts can best be explained in terms of the relations possible between the parts. The network of relationships that links elements is as important as the elements themselves (Chase 1972:121).[38]

An adequate analysis should highlight the genre and the component separate performances. The idiosyncracies should not be ignored because their presence in the discussions of both langue (implying genre) and parole (implying performance) is necessary for the fullest understanding.

The comparative study of an individual's repertoire, situated in shared genre and specific performance, can reveal how aesthetic and structural choices are made within a performance and from performance to performance. It provides a framework to study personal creativity within a larger cultural tradition and to analyze variants within one genre (see Abrahams 1970 for an American example). The genre and tradition are continually being re-created in this aural art with each performance. A new poem (focusing on performance structure) or a new performance of a poem (focusing on paradigm) has been manifested twice a week for more than forty years in Mekomba.

Textual variation may be approached through macroscopic and microscopic analyses (Biber 1988:61–63). These two approaches are mutually dependent and bring complementary understanding to the analyst. In this study, macroscopic analysis looks at the overall parameters of variation within the recorded performance paradigm of a genre. Microscopic analysis is used to determine the communicative functions of individual linguistic features and specific drum phrases in particular performance texts.

The roughly four thousand performances that Antoine has drummed in Mekomba are related, but not in the sense of an original and variants. Each performance is an original which will probably not be repeated exactly the same way. Performance 6 and the first half of performance 7 are similar, but comparison of the details shows a handful of differences in repetition of phrases (both textual and the stall pattern) and placement of pauses. These are minute details, but they do indicate that exact repetition of a drummed speech act is unlikely. Similarly, in an oral

---

[38]The structuralist view seeks the smallest significant units of a sign system. The emic emphasis of Ewondos would tend to be nonstructuralist, focused on process at formula level and higher. I have tried to integrate both approaches in this study.

speech act, any repetition of a text would also be inexact at a phonetic level. Units may be emically identical, that is, noncontrastive in context, at either a very low level according to linguistics (a set of phonetic allophones) or a very high level according to function and meaning (a set of speech acts).

Exact repetition is not a goal that is strived for in the Ewondo speech surrogate system and would not be discernible without a tape recorder. The differences between performance 1 and performance 2 are much greater than those between performance 6 and performance 7, but these greater differences are also emically insignificant. Within Antoine's paradigm of drum phrases awaiting potential use, the choosing and ordering of some phrases over others seems of little importance (except for the final stanza) and has little effect on the general meaning of the discourse. Differences would be considered significant if phrases specific to one catechist were used by another drumming catechist. Antoine said that Mekomba residents would think "a stranger is drumming" if he used drum phrases that were peculiar to Atemengue a few kilometers away.

Longacre (1983) has posited a fivefold division of discourse that can be applied to many discourse types around the world. This framework can be indicated as follows when modified to fit Antoine's performance paradigm. Each section will be examined in detail:

1. Aperture or direct address phrases
2. Stanzas: Paratactic arrangement
          Co-occurrent clusters
          Temporal linearity and nonlinearity
          Unpredictability of analysis
   2.a. Beginning stanza
   2.b. "To descendants of my father"
   2.c. Stall pattern: *ku ku ku ku lu ku ku ku*
   2.d. Use of proper names in vocatives
   2.e. Pauses: poetic line markers
3. Peak (in final stanza)
4. Poetic closure (in final stanza)
5. Finis: Rhythmic nonverbal coda

Aperture

While Longacre speaks of apertures opening narrative discourses, an Ewondo-specific term for what begins Antoine's hortatory performances would be direct address phrases, or vocatives. Each performance begins with one of the two opening phrases in (78) and (79).

(78)   *a bon be fam aladag a bon be bininga*
       to children-males in addition to children-females
       ya engokomo mvog owondzuli
       of the tree of the descendants of Owondzuli

(79)   *bekristen bese ya mekomba*
       Christians, all of Mekomba

These phrases are also repeated and used freely elsewhere in the discourses, even in the penultimate stanza of performance 10.

It has been noted that in the Ewondo speech surrogate system it is customary for a drummer to first call the name of his selected audience, then play his own drum-call name (Atangana and Messi 1919:303–6, Nkili 1975/76:129). It is interesting that Antoine never directly identifies himself as the performer, but he may refrain from doing so because it is obvious in context to all Mekomba residents. Antoine always identifies his audience as a group in the opening lines by reference either to a lineage founder or the name of the village, and both of these direct address phrases are repeated throughout the discourse.

In some Bulu/Ewondo villages the church drummer "calls the roll of drum-names as an invitation to the services" (Good 1942:74). In Good's example it took about twenty minutes to call fifty-two people by their drum names (and the drummer reportedly could have gone up to 200 drum names). This large time appropriation may be the reason why Antoine uses drum phrases to address people in groups and not as individuals.

In my analysis there is no exclusive aperture to Antoine's performances, but two opening phrases which are freely used elsewhere as well. Hence, direct address phrases seems a more appropriate designation in these speech surrogate performances than aperture. Antoine's performances have no phrase restricted to opening frame marker.

Stanzas

A perusal of the transcribed performances will quickly reveal there is not one text, but a set of ten variants or re-creations. These ten transcriptions give some insight into text change within a four-month period. If we assume that such variability has occurred over Antoine's forty-year period as Mekomba's drumming catechist, we have a total of roughly four thousand performances (one hundred a year times forty years) of a regularly scheduled but variable communication transaction. There is no way for anyone, even Antoine, to know precisely how the performances have changed through the decades or even from week to week.

Paratactic arrangement. Many discourses are nonparatactic in nature; they progress logically or temporally, such as in a narrative. In these texts, changing or omitting a section will tend to bring confusion, even incomprehensibility, to the audience. In Antoine's paratactic structure, sections and individual phrases are added, omitted, repeated, and exchanged from one performance to another with no loss of general meaning. The basic requirement is that the arrangement of the discourse make sense syntactically and semantically. The discourse is much more than an alarm clock. It is a series of persuasive arguments which do not logically build upon each other. Rather, they keep their self-contained impact together no matter when they are heard in the drummed discourse.

As an example, let us compare the use of a typical formulaic unit in different performances. The most common unit form, consisting of three aural lines marked with the bar, is given in (80).

(80) a. *mina beben a minga lig zulu metin e*
         you yourselves made promises [appointment]

      b. *a minga zu duban*
         when you came for baptism

      c. *ku ku ku ku lu ku ku ku*
         [stall pattern]

      d. *mi wulugu avol dulu a mekol e*
         you walk with quickness in the feet

      e. *mi zu kpaan zulu metin e*
         you come and fulfill your promises [appointments]

This exact form occurs in performances 1, 2, 4, 8, 9, and 10. In performance 7, the stall pattern is repeated in the middle of the textual phrases. The discourse context on either side of this unit is the same in four cases, and different before and/or after this phrase in three other cases. The unit is heard twice in four performances and is omitted entirely in performance 3.

Other forms of the unit appear as well. The formula in (80b) is omitted in performances 5, 7, and 9. Only (80a) and (80e) are used in performance 4. In performance 10, (80a), (80c), and (80d) are used, but the last one is separated from the first two by three other formulas. The formula in (80a) never appears in isolation, but no one of the other four possible formulas is obligatory to always complete it.

The formulas in this unit may be added, omitted, and repeated in diverse ways from performance to performance. Out of twelve occurrences in the recorded corpus, the unit has no single form which is more stable than another, and is changed according to the drummer's desire at the moment of performance. This structural change does not affect the meaning and theme of the discourse as a whole.

Other verbal forms built with paratactic arrangement of units include Akan *apee* praise poetry (Boadi 1989:182), Yoruba speech surrogate drumming (Euba 1991:393), Berber poetry (Harries 1973:143), Basotho migrants' narrative songs related to praise poetry (Coplan 1987:29), and some American blues songs (Jarrett 1985:163). In all of these oral arts, the poetical unit, whether line or verse, tends to be independent and can be shifted in relative position from one performance to another, or even within one performance, without emically affecting the discourse. In all of these African-based poetical forms, such unit interchange and rearrangement is the expected norm and taken for granted.

Co-occurrent clusters. In some cases phrases are combined in the same order to make a larger section. This section or unit either appears as a fairly stable unit or is omitted as a unit from performance to performance. Such a unit can be considered a CO-OCCURRENT CLUSTER shown in (81).

(81)   *a mvog tara ngogo*   To descendants of my father,
       nge mina bombo asi   if you lie in bed,
       ma mebombo asi   I will lie in bed.
       ma mena a za ebugu   For me it is what concern?

This cluster appears in the majority of performances as a unit, or is omitted as a unit in a few cases. The immediate discourse context is not always the same; this is a self-contained unit, though the initial formula is frequently used in numerous co-occurrent clusters. Within a genre's performance paradigm, certain formulas readily cross boundaries of co-occurrent clusters; in addition, some common stock formulas also readily cross genre boundaries such as 'descendants of my father'.

Another cluster which only appears as a complete unit is in (82).

(82)   *a mvog tara ngogo*   To descendants of my father,
       mot a kat wo dzam   someone tells you something,
       wo o kat manyon   you in turn tell your brother.

       ku ku ku ku lu ku ku ku

       bibug nnem wa kobo anyu te Everything the heart speaks,
       fali bise   the mouth cannot say all.

The co-occurrent cluster in (82) appears in most but not all of the ten recorded performances. Notice that two internal pauses are obligatory in this unit, on either side of the stall pattern. This cluster is usually, but not always, followed by the co-occurrent cluster in (83).

(83)   *mi zu mi wulu*   You come, you walk,
       ndenele minkumu   [nonchalantly] waving bodies [like tall
                                trees],
       mi zu wog doten   you come hear doctrine.

The tendency of some stanzas to follow other stanzas demonstrates that at the larger discourse level the ordering of stanzas is not completely ad hoc. "There is evidence that variables tend to be selected in *co-occurrent clusters*. In other words, the speaker's choice of a variable is always constrained by previous selections of variables" (Gumperz 1972:21). Co-occurrent clusters of formulas into lines, or clusters of lines into stanzas, are "one of the characteristic signs of oral style" (Lord 1960:58).

Interestingly, Antoine develops discourse through co-occurrent clusters which do not build upon each other logically, but are relatively unrelated in a paratactic fashion that is freely ordered to some extent.

Co-occurrent clusters are typical associations built through habit. In performance 10, two phrases were drummed which are common throughout the discourse. They were followed by *ekokodo ekokodo ekokodo* 'leave' with intensifier (which usually appears only in the final stanza) which was followed by three other common phrases. Altogether, the six phrases composed a unit similar to that heard in the final stanza after the discourse peak (one phrase was added and one was omitted in the early set of phrases). The set of phrases in a typical ending make up a co-occurrent cluster which, once begun early, was ended in a form closely related to its habitual form.

Studies of discourse ordering options suggest that what influences clause order in all speech forms is "prior surface information which contributes both semantically and pragmatically to the emerging text" (Schiffrin 1987:13–14). When an initial phrase is used, it will constrain subsequent development of the discourse and serve as a guide for future discourse decisions. When the beginning phrases of a co-occurrent cluster are drummed, the others will likely (but not positively) follow, with possible variations in placement of pauses and stall pattern.

The set of phrases in (84) is the beginning of a typical co-occurrent cluster used in performances 1, 2, and 9. Some phrases do not appear in all three performances and are indicated by parentheses.

(84) *(a mvog tara ngogo)*   to descendents of my father

      mot andziki lom mot   no one has sent me anyone

      ku ku ku ku lu ku ku ku   [stall pattern] (optional repeat)

These phrases are followed by the remaining five lines of the co-occurrent cluster with no variation. This cluster is in turn followed by another five-phrase co-occurrent cluster in which one direct address phrase may be substituted for another. The latter co-occurrent cluster has many potential placements in the paratactic ordering of units.

Temporal linearity and nonlinearity. Together, the principles of paratactic arrangement of units and co-occurrent clusters are what keep the poem going. The paratactic arrangement tends towards nonlinearity, co-occurrent clusters tend towards linearity. According to Kramer (1986), linearity is "the determination of some aspect(s) of music in accordance with expectations that arise from *earlier events* in the piece." Co-occurrent clusters are determined in this manner, as one phrase leads to another phrase. Nonlinearity is "the determination of some aspect(s) of music in accordance with expectations that arise from *principles or tendencies* governing an entire piece or section." The principle of paratactic arrangement of units determines the structure of the entire performance.

"Linearity and nonlinearity are the two fundamental means by which a piece of music structures its time and by which time structures a piece of music.... Virtually all music utilizes a mixture of linearity and nonlinearity" (Kramer 1986). These two forces push and pull the formulaic phrases into an ephemeral structure in performance, thereby arranging the phrases into different combinations each time the discourse is performed.

Unpredictability in analysis. The alert reader will notice that this part of the discourse analysis is full of modifying phrases. It is as etically impossible as it is emically irrelevant to declare the order and content of one version as absolute when examining the recorded performance paradigm. One section may appear in nine of ten performances, but is omitted in the last. One can speak of tendencies, but there are few absolutes as regards the evershifting arrangement of formulas through the process of composition-in-performance. Each performance in the paradigm exhibits a structured unpredictability which carries over into analysis.

Even how to mark a stanza is a problem for an analyst; looking at the use of various vocatives and the stall phrase and pauses does not provide any clear-cut form that remains constant between performances. The etic term stanza in this study refers to all the textual phrases between occurrences of *ku ku ku ku lu ku ku ku.* Since the performer sees fit to break up his discourses by this nonverbal drum phrase, so will the analyst. This analysis means there are between ten and sixteen stanzas in each recorded performance. Most stanzas may be from one to fifteen phrases long, while the opening stanza may be as long as twenty formulaic phrases.

The remainder of this stanza analysis section will compare occurrences of selected discourse features in the recorded performance paradigm including the beginning stanza, 'to descendants of my father', the stall pattern, the use of proper names, and pauses.

Beginning stanza. A typical beginning stanza keeps its form fairly consistently in eight of ten performances. The opening line can be either a one- or two-phrase line of direct address. This is followed by a twenty-phrase section which is fairly consistent, except with the alternatives that performance 4 omits one line, performances 6 and 7 switch the order of two lines, and performance 10 substitutes an alternate word.

Performances 2, 3, and 4 share the one-phrase opening line, *bekristen bese ya mekomba* 'Christians, all of Mekomba'.

Performances 1, 5, 6, 7, 8, 9, and 10 share the two-phrase opening line, *a bon be fam aladag a bon be bininga ya engokomo mvog owondzuli* 'to sons and daughters of the tree of the lineage of Owondzuli'. After the opening two-phrase line of direct address, performances 1 and 5 change considerably from all other performances and from each other.

The second half of this opening stanza contains a series of imperatives from the catechist to the congregation given in (85). The first five are in singular form, addressed to individuals. The final formula refers to the plural you.

(85)	*o man soban kpekpaaga*	You finish washing (teeth) with brush.
	o man soban mendim	You finish washing (face) with water.
	o kodo asi	You leave the bed.
	o non man ntu eyie	You take your small old cloth.
	o nga zu wawulu a zen ese	You come, you walk along the road.
	mi zu wog doten...	You come hear doctrine...

Though imperative commands appear throughout the discourse, they are gathered in this manner only in the stanza which usually appears in the beginning of the discourse. This series of imperative commands is completely omitted in performances 1 and 5 and repeated later in performances 7 and 8.

One formulaic phrase is *kidi—ndzoe elendeya hm* 'morning—the day has already dawned'. Usually appearing only in the opening stanza, it is also used in the penultimate stanza of performance 7.

a mvog tara ngogo: 'to descendants of my father'. The term *mvog* can be translated as lineage or descendants. In most drum genres the formula refers to a lineage of a specific Ewondo ancestor. Here, however, the father is interpreted as God.

The placement of *a mvog tara ngogo* in the various versions points out a pitfall of doing a standard discourse analysis on only one post-performance written text. In performance 10, the first five occurrences of the stall pattern *ku ku ku ku lu ku ku ku* are followed immediately by *a mvog tara ngogo*. An analyst using only this text could conceivably try to build a case that the latter phrase usually follows the former.

A comparison with performance 9, however, where *a mvog tara ngogo* appears after the fifth occurrence of the stall pattern but not until then, shows that no simple rules can be given. *a mvog tara ngogo* appears between three and seven times in each performance, in nonfixed nonobligatory locations, excluding the final stanza where its placement is fixed and obligatory. Two occurrences can come together with as few as three phrases intervening (performance 3) or come spaced apart with as many as thirty-two phrases intervening (performance 6).

The formula *a mvog tara ngogo* often acts as a stanza-beginning marker. Also, it often appears after *mvog owondzuli* and *mekomba* in the beginning stanzas and can follow *mba nnembe* 'name for lineage founder' and *akalan a benyia bodo mvia be fam* 'in addition to real (adult) people, pillars of men' wherever these phrases occur.

a mvog tara ngogo precedes fifteen different phrases in the recorded performance corpus, some as few as once. It is obligatory only when it occurs twice in the final stanza. Otherwise, it seems it can optionally appear at the performer's discretion. It tends to appear in the opening stanza (eight of ten times) and often marks a new stanza after *ku ku ku ku lu ku ku ku*.

Stall pattern: *ku ku ku ku lu ku ku ku*. The stall pattern appears between nine and fifteen times in each performance. The spacing of it throughout the text seems highly variable, with one to fifteen (performance 3) text phrases between the nonverbal stanza markers. It follows fifteen different text phrases, from two to fourteen times each. It is apparently obligatory for this nonverbal formula to follow eight of the phrases (but this restriction may be due to the small text corpus). After the other seven, it often appears but not always. It comes after every occurrence but one of a common closure phrase, *ake di a ke a nda* 'now it goes in the house'. In this case (performance 4), it is followed by *minga bar fe ma dzo aya* 'What other excuses will you give me?' which is usual only to complete the entire discourse.

This phrase is an example of *nkul wa kobo* 'drum it speaks' nonverbal sounds. It probably serves as an aural discourse marker, though it divides each discourse in a different way. As usual with most phrases in this corpus, a high variability exists as to when it is used within one performance and from performance to performance. Used as a floating discourse marker, it appears in groups of one to three according to the drummer's aesthetics and its necessity as a stall device in performance.

The formula's function as stall device is probably more important than its function as a discourse marker. Antoine automatically plays the rhythm phrase as a stall device, freeing his concentration to be focused on which phrase of the text will come next.

As mentioned above, there is a high variability of temporal spacing of the nonverbal stall phrase throughout a drummed discourse. From one to fifteen different textual phrases appear between occurrences of the stall phrase; in other words, it is used at highly irregular, uneven intervals. Rosenberg has aptly used the term "peristaltic" for this type of discourse progression: "several lines advance the action or idea rapidly and then progression halts ...to reflect upon the message" (1975:82–83).

This hesitation tactic is probably very necessary in speech surrogate discourse. Because a speech surrogate carries little phonetic information, an audience must concentrate much harder to comprehend all that is said. If a lengthy discourse is presented in a drummed speech surrogate mode without any stall device, the rate of new information coming at the audience can result in overload. The stall serves both performer and audience, though in different ways: the former thinks of what will be said next, while the audience reflects on what was said last.

Use of proper names. The performances use three proper names: those of the founders of the two main lineages, Owondzuli and Mba Nnembe, and the town name, Mekomba. Of these three names, Owondzuli is used most often, in seven of ten opening stanzas and nine other places. It appears in every performance except performance 3. Mba Nnembe appears once or twice in every performance but never in the opening stanza.

Mekomba is used three times; it is restricted to the opening stanza. It requires the same immediate context; the other two personal names have variable immediate contexts. The historical allusions in the text corpus are very strong; Owondzuli and Mba Nnembe appear a total of twenty-seven times in ten texts, both in almost every performance. These historical allusions may frame the body of the discourse: in performance 10, Owondzuli occurs in the opening and penultimate stanzas. In sharp contrast, the name of the village occurs only three times in the entire recorded corpus, though in a marked position, i.e., the opening line.

Pauses. Pauses are the most obvious marker of the drumming's aural structure. They are not in themselves communicatively significant as far as meaning is concerned (cf. Woodbury 1987:187), but do have a significant impact on the listener's segmentation and comprehension of the drum patterns.

The analyst expects pauses to occur in places determined by grammatical or semantic criteria. But in song and story as well as in speech surrogates, pauses may fall in unexpected and variable places. These variables of pause and line length occur in Antoine's performance paradigm.

His use of pauses in the Ewondo drumming do not show a consistent pattern from performance to performance. Compare two groups of pause breaks in one formulaic unit in (86).

(86)   *a mvog tara ngogo*   To descendants of my father,
        nge mina bombo asi   if you lie in bed,
        ma mebombo asi   I will lie in bed.
        ma mene a za ebugu   For me it is what concern?

In performance 8, each of the last three phrases is followed by a pause (marking three short oral lines). In performance 9 the entire unit is drummed as one long aural line with pause only at unit end.[39]

An analysis of the recorded performance paradigm reveals that the aural line length before a pause can vary from one word *kidi* 'morning' to the six phrases in the opening stanza of performance 1. This variability makes it impossible to report any standard line length based on where the pauses fall.

A line as marked by pause in the Ewondo performance paradigm under study is a flexible unit. One formula may be drummed as an aural line, part of a line, or containing several lines, and this may be changed from performance to performance. Formulaic phrases and aural lines are in tenuous relationship. The word *kidi* 'morning' is sometimes drummed as a two-note line bounded by pauses and sometimes as part of a longer line.

One feature found in much oral metric poetry, such as in ancient Greece or modern Yugoslavia, is ENJAMBEMENT. This is the continuation of a sentence beyond the end of the metric line. A feature found in nonmetric drum poetry could be called REVERSE ENJAMBEMENT: several complete sentences may be played without pause in a single aural line. The example in (87) is from performance 2.

---

[39]With few exceptions, a drum speech formula is not divided internally by a pause in Antoine's performance paradigm.

(87)   *bi ŋga maneya kobo*   ...they are finishing to speak.
        kidi ndzo elendeya hm   Morning—the day has already dawned.
        mot a be fe ke oyo   No one, he must no longer sleep.
        oman soban kpekpaa   You finish washing (teeth) with brush.

In Ewondo speech surrogate drumming, a pause may come after a very long utterance or in the middle of an utterance. In Antoine's performance paradigm, a pause may come after two drumstrokes or sixty-three drum-strokes (one partial verbal phrase or six verbal phrases), to measure the extremes. To use genre-specific criteria in this study, I define LINE aurally by pauses. Each line is made up of from one to six drum phrases. A phrase is defined lexico-structurally as a formula, a self-contained, tonal-rhythmic-verbal pattern that appears with little variation. Each formulaic phrase may be broken down into individual words and drumstrokes, manifested in patterns of short and long, high and low syllables.

Antoine's line lengths are not based on a regular rhythm or any other comon element of poetry, and neither do his line lengths follow the constraints of normal speech. Up to six phrases may immediately follow each other without a pause, whereas oral speech would surely include some breaks based on grammatical and semantic criteria. The example in (88) is the beginning line and stanza of performance 1 which has sixty-three drumstrokes before a pause.

(88)

a bo- nə be fam a-la-dag a bo- nə be bi- nin- ga-
    bon   bon
To children-males in addition to children-females

            ko-
ya en-go-   mo mvog o-wo-ndzu-li
of the tree of the lineage of Owono, the son of Ndzuli,

mi- ni wu- lu- gu˜ a- vo- lo du- lu a me- kol e-
            avol
you walk with quickness in the feet,

♩   ♪ ♩ ♪ ♩
♩   ♪ ♩
mi zu wo-go do- a-te- ne
    wog   doten
you come hear doctrine,

      ♪
♩ ♪   ♩ ♩ ♩
be- ke- ri- se- te- ne
bekristen
Christians,

     ♪ ♩ ♩ ♪
♩ ♩   ♪ ♪   ♩
a- ke di a- ke a n- da
now it goes in the house [church].

It seems that Antoine's aesthetic concept of musical phrases can override his sense of when to start and stop grammatical phrases. Aesthetics take precedence over easy comprehension in the case of this opening stanza of sixty-three drumstrokes, coming out of the dawn's silence without warning, to be immediately interpreted by the audience as six verbal phrases.

Peak

How does one do a discourse analysis when the discourse is a moving target? Perhaps by seeing if any part remains stationary. The concluding stanza, shown in (89) appears with minor variations at the end of each performance. It is one of few sections that is obligatory in each performance of the paradigm; it is the only section that is consistent in coming at the same place in each performance, and it is the longest stanza (eleven phrases plus rhythmic coda) of any that is obligatory in each version.

(89)   a mvog tara ngogo
         To descendants of my father,

         mot te bo na
         no one should do this:

         abog aye ke a wulu a suga bekon
         when he will go, he walks, to the end of the dead,

> *a ŋga kat kat ntondobe ofofoe na*
> he tells God, whispering over and over, that
>
> *bibug bi doten bi ne ma kokoa a mo*
> "words of doctrine, they are not in my hands."
>
> *mvog tara ŋgogo*
> Descendants of my father,
> *kodogan asi*
> [all of you] leave the bed.
>
> *ekokodo ekokodo ekokodo ekokodo*
> Leave [forever, carelessly, all at once].
>
> *mi zu wog doten*
> You come hear doctrine.
>
> *ake di a ke a nda*
> Now it goes in the house [church].
>
> *mi ŋga bar fe ma dzo aya*
> You will say to me what else [excuses]?

These structural features alone are enough to mark it as the discourse peak. Everything else may vary, but this closing stanza will be basically unchanged in every performance.[40] The final stanza in (90) includes the emotional peak of the discourse, and this three-phrase peak is the only section that cannot have anaphoric or cataphoric reference, i.e., it must appear only once and only in this place.

(90) *abog aye ke a wulu a suga bekon*
      When he will go, he walks, to the end of the dead

      a ŋga kat kat ntondobe ofofoe ne
      he tells God, whispering over and over, that

      bibug bi doten bine ma kokoa a mo
      words of doctrine, they are not in my hands

Every other phrase in the final stanza may have appeared previously. 'To descendants of my father' can potentially appear up to eight times earlier in a single performance. In stark contrast, these three peak

---

[40]This feature is also true of Atemengue's performance paradigm, though conclusions in this chapter should not be taken to represent the final stanza of all Ewondo drumming catechists.

phrases are never repeated in exactly this form; they are never drummed
in a redundant manner to ensure comprehension. They are if anything
more ephemeral than the rest of the aural discourse. They must be caught
by the audience as quickly as they are drummed.

Peak may be marked in a discourse through various linguistic devices.
Longacre (1983:39) suggests that the most frequent device used for marking surface structure peak in hortatory discourse is rhetorical
underlining. Rhetorical underlining uses such devices as paraphrase and
repetition to make the text go more slowly. Antoine's hortatory discourse
peak is strikingly not underlined in this manner; the rest of the discourse
could be said to be one long paraphrase and repetition of a single theme,
and the information load progresses very slowly from the audience's
perception. In contrast, the central three phrases of the peak stanza are
never paraphrased or repeated and pass very quickly. Part of the peak's
power comes from this structural change, and part comes from the grav-
ity of its theme: standing in the judgment, unprepared before an
awesome God, and whispering lame excuses into eternity. Both structural
and thematic evidence point to the peak in the discourse's final stanza.

Poetic closure

The body of this poem is generated based on a paratactic principle,
i.e., many parts can be omitted, repeated, and changed without loss of
meaning or impact. However, "a generating principle that produces a
paratactic structure cannot in itself determine a concluding point. Consequently, the reader [hearer] will have no idea from the poem's structure
how or when it will conclude" (Smith 1968:100). Since Mekomba residents have been hearing this drum poem for forty years, they have a very
good idea how it will end, and probably have some subjective time sense
of when it will end. The statement stands, however, that the temporal
placement of the poem's end cannot be predicted exactly from the body
of the poem. The paratactic structural principle cannot generate an ending stanza with an adequate sense of poetic closure; it can only produce
more unclosed stanzas. A paratactic structure in poetry can be closed in
various ways, but it cannot close itself (p. 102). Antoine's penultimate
stanza varies in each performance, with no clear, consistent indication
that the end is near.

A sense of closure "is a function of the perception of structure" (p. 4).
When the poem's structure changes with each performance, closure cannot be perceived until the cue is given: the formula *mot te bo na* 'no one
should do this' almost always signals the beginning of the end.

An exception to this usage can be seen in performance 2, where *mot
te bo na* signals the penultimate stanza, then is repeated a few phrases

later at the actual final stanza. Since the final stanza is the point at which structure can be most easily perceived and predicted, I would guess that the audience was as surprised as I at this uncommon placement of the formula. The cue for closure was given, but it led to a false final stanza. Aesthetic tension was set up as audience expectations were played with.

Though it contains the discourse peak, the final stanza can be seen as a tacked-on appendage, albeit one which fits naturally after the various penultimate stanzas used in the performance paradigm. This reflects Smith's observation that "one may secure closure for even the most unstructured work simply by appending to it an independently well-closed section" (1968:195). I believe that Antoine feels "I've said enough" at some point and begins to drum the final preformed stanza, which could be considered one large co-occurrent cluster.

In temporally perceived arts, formal structure and boundaries of structural units may not be easily recognized by an audience. The formula 'to all my father's descendents' signals the start of the final stanza but also appears several times previously in each performance. The initial boundary of the final stanza is only known in retrospect and cannot be predicted by what comes before (though it can be roughly predicted to come between two and three minutes into a performance).

Smith (1968) has produced a seminal study on the nuts and bolts of poetic closure (primarily in Western written poetry). A number of "terminal features" from her study can be found in Antoine's closing stanza. These include unqualified assertions; tone of authority; references to finality; sense of truth; summative phrases; and closural allusions.

An UNQUALIFIED ASSERTION "conveys a sense of the speaker's security, conviction, and authority. Since he did not guard or cover himself with implicit or explicit reservations, we assume that he did not need to" (p. 182). Antoine asserts that everyone who is a descendant of my father (God) should come with no exceptions; he also proclaims that no one should be found empty-handed before God in the judgment. These unqualified assertions are meant to be inclusive of the entire community and audience within Mekomba and to show Antoine's strong conviction about his topic and his authority to lead the village church. He is not drumming, "Wife, come and bring food"; he is drumming about the most important things in his life.

Antoine conveys a TONE OF AUTHORITY throughout the poem which does not cease in the final stanza. In a typical performance, he addresses the audience directly as 'you' and gives imperative commands twenty times, including several in the final stanza.

The reference to God's name in this final stanza alone lends weight, based on heavenly authority, to Antoine's imperative commands. Antoine is implying that if the village congregation does not gather now, they will have to answer to God for their inaction.

The final stanza, especially the peak, contains several REFERENCES TO FINALITY which are not present elsewhere in the poem. Each audience member is urged to consider his or her own personal journey 'to the end of the dead', and thereby to reflect upon his or her own mortality. Then comes an allusion to the last judgment, when each person might 'whisper to God over and over' the fact of their unpreparedness (if they do not get out of bed right now and come!). The catechist exhorts them to 'leave your beds, leave forever'. This stanza presents immediate church attendance as deadly serious through the references to finality.

A SENSE OF TRUTH is conveyed in the final stanza by the reference to God and by Antoine's final line, 'you will say to me what else?' Here he implies the people have no more excuses. Hearing this rhetorical question, the audience should have the sense that "what has just been said has the 'conclusiveness,' the settled finality, of apparently self-evident truth" (Smith 1968:152). Antoine implies he has exhausted his poetic skills to convince people of the obvious truth of his message, and they (he and God) are tired of peoples' excuses.

Another terminal feature used by Antoine in the final stanza is SUMMATIVE PHRASES. Closure effects may be brought about "when certain formal elements that appear throughout the poem (but not systematically) recur in its concluding lines" (Smith 1968:163). The phrase *bibug bi doten* 'words of doctrine' has appeared throughout the performance and neatly sums up the point of the poem.

The eight nonpeak phrases in the final stanza are all heard (in at least one performance) somewhere before this conclusion. Four of the eight (one is duplicated) listed in (91) are heard two or more times previously in each performance.

(91)   descendants of my father
        [all of you] leave the bed
        you come hear doctrine
        now it goes in the house [church]

Three other formulas, usually drummed only in the final stanza, make one early appearance each in the recorded paradigm. 'You will say to me what else?' indicates two false endings in performance 4, and 'leave forever' appears out of its usual place in performance 10. The early appearance of 'no one should do this' was mentioned above in connection with performance 2.

The four common phrases given in (91), which are obligatory only in the final stanza, certainly present the point of the poem as summative phrases. Though they are drummed with intervening phrases and pauses, they make a succinct summary of the discourse when put side-by-side and are used at least three times in each performance including the final stanza. They express the discourse theme well, existing as dominant recurring sound patterns. "In nonsystematic repetition, the terminal recurrence of sounds used earlier strengthens closure by confirming the reader's experiences, thus reinforcing the sense of the 'rightness' of the lines in question" (Smith 1968:166). The final appearance of the summative phrases not only confirms the hearers' experience of the poetic lines, but it confirms actual shared experiences: "All of you who have been coming to hear doctrine for decades, let's do it again right now." In an analysis based on counting occurrences of phrases, it could be said that these four summative phrases are the flexible backbone of the discourse, with all other phrases filling in the details.

Many poems end with INDIRECT ALLUSIONS of closure, using words such as 'last', 'finished', 'end', 'rest', and 'peace', according to Smith (p. 172). Antoine's final two lines of the poem reflect this device. 'Now it [doctrine] goes in the house [church]' implies that he has finished drumming his speech act, and that all Christians should now gather. His last phrase, 'you will say to me what else?' implies that people have no more excuses, so they should stop talking on the drum and gather together. In addition, the references to death, the last judgment, and the phrase 'leave your beds forever' all carry connotations of finality.

It seems obvious that if this final stanza appeared repeatedly in the discourse, and the earlier stanza that begins 'you finish washing [teeth] with water' was substituted for the final stanza, all sense of discourse peak and poetic closure would be lost. Antoine's skills, creativity, and experience helped him compose a concluding stanza that is aesthetically satisfying to an Ewondo audience and meets the criteria set down by critics of classical English poetry.

Smith's model of poetic closure and Longacre's notions of discourse peak bring etic insights to the study of Antoine's final stanza. The emic appropriateness of the final stanza as poetic closure and peak is probably intuitively felt by Mekomba residents though expressed in different terms.

Finis

The final rhythm phrase, without verbal interpretation, can be viewed etically from several different perspectives: as finis to a verbal discourse, as coda to a musical performance, as closure ideograph in a semiotic sense.

Both language and music often use a terminative formula, termed FINIS in discourse analysis and CODA in music analysis. The final rhythm phrase, following the final stanza, can be seen to mark finis in a verbal-based discourse analysis of the performances. "In music, the coda is a

terminal section of a piece or movement, added for the specific purpose
of securing closure and clearly distinguished from the preceeding portion
by its structure" (Smith 1968:188).

In many cultures, it can be considered rude to abruptly cease talking
to someone. "Since abrupt cutoffs are psychologically unpleasant as well
as impolite, we usually make use of some formula of conclusion to signal
the approaching termination" (p. 187). Verbal examples in English are
goodbye and amen. This concept of a conclusive formula played on the
Ewondo *nkul* 'drum' is mentioned in the earlier literature on the subject,
though authors were not very precise. For example, *si si si si si si* was
reported by Guillemin (1948:75), and "*ken ken ken* is onomatopoeia for
the three high tones with which all drum messages terminate" (Atangana
and Messi 1919:304). Antoine's closing formula is noticeably different
from either of these, implying a number of possible conclusive nonverbal
formulas for a drummed message. Atemengue, the drumming catechist of
the neighboring village, uses several forms of a closing formula that are
related to all the above yet distinct.

Semiotically, the final drum phrase can be viewed as an IDEOGRAPH
MARKER (Stern 1957/1976:134), a symbol that represents an idea (such
as closure) directly rather than a particular word. In a semiotic sense, the
drumstrokes at performance end are no longer icons in a nonarbitrary
relationship with verbal phrases; they are signals in a direct, arbitrary
relationship with a particular concept (cf. Sebeok 1976:42–45 and
Umiker 1974:512).

Syntagmatic and paradigmatic relations

Two main types of relations between drum phrases and between co-
occurrent clusters are reflected in this study. These relations can be
grouped into SYNTAGMATIC RELATIONS, that is, sequential, causal, and temporal; and PARADIGMATIC RELATIONS, that is, categorical arrangements of
similarities and contrasts.

> Words are in paradigmatic relation insofar as they can occupy the
> same slot in a particular context (or syntagm); they are in syntagmatic
> relation if they can enter into combinations that form a context (or
> syntagm). We should note that paradigmatic sense relations exploit the
> opposition or contrast existing between words and thus may be re-
> ferred to as contrasting relations, while syntagmatic sense relations
> may be called combinatory relations. (Silva 1983:13)

The two phrases in (92) are in syntagmatic relationship.

(92) *nge mina oyoa*   if you are sleeping,
      vebegan   [all of you] wake up!

The combination of these phrases forms a syntagm which serves as context in many of the opening stanzas. The phrases can be optionally separated by a pause and optionally repeated. In this study, a syntagm is equivalent to a co-occurrent cluster or part of such a cluster.

The next set of phrases shows some of the complexity involved when units are assembled into actual discourse. In (93), the middle phrases of both co-occurrent clusters are in paradigmatic relationship, i.e., either phrase can fill the middle slot of the syntagm.

(93) *mi zu mi wulu*   You come, you walk
      bela bela bebae bebae bebae   three by three, two by two by two,
      mi zu wog doten   you come hear doctrine.

      mi zu mi wulu   You come, you walk
      ndenele minkumu   [nonchalantly] waving bodies
                                               [like tall trees],
      mi zu wog doten   you come hear doctrine.

The first and third phrases of the above two co-occurrent clusters are identical and form the syntagm or context for the middle phrase. If both of the clusters are used, they are drummed in this order with intervening phrases. Only the second cluster is heard in performance 5, and neither is used in performance 10.

The first and third phrases of the syntagm are closely related to another co-occurrent cluster in (94).

(94) *mi ke mi wulu*   You go, you walk
      ewuwulu ewuwulu   walking aimlessly,
      mi tame zu bo doten   you should come do doctrine.

The seven-note drum pattern is identical for 'you come, you walk' and 'you go, you walk'. Because of these homophonous surrogate signs, the correct verbal interpretation cannot be made until the middle phrase is heard. The third phrases of the clusters have very similar meaning, but the drum patterns are sufficiently different so as to distinguish the words.

One phrase may be heard in several co-occurrent clusters. The final phrase 'you come hear doctrine' is used not only in the first syntagm in (93), but in several others as well. 'Walking aimlessly' is also used in a different syntagm.

Referencing Silva's (1983:13) definition above, the tendency of linearity pulls drum phrases into stable co-occurrent clusters (syntagms) through combinatory relations, while the tendency of nonlinearity pulls drum phrases into unpredictable paratactic arrangement through contrasting relations. One could speak of the phrases being like magnets which both attract and repel one another. In reality, of course, the phrases themselves have no power, and the combinatory and contrasting relations emerge through the drummer's compositional choices made in performance.

Phrases can be in syntagmatic or paradigmatic relation. Larger syntagmatic units of co-occurrent clusters may also be in either type of relation throughout the discourse. For example, either (93) or (94) may follow 'Everything the heart speaks, the mouth cannot say all'. The two syntagms are therefore in paradigmatic relation in the context of this proverbial phrase. The cluster in (92) commonly precedes this proverbial phrase, and is, therefore, in syntagmatic relation with the proverbial phrase (though it may be omitted).

Phrases and co-occurrent clusters may be in paradigmatic relation through an abstract semantic category but in syntagmatic relation with other phrases through discourse placement when actually performed. For example, (95) gives three forms of a direct address vocative.

(95) *bekristen*   Christians

      bekristen   Christians
      bese ya   all in
      mekomba   Mekomba

      bekristen   Christians,
      bese ya   all at
      suga movg mba nnembe   the end of the lineage of Mba Nnembe

'Christians' may be used by itself in several places. It may also be qualified by either completing locative phrase of the two syntagms. The three forms of the direct address phrase form a category of phrases which are similar in meaning, i.e., they are in paradigmatic relation. Their placement, however, is context-dependent as the phrases form syntagms with other phrases in specified contexts. The one-word form can be used in the penultimate slot of several stanzas. The first co-occurrent cluster is used only to begin the opening stanza, while the other is used only to begin other stanzas. Therefore, the three forms are in paradigmatic relation through meaning in analysis but are part of different syntagms (co-occurrent clusters) through placement in performance.

Cohesion and coherence

A single word is a form-meaning composite, and so is an entire utterance, text, or drummed speech act. "Unity of a text is achieved through cohesion in form and coherence in meaning" (Canale 1983:9). Cohesion has to do with surface-level structural relationships among text elements. In this study the perceived surface structure signs are prosodic drumstrokes; cohesion has to do with the unperceived signified text. Coherence refers to the underlying relationships among meanings and words which create a discourse that has cultural significance for the language users. "In this sense, cohesion is one factor contributing to coherence" (Tannen 1984:xiv).

Antoine's performances exhibit cohesion but in a manner peculiar to paratactic surrogate speech acts. Coherence of these performance texts is established through the same processes used in other texts, whether spoken or written. The creator's intended meaning is interpreted by the audience through the interaction of two types of knowledge: textual knowledge gained in performance and stored knowledge from sociocultural context and previous performances.

Cohesive devices

"Cohesive devices call upon a speaker's background knowledge of syntactic/semantic and sociocultural knowledge in a process of interpretation" (Gumperz, Kaltman, and O'Connor 1984:5) enabling participants to fill in any discourse gaps, make references to preceding and forthcoming discourse, and link material (including common stock phrases) to the prevailing theme.

Cohesion is established in different ways in spoken, written, and drummed discourse. In written text, cohesion is established through complex syntax and through connectives (p. 10). In spoken discourse, "prosody is among the most important of the devices that accomplish cohesion" (p. 5).

Antoine uses neither complex syntax, connectives, nor prosody in his performance paradigm of drum language. Formulaic phrases are not connected by using complex syntax, which makes it possible for them to be more easily shifted in paratactic arrangement. Similarly, only a few connectives are used to connect phrases within a co-occurrent cluster and no connectives to join the clusters themselves. Concerning prosody, it is interesting that this speech surrogate which is pure prosody of speech tone and rhythm cannot reproduce other prosodic features such as stress, tone of voice, or most forms of intonation. All of these so-called crucial contextualization cues are absent for the most part when language is represented on the Ewondo drum.

Cohesion is established in a given performance of Antoine's paradigm primarily through syntactic and semantic features at both levels of perceived sound and signified words. These cohesive devices include the use of words in the same semantic domain, repetition of key ideas, verbatim repetition of key phrases and sound patterns, reiteration of the main theme, constant use of vocatives, repetition of the stall pattern, and continuity of referents.

A chart of the primary participant referents can be illuminating as to the cohesion of performance 2. Participants mentioned in the performance include the drummer himself, the audience members, and God. 'Doctrine' has also been included on the chart in (96) as the main theme.

(96)　Primary participant referents

Textual phrase	1st pers.	2nd pers.	Vocative	3rd pers.	Doctrine	God
1			Christians			
3		you	descendants			my father
4						
5		you				
11				person, he		
13		you				
14		you				
15		you				
16		you				
17		you, you				
18		you			doctrine	
19			Christians			
20				it		
21		you, you				
23		you			doctrine	
24			Christians			
25			Mba Nnembe			
26			descendants			my father
27		you				
28		you				
30				person, he		
32		you			doctrine	
33			descendants			my father

Textual phrase	1st pers.	2nd pers.	Vocative	3rd pers.	Doctrine	God
34				person, person		
35				people		
36				person, he		
37				I	doctrine	
38				he	doctrine	
39				he		
42			children			
43			Owondzuli			
45		you			doctrine	
46				it		
47			descendants			my father
48		you				
49	I					
50	me					
51		you your- selves				
52		you				
53		you				
54		you				
55			descendants			my father
56		you, you		person		
57						
58		you, you				
60		you			doctrine	
61			descendants			my father
62				person		
63				person		
65		you				
66		you			doctrine	
67			descendants			my father
68				person		
69				he, he		
70				he		Ntondobe
71					doctrine	
72			descendants			my father
75		you			doctrine	
76				it		
77	me	you				

Major cohesive devices in this performance are Antoine's constant references to theme and to audience members either directly ('you'), indirectly ('person'), or through several direct address phrases, for a total of fifty-two audience references in seventy-seven textual phrases! Many of these audience references are in the imperative form (expected in a hortatory discourse). In performance 2, 'you' is heard twenty-six times and 'person/people/he' is heard fourteen times. The common stock vocative 'descendants of my father' is used eight times, and other vocatives are heard four times. In contrast, Antoine refers to himself only three times. The theme 'doctrine/it' is referred to twelve times. God is referred to as 'my father' eight times and is mentioned by name only once in the discourse peak. Except for one block of six phrases on the theme of morning, not more than one or two phrases go by without one of these references.

The rough ratio of these referents to participants and theme remains constant from performance to performance, but the exact proportions will vary. Constant references to participants and theme mean that each drummed discourse is cohesive no matter which phrases are actually chosen in performance or what form their aural arrangement takes.

Cohesive ties

When interpretation of one clause presupposes knowledge of information from a preceding clause, cohesive ties are established (Schiffrin 1987:26). For example, 'for me it is what concern?' can only be interpreted when the preceding phrases are known: 'if you lie in bed, I will lie in bed'. This is termed ENDORPHIC REFERENCE (Halliday and Hasan 1989:76).

At times the interpretation of a clause in Antoine's discourse presupposes information from the performance context or from a clause known from previous performances but omitted in the one heard. For example, 'you walk with quickness in the feet, you come fulfill your promises/appointment' is logically based on the preceding phrase 'you yourselves made promises/appointment when you came for baptism'. In some cases, however, the preceding phrase is only known from previous performances in this social context. Early in performance 10, the following pair of phrases is drummed without specific precedent: 'you walk, running fast, walking fast, you come fulfill your promises/appointment'. Later in the same performance, the other co-occurrent cluster of phrases on the same theme is drummed. The first set of phrases uses EXOPHORIC REFERENCE, that is, the source for interpretation lies outside the text itself. The second set of phrases uses endophoric reference because the promise/appointment was previously stated in the text. Note that the completing drum phrase of both co-occurrent clusters, 'you come fulfill your promises/appointment', is identical; whether endophoric or exophoric reference is used in a given stanza depends on Antoine's paratactic ordering of phrases and co-occurrent clusters.

An implicit term may either follow or precede its linguistic referent. "When it follows its linguistic referent, the label given to such a cohesive tie is anaphoric…. When the implicit term precedes its linguistic referent, the cohesive tie thus established is known as cataphoric" (Halliday and Hasan 1989:76).

ANAPHORA is common in most forms of discourse. Anaphoras are 'referring expressions' such as pronouns and elliptical phrases. Anaphora helps maintain discourse coherence through referential continuity (Tanehaus 1992:289). For example, *mi zu* 'you (plural) come', *o zu* 'you (singular) come', and *be zu* 'they come' all receive an identical two-note drum pattern. Which pronoun is intended by the drummer (the referential continuity) can only be determined by the preceding phrases. Every drum phrase is interpreted as text itself and as context to text that is to come (Halliday and Hasan 1989:48).

There are no real cataphoric references in Antoine's paradigm, but instead what might be called a cataphoric clarification is found in the set of phrases in (97).

(97) *mot a be fe*   No one, he must no longer
      bo bibug be koni   do things of tricks.

                    [stall pattern]

      mina beben a minga   You yourselves
      lig zulu metin   made promises/appointment
      a minga zu duban   when you came for baptism.

The referent for 'tricks' is not at all clear until the latter phrase is heard; then 'tricks' is understood to refer to making previous promises for church attendance but now breaking those promises. Again, the referent necessary for interpretation may be omitted from the performance. For example, 'do things of tricks' appears in performance 3 without any textual reference to promises. In this case, the interpretation of 'tricks' comes from outside this particular performance text. The phrase is coherent when heard here because of the audience's knowledge stored from previous performances.

Coherence relations and devices

According to Jarrett (1985:158), "context, both textual and extratextual, is the critical feature in assigning and recognizing coherence." Knowledge of the Ewondo speech surrogate system, knowledge of Antoine's usual repertoire of formulas, and knowledge of social context partly compose the frame of reference necessary for a drummed speech act to be coherent to the community members of Mekomba. Coherent discourse is constructed through integrative processes: sound, structure, meaning, and actions must be integrated with one another in message formation and comprehension (Schiffrin 1992:362).

Four types of linguistic relationships have become regarded as most significant for maintaining text coherence (Polanyi 1992:148). They are given in (98) with examples from Antoine's paradigm.

(98)   COORDINATION RELATIONS such as sequential list structures

o man soban kpekpaa	You finish washing [teeth] with brush.
o man soban mendim	You finish washing [face] with water.
o kodo asi	You leave the bed.
o non man ntu eyie	You take your small old cloth,
o nga za wawulu a zen ese	you start coming, you walk along the road.
o zu wog doten	You come hear doctrine.

LOGICAL RELATIONS such as antecedent/consequent structures

nge mina bombo asi	If you lie in bed,
ma mebombo asi	I will lie in bed.

SUBORDINATION RELATIONS such as adverbial clauses

mot akodo asi adzal adzal die nye na	Someone leaves the bed in his village, he says,
ma tam ke ake a doten	I must go for doctrine.
abog aye wog doten	When he will hear doctrine,
a nga ke a wulu	[instead] he goes walking
ewuwulu ewuwulu	walking aimlessly
a minam minam	from place to place.

RHETORICAL RELATIONS including questions

ma mene a za ebugu	For me it is what concern?
minga bar fe ma dzo aya	You will say to me what else [excuses]?

Rhetorical relations also include material repeated for emphasis, such as the co-occurrent cluster in (99) which is common in Antoine's opening stanza.

(99)	*biem bi kidi*	Signs of morning,
	bi nga maneya kobo	they are finishing to speak.
	biem bi kidi	Signs of morning,
	bi nga maneya kobo	they are finishing to speak.
	kidi	Morning—
	ndzo elendeya hm	the day has already dawned.

One device used to maintain text coherence is discourse markers. Besides marking discourse into sections, discourse markers "provide contextual coordinates for utterances; they index an utterance to the local contexts in which utterances are produced and in which they are to be interpreted" (Schiffrin 1987:326). Examples in Antoine's paradigm include direct address phrases: names of village and lineage founders, 'to descendants of my father', and 'Christians'; the thematic phrase 'you come hear doctrine'; and the common pre-pause phrase 'now it goes in the church'. Most of these discourse markers appear one or more times in every performance, serving to integrate the elements of each performance into coherent discourse. Direct address phrases frequently begin co-occurrent clusters and stanzas, while the other two phrases frequently complete co-occurrent clusters and stanzas. All of these phrases are indexed to the performance context and serve as discourse context for interpreting all other phrases drummed. Together they indicate 'who I'm talking to, what I'm talking about, and what I expect you to do about it'.

Cohesion and coherence in a well-formed text means that phrases must fit together well both by semantic and syntactic standards: 'to descendants of my father' never follows 'you finish brushing your teeth', and the latter never precedes 'all of you wake up'! Although the arrangement of phrases into co-occurrent clusters and of co-occurrent clusters into performances is paratactic in nature, the artist's freedom for choice and order of units is kept within the constraints of grammar and sense.

Implied information

Cohesion is present when drum phrases fit naturally into the discourse form; through coherence, the audience can interpret the meaning of phrases in a manner consistent with the performer's intention and the genre's theme. Implied information can then be deduced by the audience. Look at the set of phrases in (100).

(100)	*a mvog tara ngogo*	To descendants of my father,
	mot andziki lom mot	no one has sent me anyone.
	bot bete be nga zu	These people, they came [for baptism],
	ma bo dze ben	to really do what [now]?

The initial phrase is a common stock formula; the intended identity of father is known through the discourse's regularized performance context and genre. The second phrase is a simple statement of fact on the surface, but with implications for the audience's own actions (everyone should come). The third phrase is a question with implied references to past and present actions of the audience members. The audience is obliquely referred to in third person. A great deal of implied information must be inferred by audience members if this discourse section is to be properly interpreted as a call to action by the catechist. Example (101) gives my rephrasing with implied information made explicit.

(101)   To you Christians who call God your father,
        You have not come to church yet so I wait for you alone.
        You came to church a long time ago and made baptismal
            vows; was it for nothing?
        Fulfill your vows and come to church now!

Isotopies and structural ambiguity

ISOTOPIES are the principles which articulate discourse into coherent sections (Tarasti 1985:100). There are various isotopies in language and music; several isotopies in each may overlap and function simultaneously. In cases where language and music are intertwined, such as song or speech surrogate drumming, the isotopies of each may work together or against one another. This conflict of isotopies can result in structural ambiguity.

There are at least five interpretations of isotopy, two of which are relevant to the Ewondo speech surrogate paradigm. The first meaning-based isotopy is THEMATICITY, which sections off co-occurrent clusters according to the subthemes of get up, get prepared, fulfill your baptismal vows, be prepared for the final judgment of God, and so forth. The second form-based isotopy is GENRE FEATURES; for example, a particular stall pattern aurally sections off stanzas in the genre of drummed church summons (and not in other drum genres to the best of my knowledge).

In many cases these two isotopies work together to mark coherent discourse sections; a stanza is often equivalent to a thematic set of phrases. Textual genre features often coincide with thematic areas sectioned off by the stanza marker: 'to descendants of my father' and other direct address phrases frequently begin a stanza and thematic set of phrases, and 'now it goes in the church' frequently ends a stanza and theme.

The stall pattern, however, is obligatory in the middle of a few co-occurrent clusters. In these cases, the two isotopies of genre (marked in the musical form) and thematicity (marked in the verbal meaning) are in conflict, leading to structural ambiguity. When this happens, in my etic perspective, the isotopy of textual thematicity is stronger, and I make sense of this ambiguity by considering that the phrases do belong together with an obligatory stall pattern in between them for rhetorical effect, a sort of 'pause for reflection'.

When all occurrences are considered, the stall pattern is seen to have three primary functions: it serves as an isotopy to section off aural discourse sections, as a place for the performer to stall and think ahead, and as a place for the audience to reflect on what has just been said.

The three functions do not always coincide; in (102), the first and last occurrences of the stall pattern reflect all three of its functions. The middle stall pattern is obligatory in this co-occurrent cluster and used for rhetorical effect. It primarily serves as a place for audience reflection between the proverbial textual phrases.

(102)   [stall pattern]
    mot a kat wo dzam   Someone tells you something,
    wo o kat manyon   you in turn tell your brother.
                  [stall pattern]
    bibug nnem wa kobo   Everything the heart speaks,
    anyu te fali bise   the mouth cannot say all.
                  [stall pattern]

Repetition of paradigm elements

"Repetition is the fundamental phenomenon of poetic form" (Smith 1968:38). No element is formally significant until it has been repeated or perceived in a relation to another element. No formal structure can be discovered in a single word, musical note, or speech surrogate drumstroke.

Repetition "is not just a utilitarian tool, but something which lies at the heart of all poetry" (Finnegan 1977:131). It can be used as a dynamic, creative force within a performance, not only as a mechanical factor (Anyidoho 1986:28). Repetition serves several functions, including aiding of memory and learning, preservation of phrases in static surface structure form, emphasizing phrases and themes, and providing a framework for artistic expression under real-time creative constraints.

Repetition is used in Antoine's speech surrogate drumming where a phrase is usually repeated only with other phrases intervening (exceptions are commonly made in the opening stanza), and is usually not repeated more than a few times in a single performance.

Two kinds of repetition are repetition of elements within a text and repetition of elements between texts. The first type is a feature of a particular performance, the second type is a feature of a particular artistic tradition, which may or may not cross genre boundaries. Gray (1971:291–92) terms the first, FORMULA and the second, CONVENTION. In the case of Antoine's paradigm, all formulas are conventions since they recur repeatedly in the paradigm of his other performances. Some formulas are also used by other drumming catechists (such as Atemengue) working in the same genre, while use and repetition of other formulas are peculiar to each drummer's idiolect and location. For example, the word 'Mekomba' will probably not be drummed by catechists outside that village, but 'Christians' will be used by all of them.

Repetition may therefore be extensively used inter- and intra-performance within a paradigm. Within one and between many performances, a single phrase or large co-occurrent cluster may or may not be repeated at the drummer's discretion.

An example of a block of twenty-three textual phrases is used in performance 1 and repeated in performance 2. There are four types of differences between the the blocks of each performance: repetition of stall pattern, placement of pauses, change of direct address phrase (different lineage founder named), and omission of one word from one formula. This co-occurrent cluster of twenty-three phrases accounts for about a third of each performance. The differences are negligible, so it can be said that thirty percent of these two performances are identical for the most part.

In performance 1, a large part of this cluster (fourteen phrases) is immediately repeated after the larger cluster ends. Three of the changes mentioned above (stall pattern, pauses, direct address phrases) are found in this repeated section within a performance. Through repetition, the long and short form of this co-occurrent cluster account for more than half of performance 1. In performance 2, none of the co-occurrent cluster is repeated.

In performance 4, the majority of the phrases of the co-occurrent cluster are drummed but not as one contiguous unit. Instead, they are broken up into several smaller units separated by other units. Some form of some part of this co-occurrent cluster appears in every performance, but the details emerge only through performance and cannot be predicted with any certainty. Repetition serves as a major part of a performance's structure, but is different in every aural manifestation.

The redundancy in Antoine's discourses reflect "a kind of equilibrium between the unexpected and the predictable" information (Nida in Fine 1984:104). While Antoine's performance paradigm is full of repetition, it is not always predictable, and does not lend itself to the "aesthetics of regularity" (Finnegan 1977:131). Although I have used the term stanzas, this term should not imply regularly appearing stanzas of regular length. In Antoine's paradigm, we find that much repetition (with limited predictability) contributes to the emergent structural framework of each paratactic performance. This type of irregular repetition has a different kind of aesthetic potential from that of songs which have regular and cyclic repetition.

A second subdivision of repetition is verbal repetition at the surface structure level and thematic repetition at the deep structure level (Gray 1971:296). To a large extent, these are identical in an Ewondo speech surrogate performance because if a theme is repeated, it is often repeated with the same base words and drum patterns. Some themes, however, have different manifestations. In an example from performance 1 and 2, either direct address phrase (using the name of a lineage founder) was substitutable for the other in the co-occurrent cluster, indicating their thematic equivalence at the deep structure of the discourse.

Some scholars (cf. Anyidoho 1986:28) claim that each repetition of a phrase brings "modification in meaning and affect." Because the Ewondo performance paradigm under study is high-context communication, I doubt that all the repetitions of a phrase really bring different shades of meaning, or that the fourth appearance of 'leave your beds' is more affective than its first appearance.

Redundancy is present in spoken, written, and drummed language; in all cases, it "is designed to ease the comprehension process" (Schiffrin 1987:6). Redundancy reduces the rate and content of new information in a message, but it also allows misunderstandings to be detected and corrected. Speech surrogate drummers frequently impose a controlled redundancy in their messages (Arewa and Adekola 1980:194). The drumming is often so fast that the audience may not be sure of the tonal-rhythmic patterns perceived, and large-scale repetition offers an opportunity to rehear the sound patterns. According to Heepe (1920/1976:320), the drum name of the performer, addressee, and the message itself are usually repeated three times "for better understanding." Antoine's messages do not have this much redundancy, but they are more repetitive than most forms of speech or writing.

The redundancy of speech, when moved to this speech surrogate, takes a different form in that large units of phrases are repeated verbatim within a discourse. Not only that, but all of the drummed speech acts are redundant within the paradigm of one performer. Each performance quotes itself, and all performances are made up of nothing but quotes of each other.

After looking at Antoine's performances, Atemengue's performances in the same genre are less than half the length of Antoine's and have almost no redundancy except for the stall pattern (to which he ascribes textual meaning). The only intra-performance repetition is that of two word, 'Christians' and 'doctrine'. Atemengue offers no second chance to hear and interpret his drummed summons; consequently, he estimated that only about ten people in his village had good understanding of his drum language.

Contrasting sets of drum phrases

There are several sets of drum phrases which contrast the spiritual and physical realms, this life and the afterlife. Together, these phrases present images based on earthly descendants walking to doctrine in life contrasted with heavenly descendants walking with doctrine in their hands at death.

In this first set of phrases, there is one contrast between 'when you will hear doctrine' (optional) and 'when you will die' (obligatory). A second contrast is between 'walking aimlessly' while avoiding doctrine in life and 'walking' to be judged by God upon possession of that doctrine at death. A third contrast is between 'the end of the dead (spiritual)' and 'the end of the lineage (physical)' as shown in (103).

(103)	abog aye wog doten	When he will hear doctrine,
	a nga ke a wulu	[instead] he goes walking
	ewuwulu ewuwulu	aimlessly
	a minam minam	from place to place.
	abog aye ke awulu	when he will go, he walks
	a suga bekon	to the end of the dead...
		[to be judged on having doctrine]
	bekristen bese ya suga	Christians, all at the end
	mvog mba nnembe	of the lineage of Mba Nnembe

A similar physical/spiritual contrast is made between descendants of an earthly father and descendants of a heavenly father in commonly used direct address phrases like (104).

(104)	mvog mba nnembe	descendants of Mba Nnembe
	mvog owondzuli	descendants of Owondzuli
	mvog tara ngongo	descendants of my father [God]

Antoine seems keen on drawing distinctions and using these distinctions to motivate people to attend church now. "Is this world your only home?" he implicitly asks. Atemengue implies the same distinction in a set of phrases that commonly close his drummed summons seen in (105).

| (105) | mvog alanan nnama | To the lineage staying eternally in the countryside, |
| | ake di a ma ke a nda | now I go in the house [church]. |

Seven standards of a communicative text

Textual communication has seven constitutive principles, according to Beaugrande and Dressler (1981:3–11). "If any of these standards is not considered to have been satisfied, the text will not be communicative" (p. 3). Antoine's performance paradigm meets all seven standards of a communicative text. The standards are oriented toward the text itself and toward the language users.

COHESION concerns the way in which the surface structure elements are mutually connected within a sequence. Cohesion is built upon syntactic dependencies. Each unit of phrase, line, stanza, or co-occurrent cluster exhibits internal cohesion following the grammar of spoken Ewondo.

COHERENCE concerns the ways in which the surface structure of a text is connected with the concepts which underlie the text. Coherence can be said to be the outcome of cognitive processes among text users. Relations of coherence are inferred by adding one's own stored knowledge to the verbal knowledge gained through performance. For example, in *ake di a ke a nda* 'now it goes in the house [church]', the audience is expected to know which building is meant, and also that they should enter the building.

INTENTIONALITY concerns the attitude of the performer. A performance has communicated when it is instrumental in fulfilling the catechist's intention to attain a certain goal (church attendance). Antoine's intention is clearly expressed; he drums 'you come hear doctrine' at least four times in every performance.

ACCEPTABILITY concerns the attitude of the audience. A performance has communicated when it is relevant to the audience and helps them to attain a certain goal (church attendance). The residents of Mfou-villáge have even allowed themselves to be publicly insulted as a group by being called 'little monkeys' by Atemengue.

INFORMATIVITY concerns the extent to which information is expected or unexpected. The audience's processing must not become overloaded or communication will cease. Antoine's discourse paradigm has enough redundancy in a high-context communicative setting that the rate of new information is not excessive. In contrast, each of Atemengue's performances uses some phrases that only appear once in his recorded paradigm, and there is practically no redundancy except for the stall pattern and the repetition of two words. Therefore, it seems that Atemengue's new information may come at a faster rate than in Antoine's performances, though this statement is tentative since it is based on only three performances.

SITUATIONALITY concerns the factors which make a text relevant to a situation outside of the text itself. The sense and use of a text are decided in reference to the situation as in one stanza in (106).

(106) *mot a be fe bo bibug bi fongo*   No one, he should no longer do
                                            things too small [insignificant].

What these 'small things' are is never made explicit, but probably refers to staying in bed or going to farm early which are insignificant in comparison with coming to church now. The intepretation of this phrase in accordance with the drummer's intention is made through reference to the situation and to the genre's known purpose.

INTERTEXTUALITY refers to knowledge of other performances drummed previously by Antoine. A given performance communicates meaning in reference to the other four thousand or so performances Antoine has drummed in Mekomba. Familiarity with drum phrases heard before greatly increases the possibility of communication taking place. If an Ewondo newcomer to Mekomba heard the drummed church summons and could not reference the phrases to other drumming he had heard in other locations, communication would be stymied. Because common stock phrases cross genre boundaries and location boundaries, however, all Ewondo drummed texts have some relation to other texts.

Together these seven principles of textuality show that Antoine's drummed discourse is a well-formed communicative transaction, or communicative occurrence in Beaugrande and Dressler's terms (1981:3).

9

Performance Paradigm as Multilevel Structure

Textual/semantic units and hierarchy of levels

Every discourse, whether spoken, written, or drummed, is cognitively processed as a multilevel structure containing units of various sizes.

Understanding a text involves analyzing it into highly structured semantic units that are acquired, stored, retrieved, and in other ways processed as units. These semantic processing units occur at different levels, from units as small as elementary concepts, states, or events, to units that incorporate substantial portions of a text's content. The identification of such processing units is a central question both in the study of processes involved in language production and comprehension, and in the study of the form in which knowledge is represented in semantic memory. (Frederiksen 1977:58)

Various aural, structural, and textual/semantic units, arranged in a hierarchy of nine levels, will be proposed to demonstrate the multilevel discourse and semantic structure. It will be shown that the level of formulaic phrase units is the primary level used in surrogate language production by the performer, in comprehension by the audience, and is the form in which the drummed text is represented in the semantic memory of all concerned. Terms will be used here primarily as defined by Frederiksen (1977:58–59), who followed definitions introduced by Halliday.

A UNIT is "a category set up to account for segments of spoken or written [or drummed] text that consist of recurrently meaningful patterns and/or operate as components of meaningful patterns."

Units are arranged in a HIERARCHY; "each unit always consists of one or more than one of the units immediately below it in the hierarchy." The nine levels proposed in this study are represented in the hierarchy in (107), with the smallest noninclusive unit at the bottom and the largest inclusive unit at the top. The criteria for determining the units are quite mixed, based on aspects of phonology, semiotics, semantics, sound, speech act, and function. Such a mixture perhaps does not lead to an elegant theory, but I believe it leads to the most appropriate hierarchy to describe levels of the sound event in Mekomba.

(107)   genre
        performance paradigm
        performance
        stanza
        line
        formulaic phrase
        word
        syllable
        drumstroke

A GENRE is an emic unit recognized by sociolinguistic criteria related to social function. For example, all performance paradigms drummed by all Ewondo catechists as church summons make up a genre. All genres included in the total Ewondo speech surrogate system are related through common stock phrases.

A PERFORMANCE PARADIGM is a set of performances drummed by a single drummer. This unit is most applicable when the performances are regularly scheduled, for example, a church summons drummed by the catechist.

A PERFORMANCE is defined as a drummed speech surrogate act with a specific function, bounded at both ends by silence. Each performance consists of ten to sixteen stanzas, and in this context is heard usually twice a week in a particular sociolinguistic situation. A performed drum discourse of any genre is termed *foe nkul*.

A STANZA is defined structurally as a set of lines bounded at both ends by the stall pattern: *ku ku ku ku lu ku ku ku,* with the exception of a performance's beginning and end. Each stanza is composed of one to twelve lines.

A LINE is defined aurally as a set of phrases bounded at both ends by a short silence (a pause). Each line varies from part of a phrase to six phrases.

A FORMULAIC PHRASE is defined lexico-structurally (by repetition) as a formula, a self-contained tonal-rhythmic-verbal pattern. A syntagmatic formula occurs with little or no variation, while a paradigmatic formula has substitutable parts. A phrase may be bounded by other phrases, the stall pattern, or a pause. Each formulaic phrase consists of one to twenty words.

A WORD is defined lexico-semantically as a grammatical unit found in a common lexicon. Each word consists of one to four semantic syllables.

A SYLLABLE is defined as a minimal unit of speech, composed of a nucleus with optional margins and composed of vowels and consonants. It is often (but not always) equivalent to one drumstroke. Suprasegmental features of a syllable's tone and rhythm are iconically represented by one or more drumstrokes, or none where vowel elision takes place. Some false syllables may be added in controlled environments, with corresponding added drumstrokes.

A DRUMSTROKE is defined aurally as a percussive sound made by *bom nkul* 'beating the drum'. It may be short or long in duration, high, low, or both (doubled) in tone. A single drumstroke carries no semantic information or cognitive load by itself.

Syllable, word, and phrase levels, the actual units of text, may be understood within the speech community by members with receptive competency. In addition, all members of the speech community can recognize the top hierachical levels of performance paradigm (recognize their drummer by his style) and genre (recognize drummed church summons by habitual sociolinguistic context). Nonmembers and members of the speech community can recognize the levels of drumstroke, line, stanza, and performance, as these levels are all defined by aural criteria not requiring textual knowledge of the Ewondo speech surrogate system.

Hierarchical organization is essential to creating, remembering, and understanding a long text because of the limited capacity of memory. This memory restriction "is one of the most essential phenomena influencing the formation of communicational codes. This phenomenon concerns the ability of memory to store only a limited number of units not organized in hierarchic systems" (Rakowski 1985:70). Hundreds of drumstrokes unorganized hierarchically by the hearer will not result in comprehension, nor will they be remembered in any fashion. Segmentation of incoming data into structured subunits "is antecedent to any other type of cognitive processing" (Handel 1973:46).

A STRUCTURE "describes how a meaningful unit is composed of units below it in rank" (Frederiksen 1977:59). To some extent this topic remains

in focus throughout the entire book. The following is a list of chapters which
deal specifically with the structure of each level:

> How performance paradigms make up a genre, and how genres are
>   related to the totality of the Ewondo speech surrogate system, is
>   mentioned in chapter 11.
> How performances by one drummer make up a paradigm is discussed
>   in chapter 4.
> How stanzas are assembled into a performance is discussed in chapter 8.
> How lines are assembled into stanzas (marked by stall pattern) is dealt
>   with in chapter 8.
> How phrases are assembled into lines (marked by pause) is discussed
>   in chapter 8.
> How words are assembled into formulaic phrases is dealt with in
>   chapter 7.
> How drumstrokes phonologically represent syllables and words is dis-
>   cussed in chapter 6.
> How drumstrokes iconically represent syllables and words is dealt
>   with in chapter 1.

Lower-level units are assembled into higher-level units through
PERMUTATION.

> The rule of permutation means that by combining a limited number
> of lower rank elements, the elements of higher rank may be formed,
> whose number is much higher than that of the input elements. The
> process is usually repeated in turn at several levels of the code and the
> number of possible elements of the highest rank is mostly unlim-
> ited....Human memory appears very limited in storing elementary
> units of the same rank but much more capable when the information
> is coded in hierarchical order. (Rakowski 1985:66)

Permutation is the process by which drumstrokes (lowest rank) with a
tiny set of contrastive features—high/low, short/long—can be assembled
to create about a hundred formulaic phrases in Antoine's repertoire. The
phrases can be assembled into thousands of (etic) variants at the higher
rank of performance. The unit level of paradigm is limited by the number
of performers; the unit level of genre is limited by the number of functions that the society requires of this instrument.

A SYSTEM OF DECISIONS "refers to the limited set of choices available in
determining the structure of a unit" (Frederiksen 1977:59). A performance may thus be analyzed as a series of decisions governing the
structure of the units at the highest level (what genre shall I drum?)
down to the lowest level (how do I drum this word?).

For example, Antoine's discourse improvisation is a system of quick decisions primarily at the levels of line (choice and arrangement of phrases), stanza (arrangement of lines), and performance (arrangement of stanzas). Some of these decisions are made while he drums the stall pattern. Antoine's structural and aesthetic decisions are made primarily within the higher levels of the hierarchy. A particular drummer can be recognized by the characteristic decisions he usually makes at these levels, so that each village can recognize their own drumming catechist in contrast to catechists of other Ewondo villages.

Choices within the four lowest levels must be fairly automatic and consistent if the drummer wants to be understood through the speech surrogate medium of communication. The choice of genre is a decision made by the community to meet the felt need of regularly calling the church together.

Form and content of the four lowest levels of the hierarchy—drumstroke, syllable, word, formulaic phrase—must be agreed upon by the speech community, be memorized, and must remain fairly consistent to ensure comprehension. Form and content of the higher levels of the hierarchy—line, stanza, performance—are up to the individual performer's creativity and change considerably from performance to performance. These higher levels of the hierarchy are not memorized as static units, though co-occurrent clusters of phrases are memorized and played as units (with some variations).

RANK-SHIFT occurs when a unit appearing higher on the hierarchy scale is "shifted down the scale to operate as a constituent of a unit of equal or lower rank" (Frederiksen 1977:59). For example, a line can be rank-shifted down to form part of a formulaic phrase.

In 'morning—the day has already dawned', a pause can optionally come after the first word. When a pause is heard here, it makes the first word a separate line (two drumstrokes), as defined by aural criteria. 'Morning' is still part of the larger formulaic phrase, however, when phrase is defined lexico-structurally. Thus, the line has been rank-shifted down to operate as a constituent of the lower-level phrase. When 'morning' is not followed by a pause, the entire phrase is a constituent of the aural line. This choice of pause or no pause suggests that placement of pauses may not be emically significant in some cases, and any marking of an aural line by the analyst must remain fluid.

Rank-shifting also takes place in cases where the stanza is rank-shifted down to form part of the lower-level phrase. The text portion in (108) always appears as a self-contained formulaic unit. The stall pattern, which is the criterion for marking a stanza, appears once or twice in the middle of this set of lines in all but one occurrence in the corpus.

(108)   Someone tells you something, you in turn tell your brother.|
        ku ku ku ku lu ku ku ku|
        ku ku ku ku lu ku ku ku|
        Everything the heart speaks, the mouth cannot say all.|
        ku ku ku ku lu ku ku ku|

This stanza is usually bounded at the end by the stall pattern, but the stall pattern also appears in between the two text phrases. The primary function of the stall pattern at stanza end is as a place to think ahead, but the function of its internal appearance seems to be as an aesthetic device to separate the two textual lines of the entire formulaic unit. The pair of proverbs has more punch when the audience has time to reflect upon the first before immediately hearing the second. The two textual stanzas have been rank-shifted down to operate as constituents of the formulaic phrase unit. *ku ku ku ku lu ku ku ku,* which usually functions as a stanza marker, here appears with an aesthetic function within a phrase unit of two stanzas. The entire five-line unit usually, but not always, appears in this form as a co-occurrent cluster of phrases.

Ambiguity between levels

The hierarchic levels of line and stanza show the most variation within a single performance and within the total recorded paradigm by Antoine. The definitions are ambiguous when related to the level of formulaic phrase. This ambiguity is because, in addition to the phenomenon of rank-shifting between levels, formulas may be combined in various manifestations, and pauses may change position or be omitted within the line.

The four formulaic phrases in (109) may be combined into ten different manifestations.

(109)   a. you come hear (this) doctrine
        b. Christians
        c. now it goes in the house [church]
        d. you will say to me what else [excuses]?

Some variant combinations are due only to omission or changing position of pauses. Such variation does not affect meaning, but it does affect cognitive chunking (see chapter 12) by delineating single phrases or multiple phrases in a single aural line. An aural line with a single phrase is pre-chunked by the performer. An aural line with multiple phrases requires chunking into constituent phrases by the audience. Temporal segmentation at the line level provides the primary basis for organization of aural data as drummed. When pauses are not inserted after each phrase by the drummer, comprehension is more difficult for the audience.

The ten combinations in (110) may be preceded by various phrases, but all appear at stanza end followed by stall pattern (except the final stanza).

(110) a. You come hear doctrine.¦
b. You come hear doctrine, now it goes in the church.¦
c. You come hear doctrine, Christians, now it goes in the church.¦
d. You come hear doctrine. Now it goes in the church. You will say to me what more excuses?¦
e. You come hear this doctrine¦ Now it goes in the church. You will say to me what more excuses?¦
f. You come hear doctrine¦ Now it goes in the church¦ You will say to me what more excuses?¦
g. Doctrine—now it goes in the church.¦
h. Doctrine, Christians, now it goes in the church.¦
i. Doctrine—now it goes in the church. You will say to me what more excuses?¦
j. Doctrine¦ Now it goes in the church. You will say to me what more excuses?¦

Rules will now be given to explain how the four individual phrases are used and assembled into the ten combinations (co-occurrent clusters) by Antoine in performance.

Rule 1. In (109a), the majority of the line can be omitted except for the last word: 'doctrine' can function by itself as a formulaic phrase. When it appears in this truncated form, (109c) must co-occur. The word 'doctrine' can also appear in other unrelated formulaic phrases.

Rule 2. (109a) in full form can close a stanza, or appear within a stanza in other contexts, i.e., without any of the other three phrases given here.

Rule 3. If (109c) appears, (109a) (in whole or in part) must occur to give a referent to 'it'. The phrases need not be contiguous within the stanza. (109d) may optionally follow.

Rule 4. The phrases in (109a), (109c), and (109d) always co-occur in the final stanza of each performance. The placement of pauses is variable in each performance.

Rule 5. (109b) may optionally appear between (109a) and (109c), but never in the final stanza. (109b) may occur as part of two larger co-occurrent of direct address: 'Christians, all of Mekomba' and 'Christians, all at the end of the lineage of Mba Nnembe'.

Rule 6. Only three of the four phrases may occur in any one stanza.

Rule 7. Pauses may occur after (109a), (109c), or (109d), but not after (109b).

Rule 8. One or two pauses may appear within the co-occurent cluster, but not after every phrase. Each cluster (excluding (110a)) will have two or three phrases drummed without intervening pause.

The ten combinations of four phrases (forming co-occurent clusters) function as a stanza or as part of a stanza, depending on preceding material. Simultaneously, they function as part of a line, one line, or two lines, depending on the preceding material and the number of pauses. These ambiguities show the difficulty in making rules to explain every combination of every unit of every performance.

These ambiguities also show that the level of formulaic phrase units is the primary level used in surrogate language production, comprehension, and memory storage. The four formulas used in (109) keep their form and content intact (except that (109a) can be subdivided). They are arranged and rearranged differently, however, at the line and stanza level in each performance. Each formulaic phrase unit is a constant, while units at higher hierarchical levels are in constant flux. Units at lower hierarchical levels do not appear in isolation, but only as part of a phrase unit. Individual syllables and words are not drummed singly unless the word is used as a formulaic phrase unit such as 'doctrine' or 'Christians'. Cognition must occur primarily at the phrase level; higher levels change too much, and lower levels are semiotically ambiguous.

It was originally hoped to present a comprehensive generative phrase grammar to account for all combinations of all phrases used in all performances. Grammar as used here means recognition of the significant elements of a communication system "and their distribution in relation to each other and in relation to the larger units of which they are components" (Chenoweth 1972:11).

The fact that eight rules are required to cover ten combinations of four phrases, however, hints that thousands of rules would be needed to generate all possible manifestations of phrase combinations at line, stanza, and performance levels. Even if these rules were postulated, they would only cover ten performances, not the 3,990 or so unrecorded. Some of Antoine's phrases occur only once or twice in the entire recorded paradigm, while some combinations appear in nine of ten performances. It is difficult to know what phrases of his repertoire I missed completely, and which combinations are only apparently obligatory. In a truly oral/aural tradition, there is no guarantee that even the most stable co-occurrent cluster will be exactly the same in each performance (cf. Lord 1960:125).

10
Performance Paradigm as a Communicative/Aesthetic/Social Transaction

Communicative transaction

Sounds and signs reverberate through the air, around trees and houses, as one man drums at dawn while the village awakens. All the people go about their business for half an hour, then some meet in the church room. What communication has taken place? A social transaction has occurred that involves participation and intended action as well as transmission of coded information. The communication involves creativity within constraints and has a purpose which is judged successful on the basis of actual outcome. The communication is not just the sound of the drum, but it is culturally created meaning assigned to the sound by the participants.

Numerous models for the study of communication have been proposed. King (1989:52–63) has combined interaction models of communication (by Berlo, Engel, and McCrosky) with transaction models (by Barnlund and Jorgensen) to develop the fullest "music communication model." Some of the relevant elements of these models will be applied here to the catechist's drumming in Mekomba.

Communication is a dynamic process, leading to interaction for the purpose of influencing people. The term COMMUNICATION TRANSACTION is used (based on usage by Fleming 1988) to indicate that action takes place, as Nattiez would say in his tripartite analysis, on both sides of the "aural object." The communicator brings his own agenda to the transaction, including intended content and intended effect. But the audience members have the final say as to the understanding of content, its effect, and their willingness to come to church.

"Noise" may be present in any area of communication, acting to obscure the message. Noise such as birds and roosters will probably be heard in the acoustic channel; there may be noise introduced in the performance when Antoine makes a mistake; and noise may be present in the message perception since people are waking up and not giving full attention to the drumming.

In addition to internal and external noise, Fleming (1988:305) points out the elements that are more difficult to measure but still have a great impact on a communication transaction, such as shared intents, interests, attitudes, beliefs, evaluations, and background knowledge of the communicators.

Communication is more than merely producing a message, it is socially constructing meanings for the message. Drum sounds and drum meanings both emerge from the interaction among the participants in a specific context (cf. Fine 1984:70). Each person who hears the drumming will derive and assign meanings to the sound event. Everyone (even the village's few Protestants) assigns a general meaning to the performance as a whole, while some assign specific verbal meaning to the individual drum patterns. Interpretation of each aural event and its meanings are based on several factors: the sound itself, the various levels of contexts, and the personal knowledge and experiences of the individual participants.

For Nattiez (1990:18–19), the meaning of communication is found in the interaction of the three parts of his model. The sender does not transmit meaning directly to the receiver through the message; rather, through a complex intentional process of creation, patterned drummed sounds exist as a momentary aural object (the message). On the other side, a complex process of reception takes place which actively reconstructs the meaning of the sound and the intention of the sender.

All participants in a communication transaction assign meaning to the sound. The creative and receptive processes, however, rarely correspond exactly. Meaning intended by the performer may be lost (some of the verbal meaning is lost to some people each time in this performance paradigm), while different interpretations may be constructed by the audience and projected onto the sound. To the extent that the meanings assigned to the sound by sender and receivers overlap, the communication transaction is said to be successful.

The factor of unrepeatability, often mentioned concerning communication transactions, emically seems to be absent in this speech surrogate system. In the performance paradigm, the precise structure of each performance changes (which is emically irrelevant), but the components, function, and general meaning are static with identical participants and context. In contrast, in most performed interaction (whether music or language), at least some things are recognized as being changed with each occurrence. Canale (1983:4) declares that information is never fixed but is constantly changing and is qualified by such factors as context, nonverbal behavior, varying participants, choice of language form, and further information available. Meaning in communication is continuously evaluated and negotiated by the participants, according to these communication theories.

The emic view of Mekomba participants, however, is that performance meaning is constant, fixed, and repeatable. The genre-level meaning, general content, performance practice, and participants are fixed, but not the specific choice of formulas and discourse structure of the communication transaction. It does not seem likely that the performance's basic meaning has been continuously evaluated and negotiated twice a week for over forty years because the code, contexts, goals, and participants' interaction have remained constant. The specific meaning of each discourse phrase emerges as each aural line is drummed in time; the general meaning of the communication transaction as a whole has remained unchanged. Once the broad meaning of the catechist's performance paradigm was socially constructed, each performance acts to maintain that meaning rather than to create new meaning.

Another factor that is present in many forms of communication but largely lacking in this Ewondo speech surrogate system is audience feedback. As is the case in other mass media message systems, the general populace has little opportunity for input into the communication production. The audience gives little feedback except by church attendance or lack of it, but this varying attendance does not seem to influence what the drum communicates. This very limited feedback may partially account for the fact that the general meaning of the paradigm and its component phrases are relatively static; only a few drummers (and not all Ewondos) have opportunity to change things in the communication system.

Mass media message system

The Ewondo speech surrogate system can be viewed as a mass media message system (Gerbner 1985:16).[41] Collective attitudes, thought, and action in the speech community are made possible because everyone

---

[41]See van Dijk (1985b) for "new approaches to the analysis of mass media discourse and communication."

aurally perceives a drumming performance simultaneously, whether the message involves a few lines or an extended discourse. Many people in Mekomba have receptive competence to at least roughly understand any short message which is commonly drummed.

The closest equivalent of the drum as mass media in a society with more technology is the loudspeaker. All other forms of communication (conversation, print, telephone, radio, and television) usually speak to those who choose to hear or see the message. It is usually possible for people to ignore the media or physically leave it. When one of these media is forced upon someone by loud volume, such as loud music at a party, people often feel their aural personal space has been invaded. A loudspeaker or talking drum sows its message indiscriminately on unreceptive or receptive ground (referring to the audience behavior desired by the communicator). Whether regarded as relevant or not, the message's sound reaches everyone within a radius of a few kilometers and cannot be avoided.

Analysis in this study is of the mass media message system that involves relationships between drumstrokes, words, and people in the context of Mekomba village. The drummed church summons aurally actualizes these relationships in performance, and meaning emerges out of these relationships.

Numerous factors determine the effectiveness of mass media. They include what the audience thinks of the message source, whether the message is geared toward a specific subgroup, whether individuals who receive the message highly value membership in that social group, whether the media fits naturally into the existing communication patterns of the society, and whether ways are provided for the audience to act on the message (Smith 1992:209).

All of these are relevant concerns in regard to Antoine's performance paradigm. "The effectiveness of a mass media message is normally determined by factors apart from either the message or the media carrying the message" (p. 209). The attitudes of the message receptors play the largest part in whether or not people actually come to the church service (the communicative intent of the drummer). The medium (drum) will be effectively used because of its loud volume and accepted use in the society. The actual drummed message can effectively communicate depending on the audience's understanding of the verbal phrases. The sound of the drum and persuasion of the words can, however, be drowned out by the attitudes of the audience. During my time in Mekomba, I estimated that no more than ten percent of the residents attended church on any give Tuesday or Friday morning in response to Antoine's summons.

Aesthetic transaction

As well as being a communicative transaction imparting propositional knowledge and a social transaction involving community and transition, the performance paradigm serves as an aesthetic transaction involving perceptual knowledge.[42] The drum sound itself is aesthetically neutral, as are all art objects. It is the participant's strategies of creation and comprehension that determine the degree of artfulness. According to Berleant (1970:52–53), an aesthetic transaction involves an art object, its creator(s), and individuals who activate the aesthetic potential of the art.

Blacking has stated that

> The "art object" by itself is neither art nor nonart; it only becomes one or the other because of the attitudes and feelings of human beings toward it. Art lives in men and women, to be brought out into the open by special processes of interaction. Thus the signs have no meaning until that meaning is shared, so the *processes of sharing* become as crucial to the semiotics of music as the sonic product which provides the focus for analysis. (1981b:192)

Antoine's sound patterns require a great deal of effort and attention to produce and to understand. The "process of sharing" described by Blacking is quite pronounced and requires a deeper interaction between the people of Mekomba. The sound producer in Mekomba communicates a very personal message which cannot be duplicated by anyone else.

The communication mode chosen to express a message has major influence on the aesthetics which are realized. If someone in Mekomba went door to door and spoke the paradigm phrases, or left them at the doorstep in written form, the aesthetic response of people would presumably be quite different. The "process of sharing" the same verbal information would be changed drastically with changed results. Blacking claims that "our chief concern is with artistic processes rather than content, and that ultimately the effect of art as art depends on our sensitivity to the different modes of communication that are used" (1981b:193).

Writing about drum language in Ghana, Avorgbedor states that "the drum phrase, as a form of a musical encoding, affects the listener with more empathy due to the elaborate and indirect way of 'speaking' to an audience" (1986:23).

An aesthetic response may be activated by the verbal poetry of the implied phrases and/or the musical sound patterns of the drum. Musical aesthetic responses can be potentially activated by many people (including

---

[42]Aesthetics is a notoriously slippery concept across cultures. It is used here in Nketia's sense of "sensuous perception and cognition" (1984:23).

cultural outsiders), while response to verbal aesthetics presupposes fluency in the surrogate language. The potential for an acoustical aesthetic response is easily accessible as everyone in the area hears the surface structure tonal-rhythmic patterns. To activate the aesthetic potential of the verbal poetry, significantly more effort must be expended by audience members.

When the aesthetic potential of both elements is activated, the sound experience takes on richer aesthetic overlays than possible in pure music drumming or recitation of poetry. The combination of verbal poetic devices in the signified and musical sound structures in the signifier means that aesthetic potential can be activated in response to both heard and unheard sign systems.

Berleant (1970) has suggested eight qualities of aesthetic experience related to Western art forms. They have been applied by Fine (1984:78–86) as a means of distinguishing artistic verbal performance from other modes of communication. These qualities, in slightly modified form, will now be examined to see how they fit the aesthetic transaction of Antoine's drumming in Mekomba. Though they represent etic concepts, their presence or absence may indicate an underlying emic conception of the drumming.

Active-receptive. Audience members may participate as active listeners: following the flow of the drum's argument, thinking of their own baptismal vows and approaching deaths as requested, separating aural lines into component phrases, and anticipating the final stanza. This participation of the audience involves receptive competence, as listeners exhibit familiarity with the genre pattern and can understand and judge what is being heard.

It is difficult to know how many Mekomba residents really give close attention in this way. Those who actively listen are probably those with the deepest knowledge of the verbal phrases. For some, at least, the drumming is probably part of the acoustical soundscape taken for granted because of its regularity; they are passive listeners.

Sensuous. The sound of the drumming has a sensuous quality, setting up tonal-rhythmic patterns to be enjoyed at the aural level with or without verbal understanding—musical even by an outsider's standards.

Agawu (1987:403) writes of African modes of rhythmic signification. Speech surrogate drumming is one of many such modes, also including childrens' game songs, work songs, greeting formulas, formal speech, and other aurally perceived art. Even the stylized patterns of African dance drumming have some bonds with verbal rhythms (p. 417). All of these rhythmic modes have a sensuous quality in intention and perception.

Immediate. Aesthetic involvement with a performance is felt with a compelling directness; the drumming has a sense of immediacy. When a speech surrogate drummer is asked to step out of the performance mode and explain or dictate phrases, the aesthetics of the transaction are felt to be muddied in the spoken analysis which is distanced from the real event, the drumming. When the drum phrases are removed from performance context and spoken, read, or dictated, the aesthetic immediacy of pure sound patterns is removed.

Integral. Artistic form is created in performance then vanishes no less quickly than the drummed words; the aesthetic sense must be activated at the same time as verbal comprehension is gained. Aesthetic form, verbal content, and social expectations are integrally intertwined and must be found together in the perceptual experience for the fullest audience participation in the drumming.

Unique. In regard to most art forms, it is claimed that people have a unique experience with the art object at each different encounter, whether or not the art object itself changes. In the case of the drummed church summons in Mekomba, each performance is a unique sonic object but leads to essentially the same experience for participants each time it is created. Each performance is unique in its specific discourse structure, but this uniqueness is emically felt to be irrelevant. This aesthetic quality of uniqueness is related to the communication feature of supposed unrepeatability mentioned previously.

The remaining three aesthetic qualities given by Berleant—intuitive, preanalytic, and intrinsic—seem to apply less to Antoine's performance paradigm than do the other five qualities. The less applicable fit of those qualities is due to the intended purpose of the drumming. Focus in Mekomba is less on the performance for its own sake and more on the commands and persuasion of the hortatory argument. What is most important is the propositional truth that cannot be arrived at by intuition, but must come from verbal analysis of the drumstrokes. The drumming may be intuitively appreciated as pure sound, but if not analyzed and verbally understood, then it is not functional in the way intended.

The patterned sound is a musical form/language meaning composite (cf. Pike 1971:63), and the aesthetic potential may be activated for both parts. The perceived musical form can be approached in an intuitive (prereflective), preanalytic (nonpropositional), and intrinsic (focused on itself) manner. A cultural outsider hearing the drumming on tape could conceivably have these responses, as is possible for the residents of Mekomba. The meaning of the unperceived language, however, is considered the reason for a performance. If church members perceived the form and activated its aesthetic potential but did not grasp the intended meaning, the performance would be considered unsuccessful. It is, after all, a functional means to a more important end later.

Of the suggested eight qualities, four seem to be present in the aesthetic transaction of Antoines's performances. One quality is reversed from the norm in emic terms, and the subdued presence of the remaining three demonstrates in etic terms what is expected: the aesthetic aspect of the speech surrogate drumming, while present, is less important than the communicative aspect. In contrast, purely musical drumming at a dance can be easily understood to have all eight characteristics of an aesthetic transaction, and the communicative aspects would probably be deemphasized.

Social transaction

Aurally perceived performances, including music, poetry, and speech surrogates, not only exist within culture, but help create and maintain culture and its component relationships. The drumming is a context where symbols are interpreted and actions are chosen, actions of obedience or disobedience to the religious call. But whatever personal actions are chosen, Mekomba as a whole simultaneously hears the call.

Community

Antoine's drummed summons aurally unites the village, though only a portion of the residents are members of the Roman Catholic church. Even though only a portion of the membership attends on any given occasion, his soliloquy unites the entire audience as a community through numerous direct addresses. He brings together the generations, calling present Mekomba inhabitants by invoking the names of long-ago lineage founders. The current lineages are reinforced, as is Antoine's authority within the church.

Different from most aural arts, Antoine's drummed speech surrogate creates an involuntary audience of individuals, everyone within auditory range (several kilometers). Each person is in bed in the dark before dawn, then is called to unite with other individuals and to form a social unit to engage in ritual purpose (church liturgy). Each one is called to consider the impact of standing alone before God at death; this summons is the motivation to gather now in life.

Whether or not they understand the verbal text, everyone knows the basic meaning of the message. For those who comprehend the words, a rich exhortation is created in time. The catechist's drumming reinforces social relationships through sound relationships. High and low pitch, short and long duration, poetic lines marked by pauses, stanzas separated by rhythmic phrase; these musical/textual acoustic relationships call everyone to participate in community relationship in the church room (cf. Seeger 1987:6). As one drumstroke in isolation carries no meaning, message, or power until it is joined with others, so each person is called to join together now before God and the church leader.

The performance of this drumming by the appropriate person at the appropriate time reinforces the roles within the church. All congregants are basically equal before the catechist. He will soon be the physical authority in the gathering; now he is the auditory authority in the gathering command. The re-creation of leader-congregation relationships through drumming creates a social, aural context that influences other social, physical interactions (cf. Seeger 1987:93).

The church summons is what Hall (1992:229) calls high context communication: "most of the information is already known to the recipient." Because a high context communication system has much shared information between performer and audience, each communicative act strengthens the link between them more than imparts news. The speech community has shared these phrases for forty years, though many people have limited understanding. The act of religious gathering has also been shared by the community for decades. The catechist is not saying anything new, but is recreating the social relationships with his summons. The primary purpose of the communication is not to give knowledge where there was ignorance, but to implore the community's participation.

The drum phrases of the past, the current church relationships, and the future meeting with God are all united in this aural event. Sound socializes and unites the community in its shared traditions.

Transition

The *nkul* is often used to call people to move for a designated purpose. Sometimes the purpose is rather mundane: 'Wife, bring food to my farm', or the drum is used to gather residents for a community workforce such as clearing paths. At funerals, the *nkul* functions in both music and speech spheres, marking the transitions from life to death to life beyond.

A significant connection has been noted between rites of passage transition and "the production of distinctive sounds" by both oral means and percussion (Needham 1967). Percussion and ritual speech are used to signal and motivate category change (transition) in an experiential manner, to create movement (both internal and external) that is felt and physical between social categories (Knauft 1979:189).

The ritual drum speech is used to mark the transition from a collection of individuals and families into a cohesive social unit, the transition from thinking about self to reflecting on God's kingdom. Knauft writes that "percussion can easily be used for functional ends—to manage social transitions and foster collective solidarity" (p. 190). When the percussion instrument also talks (as a speech surrogate), it is a most powerful tool for affecting transitions: physical, social, and metaphysical transitions into the gathered body of Christ.

Antoine's drumming marks the beginning of a liminal period from aurally connected but separated individuals to the corporate church body. This liminal phase, begun by drummed poetry, becomes highly prosaic, as people get dressed, brush teeth, etc., and decide to assemble (or not assemble) for a sacred purpose. During this time of preparing for the day and worship, each individual is called to reflect upon his own destiny, vows, and church obligations. The "speaking" percussion instrument not only indicates 'come to church' (as do church bells elsewhere); it reasons with people, implores them to consider the past (baptism) and future (death), to make every effort to gather together for this most important purpose.

Integration of aspects in the communicative/aesthetic/social transaction

The performance paradigm has been studied from a tripartite perspective as a communicative/aesthetic/social transaction. Each aspect influences the others, and when one part is changed, ripple effects are felt through the entire paradigm. If the communicative form were changed from mass media to face-to-face speaking of the same phrases, the aesthetic and social aspects would also be drastically changed.

Any type of speech surrogate message will have aspects of communication and most have aspects of social interaction. Aesthetic considerations probably become more pronounced in longer performances because there is more aurally perceived material to work with. A thirty-second drum message of 'wife, bring food' has minimal aesthetic considerations; verbal communication and social interaction are primarily intended and understood by both participants. As a performance expands to Antoine's three-minute norm, potential features of an aesthetic transaction are more fully developed by performer and activated by the audience. A thirty-second drum call on Tuesday and Friday mornings would functionally suffice in Mekomba to summon the church; the fact that it is five or six times this length indicates that something regarded as worthwhile can be accomplished only in a longer performance frame.

The catechist's twice-weekly drumming is a transaction in which the communicative aspects, aesthetic aspects, and the social aspects all have atypical elements. The people are aurally gathered but physically separate in their own houses. A message is given through mass media, but the message instigator has more intimate knowledge of the audience than does a television announcer. The poem's structure changes twice a week but is not based on interaction with an (absent) audience or changing context. Considerable effort is put into creation but few people understand all the intended words. This type of performance, in this context, with this response, is an anomaly in regard to most speech acts, aural art objects, and social interactions. Speech surrogate drumming is like language, poetry, and music in some ways but is most clearly in a category by itself.

The artificial tripartite division developed here can bring etic insights, but it must be emphasized that a performance is one integrated sound event in the emic perspective. Agawu (1987:403) states that a distinction between functional and artistic events are ultimately irrelevant in the integrated context of African society and sound. All three aspects of the communicative/aesthetic/social transaction are created and perceived simultaneously. What binds them together is that the aspects are experienced as all-encompassing sound in performance.

11
Genre, Register, and Lects

Genre and contextual configuration

To think of text structure not in terms of the structure of each individual text as a separate entity, but as a general statement about a genre as a whole, is to imply that there exists a close relation between text and context. (Halliday and Hasan 1989:68)

GENRE[43] can be studied as the verbal expression of a specific CONTEXTUAL CONFIGURATION. This configuration involves FIELD, TENOR, and MODE in Halliday and Hasan's terms. Field has to do with experiential meanings, tenor with interpersonal meanings, and mode with textual meanings. These elements of the contextual configuration will now be examined in relation to the Ewondo speech surrogate genre represented by Antoine's drummed discourse paradigm.

The field of this genre is a summons to gather at Ewondo Catholic churches for doctrine class, which reinforces maintenance of an institutionalized system of religious beliefs and behavior. The tenor is that of a religious authority (and drum specialist) reminding and persuading a collective subgroup of the community to now attend the meeting. The audience is unseen but personally known, within hearing distance, and has an institutionalized relationship to the drummer as catechist and a

---

[43]The following section is based extensively on the social-semiotic model proposed by Halliday and Hasan 1989. Other models dealing with genre are mentioned briefly in Bex 1992:10–11.

different relationship to him as neighbor and local farmer. The mode is a system of speech surrogate formulas prescribed by the local community for this purpose. The drummer performs a persuasive monologue which is a necessary precursor to the church meeting.

When Mekomba residents awaken to the sound of *nkul* on Tuesday and Friday mornings, they quickly construct in their minds a model of the contextual configuration. They assign to it a field, recognizing that a scheduled, public communication is being drummed at dawn. They assign to it a tenor, recognizing the personal relationships involved. They assign to it a mode, recognizing specific meaning and broad intention communicated by the speech surrogate formulas. Through this mental construction of the contextual configuration, the genre is recognized, and the audience knows what action is expected of them. Even though the verbal formulas are not well understood by the majority of Mekomba residents, the field enables the tenor to be surmised with high probability, and these are sufficient to broadly identify the speech surrogate genre even without understanding all of the actual words of the mode.

The field and tenor have primarily to do with context and social interaction, while the mode is concerned with text and its texture. The three parts have a reciprocal influence on each other, and together delimit a genre in its social experience: textual meanings, interpersonal meanings, and experiential meanings.

Using language is a social activity. The contextual configuration of a specific genre points out the most significant attributes of this social, verbal interaction. Using language face to face will be very different from using language at the long-distance range of mass media drumming, and the differences can be seen by comparing the contextual configurations of each language use.

The contextual configuration is the verbal expression of a genre's GENERIC STRUCTURE POTENTIAL that is stated in terms of optional and obligatory elements in a genre and their order and repetition which are appropriate to the context. Obligatory elements in the generic structure potential particularly define a genre and set it apart from other genres. Optional elements set apart one performance from another within a genre.

From culture is derived a semiotic potential (meaning system). From the semiotic potential is derived the semantic potential (communication system). From the semantic potential is derived the generic structure potential of a particular genre. From the generic structure potential is derived the actual drummed performances (cf. Halliday and Hasan 1989:99–100).

The generic structure potential for the Ewondo genre of drummed church summons is manifested in a paratactic discourse form. This means the sequential arrangement and inclusion of units is variable and not completely predictable, though it is not random either. In Antoine's transcribed performances, some formulaic phrases and co-occurrent clusters of phrases appear in nine of ten performance texts, while a few appear only once. Since generic structure potential and genre are abstract notions, it follows that no particular text can be completely representative of a genre (Bex 1992:10). It seems possible to say that Antoine's total performance paradigm can represent one manifestation of a genre, and one performance represents one manifestation of the paradigm.

Comparative data is lacking at this point to suggest the generic structure potential for this genre as drummed by all Ewondo catechists. The following comments are based on the village-specific dialect drummed in Mekomba by Antoine, with some comparisons made with Atemengue's dialect drummed in the neighboring village.

Obligatory elements of Antoine's analyzed ten-text corpus include:

a typical opening stanza which must begin with one of two direct address phrases, and has flexibility for formulaic phrases to be omitted (even the majority) or inverted in order;

the rhythmic stall phrase used at least nine times (obligatory in some co-occurrent clusters);

'descendants of my father' used at least five times;

'you come hear doctrine' used at least four times;

'now it goes in the church' used at least four times;

at least two direct address phrases using the names of Mekomba, Owondzuli, or Mba Nnembe, one of which must be in the opening stanza;

a closing stanza with minimal variation, primarily in pause placement, wherein the three-phrase co-occurrent cluster serving as the discourse peak is only allowed to appear; and

a final rhythmic nonverbal coda where some variation is permitted.

Most other elements (formulaic phrases) are not obligatory in every performance drummed. Even the word 'Christians' may be omitted (as in performance 8). Dozens of phrases will be heard each time, but their inclusion, sequencing, and repetition are decided in performance (rapid composition in real time). The contextual configuration of a genre with paratactic discourse structure makes it difficult to predict the exact form of any particular performance.

How do people judge when a text of a given genre is complete and not left hanging? The most reliable basis is the identity and sequencing of the structural elements. The obligatory features of the genre's generic structure potential must be present before a text is considered finished (Halliday and

Hasan 1989:109–10). Predicting completion is difficult in a paratactic structure since sequencing of elements is variable. All obligatory elements of
Antoine's performance paradigm given above (except the last two) commonly make their first appearance by the start of a performance's second
stanza! After that, Antoine "plays from the heart" until his internal timing
sense says "enough" and he tacks on the two remaining obligatory elements
(closing stanza and final coda).

Differing generic structure potentials

When Antoine's performance paradigm is compared with Atemengue's
performances of the same genre, differences are obvious. Atemengue
often uses an additional stall formula, does not use any direct address
phrases with proper names, and has more varied closing formulas and
nonverbal rhythmic codas.

Conclusions drawn from only three performances cannot reveal much
about the obligatory elements of a genre; nevertheless, it is a start. The
obligatory elements of Atemengue's three recorded performances are:

a co-occurrent cluster used as the opening stanza, with minimal variation permitted;
a variant of 'you/they come hear/do doctrine' used at least two times;
'Christian' used at least three times;
'alone like a solitary bush pig' used once;
the stall pattern 'to doctrine' used at least four times;
one of two formulas used to close the discourse; and
a final rhythmic nonverbal coda, with some variation permitted.

The only two elements in common which are obligatory are a stall
pattern and a form of 'you come hear doctrine'. The performance paradigms have other phrases in common, but these are not obligatory and,
therefore, do not define the genre.

The generic structure potential is different for the performance paradigm
of each drumming catechist, but the function is the same. This genre of
drummed church summons is manifested in performance by communicative
acts which have a common public purpose within the overall Ewondo
speech community. The exact means used by each drummer, however, will
vary somewhat in each performance, and even more so across boundaries
of location or specific discourse communities. The abstract generic structure
potential must take fluid form as performed by the numerous drumming
Ewondo catechists (possibly numbering in the hundreds). The tenor and
field of the contextual configuration for church summons are probably
similar in all villages, but the mode or specific textual phrases may vary

considerably in communities only a few kilometers apart. Therefore, each drummer's performance paradigm would have a different generic structure potential, or utilize different obligatory phrases in each location where the genre is drummed.

The mode (set of phrases drummed by a catechist) serves to identify this genre in each village. A large number of common stock phrases may cross village boundaries, but only a tiny portion are used by all catechists in all performances; a single textual phrase shared by Antoine and Atemengue fits this criterion. It is therefore possible to define the genre in each village by mode but not to define the genre as a whole by a set of drum phrases which are shared by all catechists. Many common stock phrases cross genre boundaries, so it is difficult to define any genre solely by text.

Concerning this genre's contextual configuration among the Ewondo as a group, the genre of drummed church summons is marked more by common field (regularized context) and tenor (social interaction) and less by a particular mode (set of drum phrases).

Relatedness and uniqueness

How is the uniqueness of a single performance text marked, and how may it be different from, similar to, or identical with other performance texts? There are four levels at which these differences and similarities can be perceived: situation, structure, verbal surface structure, and genre (Halliday and Hasan 1989:110–12).

First, unique texts may be drummed in similar social situations, fulfilling one primary function. On the other hand, the same formulaic phrase may be drummed in different situations. The phrases 'all my father's descendants', 'leave the bed', and 'three by three, two by two by two' are all used in a funeral context (Abega 1987) as well as by Antoine in calling the church. A single common stock drum pattern can be used in various situations. Though the sound is identical, the social context, function, and discourse genre are quite distinct, providing cues for distinct connotations.

Second, two texts may be structurally identical but have verbal uniqueness. This possibility is never found in Antoine's paratactic drummed discourses with everchanging structure and is unlikely in the speech surrogate system as a whole.

Third, several performance texts may represent different possible realizations of one generic structure potential. This relationship is found between Antoine's four thousand or so performances. They have structural uniqueness and partially identical verbal phrases drummed within one genre by one performer.

Finally, texts may be unique in regard to genre. This presupposes situation uniqueness, verbal uniqueness, and structural uniqueness. This possibilty is uncommon in the Ewondo speech surrogate system because of the widespread use of polysemous common stock phrases which freely float from one genre to another.

Performances in Antoine's paradigm are bound together by sharing a generic structure potential of obligatory and optional drum phrases, assembled in real-time aural discourse through one man's habitual creative strategies. These performances are made of the same acoustic material and made in the same way, interrelated through product and process.

In the Ewondo speech surrogate system, the drumming sound disappears immediately while the textual references resonate through generations. All is simultaneously unique and related. Phrases point to other phrases, performances point to other performances, and genres point to other genres.

Speech register, dialects, and idiolects

The Ewondo language takes diverse forms through diverse media in diverse social situations.[44] Oral and written speech both have various registers, such as those involving religion or farming. In addition, some language is used primarily in certain places or by specific individuals.

The Ewondo drum language system can be regarded as a register (associated with a particular setting) with dialects (associated with a particular village) and idiolects (associated with particular language users). Any genre drummed may have diverse manifestations due to the interaction of register, dialect, and idiolect.

Defined by Halliday and Hasan, REGISTER is a "configuration of meanings that are typically associated with a particular situational configuration of field, mode, and tenor" (1989:38). The Ewondo speech surrogate register is used whenever mass media is appropriate, and is often connected (but not restricted) to public announcements about someone going somewhere: you come to church, you bring food, you go to the end of the dead, you come to communal labor, the government authority is coming, you come hunt the leopard, watch for the wife running away, you come to the wrestling match, and so on.

The function of a speech surrogate register determines when it is used in a certain setting instead of a different register (such as face-to-face conversation). A communication genre (summons) is chosen from a community's discursive practices; a register (drummed) is chosen which can best make audible an abstract genre and fulfill its social function.

---

[44]Conclusions in this section are drawn from working with drummers in only three locations (Mekomba, Mfou-villáge, and Yaoundé), but are likely to hold true throughout the Ewondo area.

The Ewondo drum language is a restricted register: it has a fixed range of possible meanings encoded into fixed surface structure drum patterns. This register provides tight parameters concerning what can be said and how it can be said. Many other registers (such as informal conversation) may be more open with fewer limitations.

The details of the register (phonological relationship between words and drumstrokes, and formulaic phrases) are not completely shared by all Ewondo drummers; each village has a dialect shared by that speech community, and each particular drummer uses his own idiolect of the speech surrogate register.

Dialect is "what you speak habitually" (Halliday and Hasan 1989:41), and what you hear and understand habitually as well. Mekomba has a drum dialect which differs to some extent with dialects of surrounding villages; certain phrases are habitually used in one place but not in another. The drummers and audience in each location share a drum dialect which is in part mutually intelligible with drum dialects of other villages. The same genres may be drummed (church summons, funeral texts, etc.) in many villages, but the actual phrases used and their discourse construction may vary widely according to drum dialects and idiolects.

Each drummer's idiolect is distinguished from others in the register by the particular mix of common stock phrases known and used, and village-specific (dialect) phrases known and used, which may have been created by the drummer. Together these create an individual's regular repertoire. The chief and the catechist of Mekomba, two of the most commonly heard speech surrogate drummers who share the dialect understood by Mekomba residents, perform different genres with different functions (calling people for church and calling them for communal labor), and use overlapping but nonidentical idiolects (vocabulary of phrases and connections).

Language users can have an active or passive repertory of verbal forms, and most Ewondo drummers probably understand more than they themselves have occasion to regularly use. Audience members in one village will not necessarily recognize phrases commonly drummed in another village. Even in ordinary oral speech, not everyone recognizes all phrases and vocabulary used by the wider speech community.

Each lengthy drummed discourse carries the identity of the drummer through habitual choice of phrases. In a brief message, the drummer usually identifies himself by drum name. A message of a few lines ('come bring food') may not be extensive enough to mark a drummer's idiolect by phrase choice. A three-minute performance, however, such as those drummed by Antoine, is of sufficient length for his idiolect to be recognized even without identifying the drummer by name.

When one traces the limited usage of a community-specific phrase such as 'descendants of Mba Nnembe', understanding comes of how the drumming dialect of a particular community is tied together, i.e., the phrase is used by Mekomba's chief, catechist, and other resident drummers.

Together these drum phrases of wide and limited use make up an individual's idiolect or repertoire. By examining the song repertoire of one singer, one can "begin to get a fuller understanding of the role played by the individual in the on-going creative process of the tradition" (Abrahams 1970:12). In a tradition-oriented speech community, creativity comes about as individual performers capitalize on community values and expectations while developing a personal repertoire and "speaking voice" (cf. p. 12). Each drummer's idiolect is related to the inclusive dialect and register, yet distinctive.

The interaction of speech register, dialect, and idiolect means that a given genre will probably be manifested somewhat differently by each drummer; paratactic discourse structure means that each performance by a drummer will probably be somewhat different as well.

12

Comprehension of the Performance Paradigm

Drummed speech is a hybrid art of musical form and language meaning. This hybrid nature affects both creation and comprehension of the
sound. The performances are not actually perceived as verbal text but as
drummed tonal-rhythmic patterns. Much research has been done on cognition of pure musical (nonspeech) patterns in Western societies; a little
research has been done on pattern perception in African music (Kubik
1977, Wegner 1989).[45] Some pertinent results will be summarized here,
comparing cognition of musical patterning and verbal patterning.

---

[45]Kippen (1987:175–76) has warned that conclusions drawn from rhythm cognition
experiments with Western musicians may not be valid in a cross-cultural setting. This
warning is appropriate; as no studies have been produced on Ewondo verbal and musical
cognition, I will make use of data and conclusions conducted by Western researchers. The
theory set forth in this chapter is at least plausible in the Ewondo context and is offered
as an initial, locally untested hypothesis. At this point, it is difficult to judge which
examples of pattern perception are culture-specific and which are unique, in regards to
music (Wegner 1989).

Auditory perception

Parallel processing of auditory and phonetic data

Speech surrogate drumming has two surface structures: that of the perceived sound and that of the unspoken words iconically represented by the sound. The sound of the speech surrogate drumming must, therefore, be processed at two levels: the perceived musical patterns which represent the base spoken phrases. According to Wood, studies have shown

a basic distinction between two levels of processing in phonetic perception: (a) an auditory level, in which an acoustic speech signal is analyzed into a set of corresponding auditory parameters; and (b) a phonetic level, in which abstract phonetic features are extracted from the results of the preliminary auditory analysis. (1974:501)

In regards to Ewondo speech surrogate drumming, an initial auditory perception takes place: the process of categorizing the drumstrokes by duration (short/long) and pitch (low/high). From this auditory analysis, phonetic processing occurs as audience members compare each drummed pattern with models of possible textual phrases which are already known to determine the correct verbal interpretation. Further phonetic and auditory processing often occur in parallel as each phrase is heard and recognized. Both levels of processing occur primarily at the phrase level since single drumstrokes cannot be categorized in terms of pitch, duration, or phonetic features represented.

Discrimination of acoustic elements and patterns

Elements of Antoine's sound patterns must be quickly categorized in terms of pitch and duration. "Musical rhythm is the discrimination of temporal patterns in sound, perceivable in terms of previously formed conceptual patterns or by repetition which gives rise to conception" (Eskelin 1971:124).

Categorical perception of incoming acoustic elements is a prerequisite for further cognitive activity. It is interesting that the perception of oral speech has a great deal to do with the articulation of consonants (Lehiste 1972:1–7) which are paramount in speech comprehension. The fact that each Ewondo consonant tends to receive a separate stroke on the drum aids in categorical perception of the sounds. The way in which some musical sounds are perceived "is functionally identical with that of the most categorical of speech sounds, namely, stop consonants" (Cutting, Rosner, and Foard 1976:368).

As the individual acoustic elements are perceived and categorized, patterns of combined elements are also perceived. The patterning of drumstrokes can be broken down into a pair of two-element patterns: short/long duration and high/low pitch. Each component pattern is perceived holistically with the other pattern; they are combined into an aural composite where pitch and duration are perceived simultaneously (cf. Preusser, Garner, and Gottwald 1970).

Perception of drumstrokes' duration

The audience's perception of each drumstroke's duration is relative to the perception of all other drumstrokes in the performance, adjacent and nonadjacent. A listen to Antoine's drumming demonstrates that the two drum tones are not merely concatenated in succession, but exist in relative timing (Martin 1972:488) to one another in a rhythmic pattern consisting of two primary durations. How are the two basic values of duration perceived? The answer may be related to an individual's "internal clock" as proposed by Povel and Essens (1985). The temporal spacing of drumstrokes follow a steady pulse for the most part, although the pulse is not organized into a meter. The pulses can determine the unit (♩) and subdivision of the unit (♪) of the internal clock. If the drummer alters his speed, the internal clock can adapt to the sequence under consideration (p. 414). The temporal (rhythmic) structure of the drumming is coded at the lowest hierarchical level in terms of the hearers' internal clock: the duration (and tone) of the drumstrokes must be perceived before chunking or higher cognitive activity can take place.

Conceivably, drumming without a steady pulse such as is used by Antoine would put more strain on a hearer's internal clock or even suspend its operation. With duration as much as with pitch, however, the relative intervals are key. The precise length or tone of any drumstroke carries little significance; what is important are the relationships between drumstrokes.

According to Abbs, a person's intention to produce a given phonological unit is "implemented by generating perceptually acceptable acoustic waveforms" (1986:202) via neuromotor activity. The exact speed and relative timing of the drumstrokes will be variable, though consistent enough that the sound patterns can be recognized by the speech community.

Structural organization

Hierarchical ordering of sound sequences

Martin points out that "sequences of sounds, speech or otherwise, that are rhythmic will possess hierarchical organization, that is, a coherent internal structure, at the sound level" (1972:488).[46]

Kubik writes that "in African music it is obvious that wherever a pattern is perceived the elements which constitute this pattern are somehow *ordered* in relation to one another" (1977:223). Relational ordering is found at all levels of the hierarchy: between drumstrokes, between phrases, between lines, and between stanzas. Temporal and tonal ordering create the levels of the hierarchy, and determine the units on each level.

Serafine also uses the concept of HIERARCHICAL STRUCTURING, "the notion that music is organized on several and successively deeper levels of structure" (1981:6). She elaborates the term to mean that "certain tones are endowed with greater weight or importance than others. These 'more important' tones compose the basic, underlying structure, and other tones of less weight or importance serve an elaborative or decorative function" (pp. 6–7). People can conceptually organize the busy surface structure of tones to a more basic, underlying musical structure. They can distinguish structurally important tones from those which are merely elaborative.

This use of the term hierarchical structuring holds true for much African dance drumming: some drumstrokes elaborate other more central strokes. With few exceptions, however, this distinction does not seem true for Ewondo speech surrogate drumming: one note is no more important than another, no notes are nonstructural (including false syllables). This structural equality of notes is one significant difference between pure music drumming and Ewondo speech surrogate drumming. It is partly due to the fact that Antoine's drumming has no regular meter or accents as in song. Speech surrogate drumming in overt musical contexts (such as speaking to dancers) in other African cultures may exhibit Serafine's suggested difference in weight of notes.[47]

Language also has some words which are more important than others: for example, *book* is more structurally important than *the* in a noun

---

[46]I have proposed a hierarchy of elements in chapter 9, but this does not lead to a hierarchically organized structure of transformational rules. "Pragmatic variations on repetitions, deletions of expected phrases, associative clusterings involving a large amount of historicity can be sharply distinguished from hierarchically organized rule structures" (Pribram 1982:31). Antoine's paratactic poetry fits with the first set of criteria.

[47]For example, at the Damba festival in northern Ghana, a Dagbamba drummer may "sweeten the rhythm" by doubling the drumstroke (Locke 1990:106).

phrase. In a speech surrogate, however, understanding is much more difficult if even a few drumstrokes are omitted. When cognition occurs at the phrase level, and a phrase can be as short as one word (bekristen), few drumstrokes can be merely elaborative or nonstructural. All of Antoine's drumstrokes are equal in cognitive importance, from musical and textual perspectives.

The only exceptions are the optional vowel prolongations in a few words at line end. These prolongations can be said to be elaborative and nonstructural, drummed for aesthetic reasons. It is important, however, to note their potential placement: only when the entire phrase has been heard and before a pause. They are not placed to interfere with textual comprehension.

Units of music and text

Serafine writes about UNIT CONSTRUCTION in music as "the creation of short, coherent, memorable units" (1981:6–7). The creation of such musical units is analogous to the creation of formulaic phrases from the textual perspective. These units can then be joined together in unit chaining (analogous to textual lines). UNIT CHAINING produces larger units that are more coherent and memorable than random collections of random notes, or units of notes joined in a random manner. Tonal-rhythmic phrases joined together in an aural line are coherent and memorable. Large-scale units are also constructed in music on a level known as PHRASE GROUPING. The phrase-grouping unit is similar to stanza from the textual perspective. Since most speech surrogate patterns are verbally based, the meaning and grammar of the signified words provide the main restrictions on unit construction (phrase), unit chaining (line), and phrase grouping (stanza).

Chunking by phrases and pauses

According to Kramer, "most music is patterned—chunked—in some manner" (1988:336). Some of Antoine's lines are long—up to sixty-three drumstrokes without a pause—and the notes must be chunked in some manner for the audience to cognitively process the aural line.

The chunking mechanism may be that of musical contour and/or verbal phrase. In both cases, the unit used in cognition is not the individual note or word, but notes or words chunked into larger self-contained coherent units.

Chunking in music is "the psychological mechanism that responds to music's rhythmic groupings" (Kramer 1988:339). A chunk is defined as "a stimulus pattern or sequence that the memory system recognizes as a

familiar single unit for which an internal code already exists in memory"
(Bower and Cirilo 1985:75). If a person has no previous understanding
of the musical system or grouping principles, only individual notes can
be perceived.

Musical notes may be temporally grouped by a hearer in two different
ways: by musical phrase or by musical meter. These two grouping
mechanisms are in contradistinction, as musical phrases may frequently
cut across metrical units (Longuet-Higgins and Lee 1982:116). As there
is no meter in Antoine's drumming, the notes can only be grouped by
verbal phrase (requiring text understanding of the audience) and/or
grouped by musical line and stanza (aurally grouped by performer).
Temporal grouping of drumstrokes in a dance context may take place by
musical meter as well.

When some understanding of the musical grouping system is acquired,
writes Kramer,

> We hear and remember not simply a series of individual notes but
> a melodic line consisting of notes and relationships between them.
> Some of these relationships become memorization cues.... This is
> one reason we hear melodies as ongoing entities rather than as
> successions of single notes. (1988:336)

When the verbal basis of the drumming system is understood by an
audience, the tonal-rhythmic patterns are perceived as speech and not as
a succession of single drumstrokes. In oral speech, cognition can occur at
the level of an intonation unit that is likely to be a single clause with a
single intonation contour, followed by a pause (Chafe and Danielewicz
1987:95). In Ewondo speech surrogate drumming, however, each clause
is not necessarily followed by a pause, minimal intonation is present, and
several clauses are often strung together into one line. Therefore, the
criteria of intonation unit does not apply.

More so than in speech, the hearer of the drum must work at providing a usable chunking mechanism. Listening effort must be invested to
chunk a line into its component phrases, because "cues for the boundaries of chunks are not unequivocal" (Kramer 1988:336). In Antoine's
performances, a phrase may be aurally equivalent to a line or part of a
line, or a line may be part of a phrase, depending on context and the
insertion of pauses into the text. If he drummed each formulaic phrase
separately and paused, much chunking would already be accomplished
in performance and it would be easier to understand. Because the same
phrases are aurally chunked differently in each performance, however,
the listener has to work harder at quickly chunking cognitively at higher
levels as the performance progresses. The drummer prechunks his drumming only partially; the rest is up to the audience.

The performer provides aural chunking at line and stanza structural levels by means of pauses and the stall phrase. Verbal comprehensibility, however, mainly occurs at the phrase level, which must often be chunked by the audience without aural cues (pauses), only by previous knowledge of the verbal phrases.

This previous knowledge of phrases is related to what Kubik (1977:234–35), in reference to African music, calls a "scanning pattern" in the memory of the hearer. If a sound does not match a preconceived mental pattern, disorientation occurs, and the hearer perceives only a chaos of drumstrokes. When verbal phrases are recognized against sound patterns, cognitive chunking occurs.

The number of chunks that may be retained in short-term memory is limited to about seven (cf. Pressing 1984:360). If the sixty-three drumstrokes which begin performance 1 are conceptually unassociated, they cannot be remembered or carry any verbal meaning. If these same drumstrokes can be conceptually chunked into six phrases by the audience, the aural line can then be understood and remembered. Note that Antoine drums no more than six phrases in any given aural line, perhaps unconsciously aware of this chunking limitation in human perception.

The variant insertion of pauses into the text does not affect meaning, but it does affect cognitive chunking. In one music cognition experiment, it was found that "pauses aid memorization and recall when they are inserted between the melody's natural chunks...and hinder encoding when they are inserted elsewhere" (Kramer 1988:339). Musical sequences that are temporally segmented according to their inherent (in this case textual) chunking are recalled best by a hearer. When structured sequences are not temporally segmented (as are, for example, Antoine's six verbal phrases in one aural line), they are not recalled as well. "In most tasks, it appears very difficult not to allow the temporal spacing to dominate organization" of incoming sound patterns (Handel 1973:54).

Physical and structural phrase markers

In spoken and written language, performed and notated music, the phrase is a unit of particular importance in cognitive grouping of data (Sloboda 1977:118). In language and in music, some units are defined by physical markers such as punctuation, word space, or aural pause. Other units are defined by structural markers. For example, a written syllable is marked by phonological rules, and oral speech elements are organized into groups by means of intonation. Included as structural markers are the unheard boundaries which mark Antoine's formulaic phrases in a lengthy line or stanza. A linguistic or musical unit may be marked by both physical and structural markers; they are not exclusive (p. 117).

Spoken language has fewer physical markers than written language (p. 117). Spoken words, for example, are not heard separated on each side by space, though they are written that way. In Antoine's speech surrogate, the performer places physical (aural) markers at the line, stanza, and performance levels to mark bounded units. Structural markers at the phrase level are equally needed for comprehension, but they must often be supplied by the hearer's previous knowledge and conception of the formulaic phrases and their possible combinations.

In a test of reading music notation, results showed that music readers use structural as well as physical cues in the analysis of music. This "suggests analogies between music and language processing at fairly high levels of abstraction....Musical cognition may be a non-verbal skill which has the kind of characteristics usually associated only with language" (Sloboda 1977:123). Probably the people of Mekomba use closely related cognitive skills to make sense both of perceived drumstrokes and of signified verbal text.

For readers of language and music, the presence of both structural and physical markers causes cognition to extend exactly to a phrase boundary (Sloboda 1977:117). This phenomenon may be true of hearers as well. It would suggest "that the time course of analysis progresses in leaps from one boundary to the next rather than in a continuous flow" (p. 122). Anyone who listens to a drum performance can easily hear the aural boundaries (indicated by physical markers) of units at the levels of line, stanza, and performance. Those who know what the drum is saying, however, hear not a flow of irregular drumstrokes in each line, but recognize the boundaries (indicated by structural markers) of each phrase unit within the line or stanza.

Each of Antoine's formulaic phrases remains identical in surface structure form for the most part. Therefore, when a hearer recognizes the beginning boundary of a phrase (which may take up to seven drumstrokes), he will know the entire phrase. The beginning phrase boundary acts as a memorization/cognition cue for the entire phrase. The hearer must then concentrate on the next phrase boundary, indicated by structural markers. The physical marker of a pause may or may not be present.[48]

In reading, recognition of only the beginning part of a word can bring recognition of the whole word. Similarly, recognizing the initial part of a drum phrase can bring recognition of the entire phrase. "The fluent reader passes over letters, and even words, in favour of larger meaningful units" (Cole 1974:23). This phenomenon also seems to be true in aural recognition and comprehension of speech surrogate drumming. The fluent hearer can

---

[48]For a brief bibliography on pauses in verbal cognitive processing, see Scollon 1981:337–38.

pass over individual drumstrokes and words and recognize the phrase as a unit.

In pure music, the ending of a phrase unit is often marked structurally by a cadential sequence of notes (Sloboda 1977:119). Antoine's tonal-rhythmic-verbal phrases do not have any sort of cadence or structural marker that the phrases are about to end, though the intonation pattern of vowel prolongation can mark the end of some aural lines, somewhat like a musical cadence. Knowing the verbal base is the only way to predict the boundary of a musical phrase, line, or stanza.

Role of memory

Memorable sound patterns

The drum patterns are most fully memorable when the underlying text is known. Even at the lowest hierarchical level of drumstrokes—pure sound—many phrases, however, are rhythmically coherent and memorable in a western aesthetic sense, and are easily recognizable at this lowest nonsemantic level. For example, the pattern 'to sons and daughters' is a common opening line. Pulses are indicated by dots in (111).

(111) . . . .

♩   ♪ ♪ ♩   ♪   ♪ ♪ ♩   ♩   ♪

♩   ♩   ♪ ♪ ♩   ♪   ♪

Even a foreigner, after hearing this pattern a few times, would be able to recognize the rhythm (not the text) because it is so well balanced and memorable in a musical sense. For me as a Western-trained drummer, each of Antoine's drum phrases is unique enough to be identifiable (in isolation), even as pure sound without text. Each phrase also brings out a subjective, aesthetic response so that Antoine's drumming can be enjoyed on the level of wordless sound.

Some scholars state that tonality is more important than rhythm in recognizing the actual words of speech surrogates. Rhythm has been said to come into focus "especially to distinguish otherwise homophonous signals" (Stern 1957/1976:139). In the Ewondo system, rhythm and tone seem to be of equal value in creating recognizable, memorable sound patterns.

Since the drumming carries only prosodic linguistic information, the stylized rhythms become even more important for cognition than in speech. According to Martin, "there is a great deal of evidence that

rhythmic patterning carries a heavy information load in ordinary connected speech. This is particularly evident in cases where speech remains
intelligible when segmental information has been distorted or destroyed"
(1972:500) as is heard in a speech surrogate system that only represents
suprasegmental information.

Both time and tone contribute to the perception of the drummed
pattern, and thus to the verbal phrase. A single drumstroke has duration
and pitch, but only in contrast with other drumstrokes. The cognitive
patterning of drumstrokes leads to the perception of textual phrases and
meaning, and these patterns are maintained in the memory of participants from performance to performance.

Forms of information coding in memory

In a cognitive sense, CODING "refers to what is stored in memory during
learning" (Rubin 1981:174). There are at least seven forms of coding,
and six of them are pertinent to this study: echoic, rhythmic, linguistic,
motor, musical, and notational. The seventh form of coding, naming, is
not as relevant and will not be discussed.

ECHOIC CODE is "a temporary mechanism needed to hold incoming
sound while other codes have a chance to be formed" (p. 174). This
retention is necessary for the retrospective patterning which takes place
at all hierarchical levels of the performance. Sound is stored in an unana-
lyzed form for a brief time until grouping and comprehension comes into
play (or when no grouping and no comprehension occur and the sound
is forgotten).

RHYTHMIC CODE is "a way of setting up reference points on which words
can be placed. In fact, learning a rhythm and words is often easier than
learning just the words.... Rhythmic structure often coincides with linguistic structure" (p. 175). Martin points out that "speaking and listening
are dynamically coupled rhythmic activities, such that linguistic information is encoded rhythmically into the signal by the speaker [or drummer]
and decoded out of it on that basis by the listener" (1972:489). Temporally patterned speech sounds can be "redundant with respect to
linguistic message elements to a far greater extent than sounds that are
only concatenated" (p. 488).

LINGUISTIC CODING usually preserves only the meaning of speech, while
the surface structure, the actual sounds, go into echoic coding and are
soon forgotten. One cognition test showed that "by the time 80 syllables
had passed only changes in meaning could be detected with any accu-
racy" (Rubin 1981:176). The surface structure was not retained.

If a text is rhythmically coded, however, the linguistic surface structure will be better remembered. As Rubin notes,

Rhythm can aid in recall. This can occur, however, only if the exact number of words, or rather syllables, is recalled, and not if a paraphrase that loses the rhythmic structure is recalled instead. If the rhythmic or intonational structure matches the semantic structure, then recall is greater than if rhythm were not present...*Thus where rhythm is present there are forces acting to preserve the exact form as well as the meaning.* [emphasis added] (p. 179)

Antoine's dictated version is an example of the recall of a paraphrase without rhythmic encoding. Because he said it without the drummed formulaic rhythm, he dictated surface structure variations not found in drummed performances. When rhythmic encoding was not used, the exact formulaic phrases used in drumming were not always dictated and surface structure variations were spoken.

MOTOR CODES are similar to linguistic codes. Motor skills are "hierarchically organized, rule bound, and productive in the same way that language is. The analogy is strongest, however, for the complex motor skill of speech" (Rubin 1981:178). Because it is rhythmic and related to speech, the motor coding in Antoine's hands reproduces exact formulaic phrases in an automatic manner.

MUSICAL CODING has a lesser effect on speech surrogate drumming. Two pitches are used, but not in a tonal manner as in the song system. The tones are connected to speech more than to music. Each tonal-rhythmic pattern does have a musical sense, however, and the musical aesthetics of drumming have some impact on how the underlying verbal texts are manifested. "Redundancy is added to drum and whistle messages by the orchestration of the transferred verbal structures with musical rhythms....The superimposition of musical structures upon verbal ones...not only increases the intelligibility of messages but may serve certain aesthetic goals as well" (Sebeok 1976:197).

NOTATIONAL CODING is a form "that allows for the use of external memory aids...[It has] virtually no limitations on capacity" (Rubin 1981:179). Notation was necessary for me as a cultural outsider to learn the speech surrogate system and necessary for transcribing, comparing, and analyzing a series of performances. Notation lessens the need for echoic coding; sound (or rather a representation coded on paper) will stay in space when it will not remain in time.

Object memory and process memory of participants

Antoine and his audience utilize both OBJECT MEMORY and PROCESS MEMORY in discourse creation and comprehension. First, specific phrases, or discourse building blocks, are entered into object memory in various codings including rhythmic, linguistic, and motor codes. Second, composition techniques of phrase juxtaposition and preferred combinations (co-occurrent clusters) are used each week and form the basis for process memory (cf. Pressing 1984:355). Object memory has to do with the bones of the performance skeleton while process memory has to do with the joints.

It has been said that "remembering is a process not of reproduction but of reconstruction" (Treitler 1974:344). The creation and comprehension of the drum messages involves reconstructing the skeleton in a new way in each performance. Going beyond speech surrogate formulas, it has been suggested that all language is more a matter of arranging and recognizing preformed phrases and utterances than of arranging single words (Tannen 1992:11).

The terms of object and process memory are related to those used by Austerlitz (1983:5–6). Members of the speech community have SPECIFIC MEMORIES of utterances (parole) and SYSTEM MEMORIES of how the speech surrogate system works in general (langue).

When Antoine begins to drum a discourse, through object and process memory he recreates the general content and structure which are typical of his performance paradigm. A person who remembers an incident or performance text "has it before him in some sense in its totality before he begins to verbalize it" (Chafe 1977:42). A speaker or drummer organizes his memory of the text in chunks and communicates in chunks, according to patterns already established in his mind. These patterns, or SCHEMATA, would primarily consist of co-occurrent clusters in the case of Antoine's performance paradigm. Through the process of forming schemata (p. 46), a paradigm of lengthy discourses is chunked in Antoine's memory in units which can be easily expressed on the drum in terms of phrases, lines, and stanzas forming co-occurrent clusters.

Memory: Short-term, intermediate-term, and long-term

In the initial perception of sound patterns, a stimulus event is heard and laid down as a fleeting memory in an auditory sensory buffer. Features such as pitch, duration, and silence are detected and

> an identification stage ensues during which the system tries to classify the stimulus. Roughly speaking, pattern recognition is assumed to involve a weighted matching of the current feature list against a likely set of protoypes (idealized patterns) [already extant in long-term memory]....Accuracy of identification depends on the quality of sensory information extracted [how well did the drummer perform and how well did the audience hear] and how many alternative prototypes [and other similar formulas] are under consideration. A word will be identified more readily if it is probable and expected in the context. (Bower and Cirilo 1985:74)

Short-term memory "tends to preserve the surface perceptual properties of the stimuli as well as their temporal order" (p. 75). It has been pointed out that rhythmic encoding of the perceived surface structure drumstrokes in a particular patterned order aids recall of the signified verbal formula. In the case of many speech surrogates, the surface perceptual properties must be stored in long-term memory as well as in short-term memory.

Short-term memory has a severely limited capacity for processing unrelated information units, usually no more than seven (cf. Pressing 1984:360). This limit of seven coded items is significant at two levels of the hierarchy. First, one contrastive pair of phrases are homophonous for the first five drumstrokes. It means that at least six drumstrokes must be kept in short-term memory to distinguish the two phrases. Second, up to six phrases may be drummed in a single aural line and must be kept in short-term memory in order for the sense of the entire line to be understood. If two formulaic phrases were identical for more than seven drumstrokes, or if an aural line consisted of more than seven phrases, the short-term memory would likely be overloaded and cognition would be impaired.[49]

If a listener had to hear fifteen drumstrokes before recognizing and identifying a phrase, the earliest drumstrokes would probably already be forgotten. If Antoine chunked as many as a dozen formulas into one aural line, it would be very difficult for the audience to keep up with the discourse flow. Therefore, the limit of seven coded items in short-term memory is an important restriction which is followed in Antoine's idiolect of drum language. More research is required to determine if this restriction is followed by all speech surrogate drummers.

As well as short-term memory, which can manage a few phrases, and long-term memory, where prototypes of all formulas are stored when not in use, the cognitive system uses intermediate-term memory, or working memory. Working memory "constructs and maintains an internal model of the immediate environment and events of the past few minutes" (Bower and Cirilo 1985:76). This memory level is constantly updated with new information as a performance progresses, and can hold all of Antoine's drummed message, which lasts usually less than three minutes.

All three memory levels are utilized simultaneously throughout the conception and perception of each performance. For the audience, surface structure patterns are identified in short-term memory, matched against verbal formula prototypes in long-term memory, and built into a coherent discourse through intermediate-term memory.

---

[49]In all of these cases, immediate discourse context also helps in distinguishing phrases, and could possibly override the seven-item limit.

For the performer, formulas are retrieved from the stock in long-term memory. In short-term memory, the phonetic features of the drum patterns are computed and stored as an ordered string in an output buffer. The phrase is then translated into neuromotor commands (cf. Allen 1975:84). The relationship and discourse ordering of phrases into lines and stanzas takes place in intermediate-term memory. This working memory "holds the plan that the person is following in performing some task. The plan is typically a hierarchically structured set of goals, subgoals, and anticipated actions" (Bower and Cirilo 1985:76). Working memory structures each performance in a different way to achieve a single standard goal and action: a well-made discourse to encourage church attendance.

For Antoine, what goes on at the levels of short-term and long-term memory must be fairly automatic. He does not consciously compute the drumstroke pattern for each phrase, nor consciously select from a stock of formulas. The conscious creative speech act of each performance takes place predominantly at the level of intermediate memory, just as in speech we do not consciously compute all phonetic features or think of all the words we can choose from. We "just talk" in a manner similar to the way Antoine "just drums."

> For listening comprehension to occur, numerous cognitive tasks must take place in a brief period of time, and they all require attention. When listening, the activities which require attention include segmenting the speech stream into morphemes and syntactic units, holding idea units in memory, identifying anaphoric terms, finding the referent for those terms, and integrating information from the speaker with knowledge stored in the memory of the listener. (Samuels 1987:299–300)

Because attention must be given to all of these tasks simultaneously at a high rate of speed, some of these cognitive tasks must be performed with as little attention as possible, or automatically.

The performer's conscious attention is given to choices at the discourse level, while precoded motor movement sequences necessary to reproduce formulaic patterns receive automatic attention (cf. Pressing 1984:356). At the discourse levels of line, stanza, and higher, decisions are made in real time. Decisions at the lower hierarchical levels were made long before through the performer's habits (task rehearsal) and the consensus of the speech community. It would not be feasible for a drummer to decide during a performance how to handle vowel elision or consonant clusters; phonological decisions would greatly slow down a performance. In oral speech as well, unconscious attention is given to phonological phenomena while conscious attention is given to ordering an utterance.

Recognizing mistakes in performance

Whether spoken or drummed, errors are not uncommon in normal speech (cf. Laver 1970:75). A transcription of performance 7 shows three occurrences where tones were inverted by accident, in these cases shortly before a pause. These mistakes probably came about through errors of motor action (striking the wrong drum side or holding the stick at an incorrect angle) and not through errors of thought. Tone mistakes are probably not uncommon in speech surrogate drumming (see Arom 1976:128 for a tone mistake on a Banda talking drum).

In some cases it appears that Antoine corrected himself, especially at the beginning of an aural line. In performance 10 a set of four low tones were drummed, but the third should have been a high tone to represent *mòt à bé fé*. Antoine recognized his tonal mistake and quickly stopped and restarted that phrase. The study of speech errors has provided "clear testimony to the presence of an error-correcting code operative both in speaking and listening. Speakers pre-edit their linguistic programs both covertly, in the planning stage, and overtly in their execution, so as to secure efficient and optimal speech communication" (Cohen 1986:528).

While drumming the stall pattern, Antoine plans or pre-edits his next wave of drumming (aural line) up to a pause. If a mistake occurs near the beginning of a line, he is likely to stop and start over. If a mistake occurs well into the line, he does not stop to correct it.

Cognition

Cognition and contexts

Appropriate meanings for drum language are determined through the performance and discourse contexts. When interpreting discourse of any type, the hearer must select the appropriate model of interpretation according to the situation (Cushing 1984). In the case of the drummed church summons heard in Mekomba, the hearer selects the interpretive model that applies to formulaic phrases drummed regularly in the performance context of Tuesday and Friday dawn, as opposed to a model to account for discourse spoken face-to-face later in the day. The latter model must theoretically cover every potential utterance. The model for perception of drummed discourse in this restricted environment must account for only about a hundred formulaic phrases.

Discourse context also has an effect on processing strategies. In studies of English material presented aurally, discourse context was found to

influence the immediate cognitive processing and organization of a subsequent clause; as well, listeners made certain types of context-based
inferences prior to the end of a sentence. As pointed out by Tanehaus and
Seidenberg, "the initial processing and representation of a sentence in
discourse may differ from those of the same sentence presented in isolation...[C]lausal processing strategies can be affected by discourse
context" (1981:211).[50]

When a phrase is used in various performance and discourse contexts,
the model of interpretation will vary according to those contexts. "Text
structure can lead to different processing strategies...Conversations are
listened to differently from lectures and lectures differently from dramas"
(Danks and End 1987:273). Most Ewondo verbal interaction does not
consist of a long-distance monologue of pure prosody composed of assembled formulas. The phrase 'all my father's children' will be processed
somewhat differently depending upon the performance and discourse
contexts in which it is perceived.

Cognition and contextual elimination

Nketia (1971a:730) points out that there are two main factors that
influence an audience's efficiency in decoding an implied verbal text
from tonal-rhythmic patterns. Both require significant effort by the
hearer. The first factor is familiarity with the text, which comes from
repeated listenings and an initial verbal explanation by someone in the
speech community. The second factor in decoding is the contextual elimination of phrases sounding similar or identical.

The textual identity of a tonal-rhythmic unit "is defined both by what
precedes and what follows it. Thus identical rhythmic groups may be
given different verbal interpretations depending on their position in sequences of rhythmic groups" (Umiker 1974:511; also cf. Nketia 1968:35).
Often the first few notes following a phrase boundary are not enough to
ensure comprehensibility. Retrospective patterning is used at the line and
stanza level, therefore, to check the context of a phrase to see whether it
makes grammatical and semantic sense. This necessity of making sense
seems also to be the main restriction Antoine has in ordering the phrases
within each performance.[51]

The acoustic elements of a performance must be connected in an
agreed-upon, coherent manner to carry the intended meaning. These
connections must fit the drummer's aesthetic, musical sense as well. In
the drummed speech act, the sequencing of drumstrokes into phrases,

---

[50]For models of discourse processing, see van Dijk 1987.

[51]The idea of a message "making sense" constrains a communicator at every moment
and is invoked by the listener in interpreting the message (Fry 1970:31).

phrases into lines, lines into stanzas, and stanzas into performances must satisfy all syntactic, semantic, and aesthetic constraints. These constraints are equally valid for the drummer's creative act and for the act of interpretation by the speech community, i.e., audience members expect the drummed message to be in proper grammatical form, to make sense, and to meet certain aesthetic standards.

Prediction and retrospective patterning are common strategies used to process speech. Perception of drum speech is a form of pattern recognition, that is, phonological, grammatical, and aesthetic interlocking patterns which are repeated inter- and intra-performance. Each of these patterns is an arrangement of acoustic cues (cf. Fry 1970:35). Recognizing some cues of a stereotyped phrase means that feedback and feedforward can occur, processing what has been heard and predicting what will be heard (cf. Martin 1972:503).

In most cases of communication, unconscious predictions are made concerning what will be said next. Any surprise will usually be within the broad framework of something that is expected (Halliday and Hasan 1989:9). Fluent use of a language involves "knowing a great deal about what is likely to follow at any point in a spoken language, that is, a knowledge of sequential probabilities on all levels of the language" (Fry 1970:31). The actual acoustic information perceived is combined by the hearer with what he expects to hear.

In the case of perceiving homophonous surrogate signs which are ambiguous, retrospective patterning is used not only to adjust expectations concerning the future items, but also to adjust perception of the preceding ones (Smith 1968:13). For example, the pattern of five low contiguous long notes in (112) is acoustically very striking, but has two different verbal interpretations. The proper interpretation is determined both by what precedes and what follows the five notes.

(112)

e- wu- wu- lu~e- wu- wu- lu a mi- na- mə mi- nam
walking aimlessly from place to place

be- ke- ri- se- te- ne a- ke di a- ke a n- da-
Christians, now it goes in the house [church]

Prediction of items based on context is not limited to word level and higher. In decoding speech, all phonemes in a language system are not equally probable at the same point in an utterance. This limits the possibilities that must be scanned in the acoustic processing to those phonemes that are most probable (Fry 1970:48).

In decoding a drummed speech surrogate, no actual phonemes are heard; the drumstrokes carry only the prosodic information of tone and length. Feature detectors exist, however, in human cognition for nonlinguistic sounds (such as drumstrokes) as much as for phonetic features in speech sounds (Cutting, Rosner, and Foard 1976:374). When the initial part of a drum phrase is recognized, the completing drumstrokes can be predicted to a large extent since they are chosen from the few patterns that are most probable.

As Tarasti points out, "earlier musical events [motifs in the piece] are stored in the memory of the listener and thus continuously influence the way any event heard in the 'now' moment of music is experienced" (1985:111). Acoustic elements of a temporal, musical chain are constantly compared with preceding elements, both those which are contiguous and those which have been repeated elsewhere, and a paradigm of memory is increasingly developed as a piece continues.

There is also a paradigm of expectations, made up of compositional choices considered probable by the listeners. "Where the paradigm of memory has a continuous tendency to grow, the paradigm of expectations, on the contrary, continuously decreases as the work proceeds, and the possibilities of choice diminish as the work finds its own line determined by its choices" (p. 112). The end of a performance is found in the beginning to some extent, although as pointed out, a section of the typical opening stanza can be repeated as late as the penultimate stanza. Both memory of past motifs and expectations of future motifs help guide audience members in following a performance, and both are determined through the "collective musical memory of a given tradition, style, [or] community" (p. 113).

According to Poyatos (1983:77–78), there are four possible ways of decoding the meaning of signs: (1) SHARED DECODING when meaning is common to a group; (2) IDIOSYNCRATIC DECODING when association of the sign and its meaning is peculiar to an individual; (3) FALSE DECODING when the sign is given the wrong interpretation; and (4) ZERO DECODING in which signs are not decoded at all. All of these are possible responses to the speech surrogate drumming.

Individual cognition

There are various levels of receptive speech competency among members of the local speech community. When I was practicing the drum patterns, about ten Mekomba residents walked in off the path at different times, heard me duplicating Antoine's phrases on a drum, and repeated them to me verbally. They all recognized some of the phrases, but no one recognized them all. Individuals have different degrees of understanding gained through more or less developed cognitive skills, but there is a common agreement as to what the sound patterns mean.

According to Fine,

> Language use is a creation of cognitive forces as well as social forces. Cognition, unlike social structure and interaction, is not a source of meaning or a source of systems of meanings. Cognition is inherently individual, whereas meanings must come out of negotiated interactions for which individuals must agree with each other what and how language means . . . The abstract systems of language are actualized in specific situations for specific social purposes. Generalizations are thus derivable from how groups of speakers have agreed to interact. (1988:180–81)

Structural and functional perception

Perception takes place in two stages, according to Smith: "structural (the physical reception of signals by the sense organs) and functional (the mental interpretation of those signals). Functional perception is usually the critical element in achieving effective communication" (1992:284). Even when the acoustic elements are heard and adequately categorized in terms of sound patterns through structural perception, it is only the first step in full comprehension.

Smith (pp. 271–84) gives six axioms of functional perception:

Perception operates from experience. The more experience one has had in decoding a paradigm of performances, the easier it will be to interpret the next one.

Perception depends on social configurations, especially when structural perception is unclear. This axiom harks back to Halliday and Hasan's description of a speech act's field, tenor, and mode. Even if perception of the sound is unclear, or the textual phrases are completely unrecognized, the performance situation and social configuration provide sufficient cues for proper interpretation of the general meaning intended.

Perception is always selective. People functionally perceive that which promises to meet a felt need. Members of the Roman Catholic community in Mekomba have agreed to use a speech surrogate drum to serve as a wake-up call and persuasive reminder of church meeting dates. All residents perceive the drumming as sound, though the message is not relevant to noncatholics. The minority who understand much of the drum language can choose to focus on perceiving the sound at the textual, semantic level as well.

Perception seeks to reduce surprise. As each performance is built up by formulaic phrases, aural lines, and structural stanzas, new sound stimuli are related to patterns which are familiar or similar in the listeners' memory. Antoine intends to drum no surprise phrases ("or they would think it was another catechist"), and the audience expects to hear none. When the speech surrogate phrases are already known they may be more easily understood and assimilated.

Parts are perceived as parts of a whole. Drumstrokes and drum formulas are not perceived in isolation but as part of an entire performance paradigm. Recognition of only the essential parts of a word brings recognition of the whole word (Cole 1974:23); similarly, recognizing the essential parts of a drum phrase brings recognition of the entire phrase.

Items close in time and space are perceived as parts of the same structure. Lines, stanzas, and co-occurrent clusters are perceived in relation to each other within the entire surrogate speech act.

Factors influencing comprehension

Samuels (1987:296–309) divides factors which influence aural comprehension into "inside-the-head" and "outside-the-head" factors. The former have to do with the hearer, the latter have to do with the speaker (or drummer). Inside-the-head factors relevant to this study include:

> the listener's ability to recognize words and formulas and to segment and chunk the speech stream into its component parts;
> the listener's accurate understanding of Antoine's idiolect of drum language; and
> the listener's ability to follow cohesive ties, make appropriate inferences, and understand the implications of common stock phrases in this discourse type.

Outside-the-head factors in this study include:

> the drummer's presentation of too much information;
> the drummer's too rapid presentation of new information;
> a clear and well organized presentation of the message; and
> an unimpeded hearing of the sound of the drum.

A listener in any speech act has little control over speech rate and no continuing access to what was said except through asking the speaker to repeat. Listeners are "forced to process the signal immediately regardless of whether they are prepared to receive new information or whether they are still processing the immediately preceding signal" (Danks and End 1987:276). In most listening situations, however, the speaker and audience typically interact face-to-face so that the listener has some potential control over the communication and can give feedback. In contrast, the listener in many drummed speech acts is out of sight of the speaker and has no input at all into the distant monologue. Besides visual cues, aural cues such as intonation and stress which aid in proper parsing of material are also missing.

Together, all of these factors mean that comprehension as much as creation of drum speech is dependent on individual skills combined with communicative standards of a community.

13
Orality, Literacy, and Aurality

An interactive continuum

Some scholars[52] have set forth the Great Divide theory between orality and literacy, focusing on the opposing world views they supposedly predetermine and their distinct effects on verbal arts and ways of thinking. Others[53] have critiqued this model, seeing orality/literacy as a dynamic and reciprocal complex of interrelated, interactive, and interpretive practices representing the norm in many cultures (George 1990:4).[54] Concerning the effects that oral versus written media are said to have on culture, Finnegan states, "once-confident assertions about the supposed differentiating features of oral and literate cultures are now exposed as decidedly shaky" (1988:13–14).

---

[52]See Maxwell 1983:xiii for a list of members of "an Anglo-American oralist school of cultural studies," including Ong and McLuhan.

[53]For several Great Divide critiques dealing with language, see George 1990:4, Bauman 1986:9–10, and Finnegan 1977 and 1988. See Finnegan 1986 and Feld 1986 for critiques of the Great Divide theory from an ethnomusicological perspective.

[54]Literacy and orality are said to interact in complex ways according to community, genre, and tradition; cf. George 1990. This interaction is clear in the case of Mekomba. For detailed studies of orality/literacy interactions within specific cultures, see the *Cambridge Studies in Oral and Literate Culture* series. This fine series goes beyond the simplistic dichotomy of earlier years.

A huge amount of paper and discussion has been generated concerning the differences between written and spoken language.[55] Numerous generalizations have been proposed, but also numerous exceptions. Recent conclusions have been moving from a simple dichotomy to an interactive continuum between orality and literacy, recognizing that any discourse type within a culture will have a complex of characteristic features. In a single discourse genre, some features may be commonly labelled as indicating "oral" and others as indicating "literacy."

Horowitz and Samuels (1987:9) present a chart of the stereotyped oral-written dichotomy.[56] The characteristics found in the speech surrogate performance paradigm are split evenly on each side of the supposed dichotomy. On the oral side, we find that the performance texts are: action oriented (towards receptors), situated and bounded here and now, sharing numerous contexts, interpersonal, repetitive, fleeting in the sense of sound, and made of simple linear structures in paratactic patterns.

On the literacy side, we find limited reciprocity between communicators, artificial communication which is formal and argument oriented (towards sender), explicitness in text, cohesion through linguistic cues, permanence in the sense of memory, hierarchical levels, and conscious planning. The communication via drummed sound patterns is not face-to-face or face-to-text, but could be regarded as hand-to-ear.

Often the point is made that written texts provide fewer communication cues than oral communication: paralinguistic elements such as gestures, intonation, tone of voice, and emphatic phrasing are absent from written texts. In this regard, the drummed performance paradigm offers fewer communication cues than are provided through writing, which at least gives consonants and vowels.

A primary communication cue that the drumming does have in common with oral communication is the immediate context of performance. Even for Mekomba residents who do not understand any of the drum's implied verbal phrases, the general meaning is obtained through context, which is less likely in a written text in a language not understood. Situationally constructed meaning is most important for interpretation of meaning in oral discourse (Watson and Olson 1987:329). Written texts are generally produced for future reception, and meaning is less easily constructed and confined to only one situation. In the case of Ewondo speech surrogate drumming (though not in the case of membranophone speech surrogate drumming at a dance), the personal interactional context is missing (similar

---

[55]See Luetkemeyer, van Antwerp, and Kindell 1984 for an annotated bibliography on this topic. See Clark 1984 for a helpful summary of various academic perspectives on the matter.

[56]The authors clearly say that this dichotomy, based on the work of numerous scholars, "begs for research" and point out a high degree of overlap between the two media.

to written communication) while the regularity of performance context is sufficient for general meaning to be inferred. This inference can take place even without precise understanding of the words (sometimes possible in face-to-face communication).[57]

Even though communicators share an immediate context, it is not interactional in the same way that face-to-face oral communication is. The drummer is, like a writer, "detached from direct personal interaction" (Chafe 1982:52) and has very limited control over who may receive the message. The unseen audience has little opportunity for direct feedback in the communication transaction. The drummer is unlike a book author in that he has intimate personal knowledge of his audience, more common in conversation (or personal letter writing, for that matter). All of these factors combined mean that this type of communication transaction is unlike any other type, be it oral, written, or electronic mass media.

All five of the speech surrogate drummers I worked with are literate, though the literacy skills seemed to have no effect on their process of drum communication, either at the phonological level (such as eliminating vowel elision) or at the discourse level (such as a fixed text). I suspect they kept these communicative systems compartmentalized in their minds as the visual and aural sign systems are kept separate and given different functions by society.

Literacy has had a direct effect on the content of the performance paradigm. The genre of drummed church summons has only been in existence since missionaries introduced Christianity and literacy to Cameroon about a hundred years ago. A "religion of the Book" (Goody 1987) gradually became primary in Mekomba and brought a new use for the speech surrogate system. The aurally perceived communication already in use took on new content, form, and context as the drum was used to call together the congregation. The community at large still relies heavily on aural communication: the catechist is often the only person present with a book as he leads the meeting, while most other participants answer according to their memory and as orally cued by Antoine. Without literacy and the Bible coming to Cameroon, Antoine's performance paradigm would not exist (except for the common stock phrases already extant); it would lose its reason for existence. Without the aurally perceived drumming or even a bell, however, the congregation would not be gathered so easily (or persuasively). The catechist's summons is the most common speech surrogate drumming heard in Mekomba today. It may be ironic that it owes its continued existence to the acceptance of a

---

[57]It is possible for either context to be present or absent in other genres: the interactional context is present when a speech surrogate speaks to a dancer or recites royal genealogy at court, while in some cases the performance context of drumming is insufficient for general meaning to be inferred (such as announcing a death from another village).

religion built on a book; *bibug bi doten* 'words of doctrine' is the key to
the drummed discourse.

Ewondo society in Mekomba uses a mix of communicative media as
does Ewondo society in Yaoundé, though the media mix will vary from
rural to urban areas. Radio, written materials, and face-to-face communication are plentiful in both places. There is no place here to posit a
simple primary oral culture in world view or use of language. Communication in Ewondo culture is oral plus aural surrogate (drum) plus visual
surrogate (writing and print) (cf. Goody 1987:xii).

Communication is a dynamic process, "a socially interactive and inter-
subjective process of reality construction through message production
and interpretation" (Feld 1984:2). Every communicator possesses a repertoire of resources and devices "which are combined in varying mixtures
depending on the context, the purpose, and the subject matter of language use. In other words, language adapts to its varying environments"
(Chafe and Danielewicz 1987:110). In regard to speech surrogate drumming, the verbal language is adapted in sound and structure to be most
useful as a mass medium, and preexisting drum language phonology,
phrases, and function were adapted to church use as Ewondo society
changed.

Six oral/literate dimensions of communicative acts

Orality, literacy, and speech surrogate drumming are all used in the
church's communicative repertoire; language is adapted as needed. Biber
(1988) has proposed an analysis of communicative acts using six dimensions, each on a continuum of linguistic variation. Any genre or
individual speech act can be plotted on these continuums, specifying the
extent to which it shows characteristics of stereotypical orality or literacy. Comparisons should be made on the basis of all six dimensions. In
English, written and spoken texts overlap in every dimension (Biber
1988:160) as various genres are weighted in one direction then in the
other along the six continuums. "No absolute spoken/written distinction
is identified in the study. Rather, the relations among spoken and written
texts are complex and associated with a variety of different situational,
functional, and processing considerations" (pp. 24–25). To this I have
added production considerations, keeping in mind the basic tripartite
analysis (performer production, situated sound, and audience processing)
used in this study.

Biber's approach to macroscopic textual variation in a language would
bear the most fruit when applied to different communicative media and
genres within a single culture. For example, this model would be a good

base to analyze differences and similarities between spoken language, written letters, radio, and drum speech in Mekomba. In addition, different genres such as memorized church liturgy and drummed church summons could be succinctly compared. Unfortunately, this full communication ethnography would require significantly more time and effort than I had available during field research. I will gauge the relative position of the Ewondo drummed church summons genre along these six dimensions, and someone else may be able to use these findings in comparison with other forms of Ewondo communication, or in comparison with other speech surrogate systems. The conclusions are not surprising; Biber's analytical method makes it possible to be more precise as to why certain conclusions were reached.

1. Involved versus informational production. Antoine's performance paradigm exhibits frequent occurrence of present tense, second-person pronouns, and emphatics. It has few nouns and much repetition of vocabulary. These combined elements show that the drummed speech acts focus on interpersonal and affective content rather than on strictly informational content. Unedited discourses produced under strict real-time constraints (such as composition in performance) generally have low informational densities.

2. Narrative versus non-narrative concerns. Besides content, some linguistic features that mark this non-narrative, hortatory discourse are infrequent occurrences of past tense verbs, third-person pronouns, and present participial clauses.

3. Explicit versus situation-dependent reference. Personal referents are explicitly identified through the names of lineage founders and the village's name in direct address phrases repeated throughout a performance. The temporal reference is likewise made explicit: it is dawn, come now quickly, the doctrine has already entered the chapel. Even though the broad social and immediate performance contexts are known to all, Antoine's drum speaks very explicitly and directly when referencing people, places, time, and things. Someone hearing or reading a performance for the first time even out of context would have little trouble identifying all referents. Clues for comprehension are verbally given and not dependent on the situation.

4. Overt expression of persuasion. These drummed monologues seek to strongly convince hearers to take a certain action based on the superiority of the position claimed by the authority. Many of the phrases in a given performance can be categorized as directly persuasive, with the remainder indirectly persuasive or setting up the context for persuasion.

5. Abstract versus nonabstract information. Discourses such as these which present nonabstract information generally feature active agents and little technical terminology.
6. On-line informational elaboration. When information is added and elaborated under real-time production constraints, it may be presented in a fragmented manner by tacking on additional clauses, rather than by packing information into more high-content words and phrases. Explicit marking of an individual's stance, including personal opinions, attitudes, and statements, is frequently found in genres that rate high in this dimension. All of these features appear strongly in Antoine's performance paradigm.

Together, all of the features highlighted in these six dimensions are apparently well suited to the combination of communicative demands of Ewondo drummed church summons (cf. Biber 1988:160). Plotted on continuums of all six dimensions, the graph for the Ewondo drummed church summons genre is unlike any graph for any English language communication genre in Biber's study. This conclusion is not surprising; English does not have this combination of communicative demands or resources: an individual's persuasive, reference-specific, non-narrative, interpersonal and affective, nonabstract discourse produced as pure prosody under severe real-time constraints on a musical instrument in mass media format twice a week. Mekomba does have this combination of communicative resources available, and Antoine's drumming has served well for over forty years.

Biber (1988:162–63) characterizes "stereotyped oral or literate discourse" by means of a range in dimensions 1, 3, and 5. In dimensions 1 and 5, the Ewondo drummed performance paradigm of this genre rates very high on the oral side of the continuums: it has a low informational load but high interpersonal, affective, and nonabstract content. The referents in the drummed discourse, however, are repeatedly made explicit (dimension 3), which in Biber's analysis is a feature of stereotypical written discourse such as official documents. In the case of the Ewondo speech surrogate drumming, these explicit referents seem to be present for stylistic reasons of ritual speech. They are not really essential for the audience's understanding since everyone within hearing range knows that the catechist is calling them. The names of the village and lineage founders are frequently repeated to emphasize a sense of community responsibility more than to remind listeners of their location. It is possible that a high rating of explicit referents on this dimension would be a better indicator of the formality of language rather than of written discourse.

These three combined characteristics mean that the performance paradigm does not neatly fit on the stereotypically oral side of communication media according to Biber's framework. This drum language paradigm cannot serve as a "paradigm of primary orality," as Ong (1977:97) claims for Lokele talking drums. Ong provides a list of seven salient features of a primary oral culture which are emphasized on talking drums.[58] All of these features are not noted in Antoine's performance paradigm, though they may be present in the Ewondo speech surrogate system as a whole when other genres such as drum names, funeral texts (esana), and transmitting news between villages are included.

It is important to note that a particular combination of Biber's characteristics is found in this genre as drummed by this performer. Other speech surrogate genres, however, such as news transmission have very high informational loads with little affective content (see dimension 1) and would receive a different rating when plotted on continuums of the six dimensions. It is risky to make generalizations about talking drum communication even as used by one culture, not to mention an entire continent.

Dimensions 2, 4, and 6 identify other parameters of textual variation, but can apply to either spoken or written discourse. In all three of these dimensions, the drummed church summons genre is again rated high at one end or the other of the continuums. The only place in a performance which approaches narrative is the three-line peak in the final stanza, marked by dropping the second-person pronoun often used previously (dimension 2). The discourses' stated function is practically entirely persuasive, although other related functions are present (dimension 4). And the paratactic discourse structure certainly evidences the unconnected, fragmented manner in which information is produced under severe real-time constraints (dimension 6). It seems that regarding all six dimensions, the drum poem paradigm is strongly this or that with little intermediate rating. When the this or that of all six dimensions are combined, the drummed performance paradigm is found to be both like and unlike stereotypical orality and literacy in differing ways. It is a third manner of constructing reality through language. Antoine's performance paradigm is most truly a paradigm of speech surrogate drumming and not of orality or literacy.

Complexity is one feature which has different emphases in different genres produced through different media. Complexity in language has to do with ease of comprehension. To oversimplify, "the complexity of written language is lexical, while that of spoken language is grammatical" according to Halliday and Hasan (1989:63). The drum language of Antoine's performance paradigm utilizes a small, simple set of lexical items (which are easier to memorize) connected by fairly simple grammatical patterns (which make

---

[58]For comments on Ong's seven features applied to Xhosa oral poetry, see Opland 1983:182–93.

it easier to connect units in paratactic fashion). The complexity of this drum language is not lexical or grammatical, but has to do with the comprehension of the surrogate signs. Since only prosodic features are heard (and those very fleetingly), much attention of the audience must be devoted to recognizing the drum patterns and the base words. If the base text was full of complexity in grammar or vocabulary, the chances for communicative success would be lessened considerably.

Performance paradigm as oral literature

There are four presuppositions (Finnegan 1988:88–89) concerning oral literature which are generalized by some scholars to manifest the typical form of oral literature in oral cultures. It has been shown that all four presuppositions have exceptions somewhere in the world and that they should not be taken as universals. It is worth mentioning, however, that Antoine's performance paradigm does share these four characteristics with some important modifications of the first three due to the special nature of speech surrogates.

1. The text of oral literature is variable and dependent on the occasion of performance, unlike the fixed text of a written book. The discourse structure of the drummed church summons genre is variable and not fixed, but is not dependent on the unchanging performance situation. The phrases themselves are fixed for the most part and remain that way in various performance contexts across genres.
2. The form of composition characteristic of oral literature is composition-in-performance, i.e., not prior composition divorced from the act of performance. Let us emphasize composition of discourse structure in performance. The content (formulas) exists before performance; the choice of formulas and their structural form combined into lines and stanzas is not decided until the drumming begins.
3. Composition and transmission of oral literature is through the process mentioned above and not (as we once thought) through word-for-word memorization. The discourse is not memorized as a whole, but the component phrases and co-occurrent clusters are memorized and transmitted as individual units.
4. In oral literature, there is no concept of a "correct" or "authentic" version. This is certainly Antoine's emic view: all performances are created equal in function and meaning, and one is no more correct than another.

These statements show that the speech surrogate performance paradigm is related to stereotypical oral literature. Most of the differences are
due to the constraints of the drum in replicating speech: formulas must
be memorized with static form. At the discourse level, the drummed
speech acts behave more like other stereotypical oral poems as far as
being not fixed, unmemorized, and composed in performances regarded
as equally correct. The difference of textual change not being occasion-
dependent is fairly rare, as most other performances of oral poetry
involve face-to-face contact and/or situations varying in some manner.

Antoine's performance paradigm also fits the definition of oral (as
opposed to written) poetry in the three ways earlier suggested by Finnegan (1977:17): composition, transmission, and performance.

Enphrasing in drum language

Ong (1977) has claimed much about orality based on Lokele talking
drum language. One linguistic feature from which he infers much about
orality and culture is ENPHRASING, or expanding a spoken word into a
drummed descriptive phrase. Much importance has been given to the fact
that in Central African surrogate languages, a single word is often accom-
panied by an obligatory descriptive phrase. "In spoken Lokele the word
for 'banana' is likondo. The equivalent drum-language phrase is likondo
libotumbela, which means 'bunch of bananas propped up'" (Carrington
1971:92). 'Manioc' and 'plantain' are drummed with similar expanded
descriptive phrases in Lokele. This feature of enphrasing is minimally
used in Antoine's performance paradigm.

Carrington (1949b, 1971) and Ong (1977) report this enphrasing as
an essential feature of Central African surrogate languages. Carrington
uses a formula developed in information theory and calculates "that
about eight gong-phrase syllables are needed for every syllable in a
spoken word" (1971:93) to provide the necessary redundancy and identification of each phrase. This enphrasing is required because linguistic
segmental features of consonants and vowels are not produced on the
drum, but only suprasegmental features of speech tone and rhythm.
Carrington notes that although eight drum syllables are needed in theory,
Lokele drummers do not go that far in practice.

Following Carrington's method, I calculate that Ewondo has at least two
hundred eighty theoretically possible syllables: twenty consonants times
seven vowels times two basic tones.[59] This number is close to Carrington's
total of two hundred sixty-six syllables available to be spoken or drummed

---

[59]This total does not include other syllable types, such as V or CCVC, or the
downstepped mid tone, which were omitted by Carrington in his method of calculation.

in Lokele. The information theory formula predicts that about seven drum-strokes are needed (through enphrasing) to provide enough redundancy for one oral syllable to be identified in the Ewondo speech surrogate system. But in fact, all performance texts transcribed and analyzed usually present only one or two drumstrokes per spoken syllable, with a few exceptions such as line final vowel prolongation in (113).

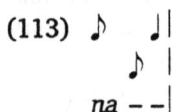

(113) ♪   ♩|
         ♪ |
    na – –|

The expanded, obligatory, adjectival phrases noted by Carrington and Ong are largely missing in Antoine's performance paradigm. Most nouns are drummed in single word form as they are spoken: *kidi* 'dawn', *kpe-kpaa* '(tooth)brush', *mendim* 'waters', *asi* 'ground', *doten* 'doctrine', *nda* 'house', *bekristen* 'Christians', and *ese* 'road'. None of these words are drummed with expanded descriptive phrases.

A few nouns are expanded within Antoine's performance paradigm with diminutive descriptions: *man ntu eyie* 'small old cloth' and *man etug nkul* 'small, old, broken drum'. The word for 'village' may be drummed *dza* or expanded to *otutu dza* 'poor little village' or *otutututu dza* depending on which formulaic phrase it is part of. This use of DIMINUTIVE ENPHRASING is found in other genres as well. Here is a drum message as reported by Guillemin (1948:77), with diminutive enphrasing in italics: "Come cook me a *tiny piece of manioc in your little old pan*. Come give me a plate of *little unripened bananas*. Come eat a *little something cooked, a little piece of manioc stick*. I want to eat a *little plate of cooked manioc leaves*. Come bring me a *tiny calabash* of that which sways the dry trees [palm wine]." In this message, the final noun phrase is represented through a metaphorical typical example of enphrasing. Seven other noun phrases in the message are expanded through diminutive enphrasing.

Enphrasing, whether by metaphor or diminuation, may be prevalent in other genres of the Ewondo speech surrogate system. The short spoken word *zog* 'elephant' is replaced on the drum by the phrase *akud tsid tugulu tugulu* 'the animal that turns everything upside down' (Marfurt 1957:29). Other examples of enphrasing are found in Heepe (1920). The striking lack of enphrasing in Antoine's performance paradigm means, however, that this technique is not essential to drum language communication. The information theory formula does not seem to apply in this case. Redundancy is plentiful in Antoine's performance paradigm, but as repetition of entire phrases, not as expansion of a single word to a phrase. Identification of each phrase does not require seven drumstrokes for each spoken syllable.

Identification of verbal phrases

Simmons has calculated that in Efik (Nigeria) surrogate speech, a four-word tone pattern could be filled by almost three billion possible phrase constructions of morphemes put in a line with the single tonal contour, when sound and not grammatical sense is the criterion for filling the tone pattern. For a genuine six-word drum message, "over 113.2 trillion phrases can be constructed which possess the same tone pattern as the signal message" (1960:805).

These are large numbers, but there are limiting factors to help hearers choose the intended verbal interpretation. First, the entire phrase must make sense by itself (have correct meaning in isolation). Second, it must make sense in its immediate context in relation to other phrases (have correct coherence in discourse structure). Third, it must be a phrase already agreed upon and understood by the local speech community (have correct sociolinguistic preparation and maintenance of meaning). Fourth, the verbal interpretation must be applicable to the performance context (have correct immediate situation meaning). Fifth, rhythm can be as important as tone in distinguishing between verbal interpretations; identical tone patterns are likely to have different rhythms (have correct sound structure).

When these limiting factors are brought into account, the number of possible verbal interpretations which match a single tonal-rhythmic pattern on the drum falls from the trillions to usually one or two. When Simmons analyzed sixty-one actual Efik surrogate phrases, only two possessed the same tone pattern as opposed to the large number theoretically possible. If a drummer produces only patterns that meet the above five qualifications, semiotic signs (tonal-rhythmic patterns) are not needed for trillions of other theoretical phrases which are never drummed. In Antoine's performance paradigm, no two entire phrases have identical drum patterns, though portions of phrases are occasionally identical as partially homophonous surrogate signs (see chapter 6).

Antoine's dictated text

When asked for a text, Antoine dictated one without reference to a specific performance, one phrase at a time. Innocent wrote it down then read it back to Antoine, who drummed it phrase by phrase.

A study of Antoine's dictated text shows very little internal repetition in the dictated text unlike in a performance. For example, *mvog tara ngogo* 'descendants of my father' appears only once in the text's body and is omitted completely from the last stanza. In a drummed performance this phrase appears between five to nine times, plus two obligatory occurrences in the final stanza.

Not surprisingly, the nonverbal stanza marker phrase was omitted. It was not needed as a stall device since Antoine could think ahead as Innocent wrote the previous line. The omission implies that the main function of *ku ku ku ku lu ku ku ku* is a pause, and that it is not essential to Antoine's emic conception of the discourse, though it is essential to each performance drummed in proper context.

The discourse was dictated primarily at the formulaic phrase level; stanzas were not marked because of the complete omission of the stanza marker phrase. This omission is to be expected; Antoine would undoubtably find it ludicrous to repeatedly speak nonverbal sounds. It would also prove difficult to properly place this stanza marker out of performance context.

In the final stanza, which includes the discourse peak, the dictated version omitted several descriptive words that are peculiar to (and obligatory in) the drummed performances: *anga kat-kat Ntondobe ofofoe na* 'to say to God, whispering over and over' became *anga kat Ntondobe na* 'to say to God' even though when read back to Antoine, he drummed the longer standard version of the phrase. The phrase *ekokodo ekokodo ekokodo ekokodo* 'leave forever [all at once]' was omitted entirely.

The dictated text showed several word variations that did not appear in the transcribed drum performances or that were changed or omitted from the dictation. Some examples are given in (114), indicated in bold.

(114) **babe dzan bese** (used only in dictation)
    all my brothers

    *o zu wog **bibug bi** doten* (changed in dictation)
    you come hear **words of** doctrine

    drummed as *o zu wog doten*
        you come hear doctrine

    *bot bete be nga zu ma **koe totoa*** (changed in dictation)
    those people, they came **and found me sitting up**

    drummed as *bot bete be nga zu bo dze ben*
        those people, they came to really do what?

    ***mot** abe fe tobo a tobo tobo tobo*
    person do not stay too long (omitted from dictation)

In general, these variations are minor. The omitted internal repetitions demonstrate the biggest difference between dictated and drummed versions: there is a total of forty-one spoken phrases in the dictated version as opposed to more than eighty textual phrases in each drummed performance. Redundancy is common and important in the drummed message but omitted from the spoken version.

Lord (1960:125–28) has pointed out that dictated texts of oral epic poetry are inherently different from sung texts. He attributes this difference to two factors: the rhythmic structure of each formula and stanza is broken by dictation, and the performer is forced to assemble his lines much more slowly than usual. "Clearly he has time to plan his line in advance, but this is more of a hindrance than a help to a singer who is accustomed to rapid-fire association and composition" (p. 128).

This difficulty in dictation was found to be the case with Atemengue, the neighboring catechist, as well. Immediately after recording a drum performance, the tape was played back, and he gave verbal interpretations. Later these verbal phrases were checked by Innocent and me in great detail as we tried to match every syllable to a drumstroke. It was found that when speaking, the drummer omitted phrases, changed word order, and used variant phrases. There seems to be a different way of thinking about the formulaic phrases dependent on the medium used: a different way of producing, remembering, and recognizing phrases connected with the presence or absence of static surface structure.

It is striking that even the final stanza of Antoine's performance paradigm is noticeably different when dictated than in drummed performance context. Normally this is the only discourse section which can be predicted with much assurance. In a number of cases throughout the dictated version, the formulaic surface structure pattern (exact wording) is lost when the rhythm is not present and when the stanza is not played quickly at a fairly automatic level. The changes from aurally perceived performance in context to oral literature out of that context are noticeable and point out that static surface structure patterns of formulas, repetition of formulas, and rapid composition are integral parts of the performance paradigm when drummed and not dictated.

Reflective thoughts on aurality and literacy

To some extent, different modes of learning and thinking are connected with different media. Antoine is literate in Ewondo, and half an hour after drumming the church call he would lead the doctrine class occasionally with the aid of a written liturgy. He is certainly not in any so-called pure oral state, untouched by literacy. He is able to make use of drummed, spoken, and written communication channels even with the same audience. One channel is simply more useful in a certain context.

The method of learning drum speech for an Ewondo person involves learning each whole phrase aurally. My method of learning required paper (and tape recorder) and involved a note-by-note, syllable-by-syllable process.

To Antoine, his drumming was an aural call to action; to me, it was a subject for scientific study. Aurally, the performances are a local, fleeting phenomenon. With publication of this study, the recorded performances and written translations become permanent and reach an international audience.

The speech surrogate system replicates the manner in which words are heard, not the way in which they are written down. The aural surrogate is noticeably different from the visual surrogate; it is closest to the dominant communication system. If oral speech has vowel elisions, so will drum speech.

As is not uncommon among Western scholars, I began this study with "the assumption that there must be a consensus, 'a consistency of all versions in all parts'...[and] presuppositions of consistency which were based upon written models" (Goody 1987:298). Antoine did not share these presuppositions.

No one in Mekomba would ever try to memorize details of a morning's performance and compare them with the next week's performance. My emphasis on linguistic details and a comparative analysis through time were viewed as culturally irrelevant. Mekomba residents were only interested in my performance abilities: could I make the drum speak like Antoine did? I did manage to produce an acceptable performance, but only by reading my musical transcriptions from my notes.

I never came close to producing sound through Antoine's process of combining formulaic phrases under real-time performance constraints, though that could be possible with a few years' practice. I only managed to repeat a static structural form that Antoine himself would never repeat in exactly the same way. I was able to adequately drum an example of what he said without duplicating how he said it. As Stone points out, "It is quite possible to perform in a manner acceptable to a group of musicians while applying one's own particular code to organizing and making sense of the sounds" (1982:28).

To Antoine the question was, could I say what he said on the drum? To me the question was, what exactly did we just say and how did we say it? Antoine of course recognized verbal patterns in the sound, while I initially recognized only tonal-rhythmic patterns in the same sound. Antoine's interest was in my mimicry, that is, the production of drum phrases he could understand. I think he never fully understood my painstaking matching of each transcribed drumstroke to a verbal syllable and constant rechecking. I am sure I do not fully understand his playing from the heart—his ability to pick up two drumsticks and be creative in a communicative/aesthetic/social transaction that was at the same time very new and very old.

It can be seen that speaking, reading, and hearing have different effects on most areas of this study, including conceptualization, learning styles, performance practice, prospective audience, and performance purpose.

Because there are different levels of speech competency in the speech surrogate system, there are different possible levels of understanding Antoine's performance paradigm. Cultural outsiders can gain one kind of comprehension through literacy. When this reading knowledge of drumming is added to the performance's sound on cassettes, an outsider could perhaps gain more of one kind of detailed knowledge than a Mekomba resident has gained through aurality alone. Of course, this more detailed knowledge would be considered irrelevant by most Mekomba residents, just as most mother-tongue speakers of any language find a phonological analysis of their language to be irrelevant and unnecesary for communication. The level of understanding really depends on how much effort a person puts into comprehension, either an outsider reading this study, or an insider asking Antoine to explain the drum speech to him.

Where, then, is the emic viewpoint? Is it that of Antoine, who alone fully knows every word, and that only during performance? Is the emic viewpoint that of Mekomba residents, many of whom know the message's theme only by context? In Mekomba, there is a plurality of related but graded emic understandings. The different levels of specialist versus nonspecialist communicative competency enter into play here, suggesting that what is aurally, significantly contrastive for one person may not always be so for his neighbor. Through literacy, however, all nonspecialist readers probably see the same contrasts in the data because it is overtly pointed out and can be seen many times.

Comparative analysis, made possible by the technology of tape recorders[60] and by writing, has given cultural outsiders a different type of understanding than is gained by growing up in Mekomba. Charts have been made, general rules proposed, exceptions noted, theories applied, comparisons suggested; this understanding through formal training substitutes for our presence at performances.

Many voices have been presented in this volume: Ewondo catechists, residents of Mekomba, myself, and numerous other scholars. Those who drum speak for themselves and are recorded on cassette tapes. The rest of us speak and write what we think about the drumming. Their understanding and hermeneutics are different from our understanding and hermeneutics

---

[60]See Shelemay 1991 for comments on cassette recording making possible this type of comparative study.

(cf. Apter 1992:224–26), even if we stay in a place long enough to act as insiders.

The performances are valuable to cultural outsiders who have understanding by sight and sound out of context. They are valuable in a very different way to Mekomba residents who have understanding by sound alone in context.

Antoine and others are the artists and keepers of knowledge in context. I am a scribe and presenter of knowledge out of context. This written ethnography of drum speech, this surrogate analysis of surrogate language, is quite different from the aural reality of drum speech. That does not mean, however, that this ethnography is hopelessly removed from the reality or that it has little value even from the local perspective; Antoine thought it was good to record and transcribe the drum call since it is a dying art.[61]

The difference between drummed reality and surrogate analysis means that this study presents the sound and social realities through a Western academic grid of oral formulas, semiotics, semantic units, poetic closure, and so forth. Mekomba residents create, hear, and interpret the sound reality through a grid of social relationships with their neighbors and with their God.

---

[61]Antoine and other drummers would have much less use for the analytical parts of this study. His main interest was in preserving the drum phrases so that they could be learned by another catechist even after his death—a community-based functional reason.

14
Final Matters

A word should be said about the abundance of models used in this study and the large number of analytic perspectives thereby gathered on different aspects of drumming. Dozens of models from different disciplines have been tried. How well do they all work? Most models have been modified in the details to better fit the Ewondo speech surrogate while the broad outlines of the models have been retained. I believe all the models have been useful in providing different ways to hear and understand the drumming. Brought together, various models account for various facets of the performance paradigm. It is hoped that other scholars will find some of these combinations of models equally applicable to studies of other speech surrogates, or even music and language in general.

A combination of some of the primary models used in this study can be seen in the diagram in (115). The total truth is oversimplified in this tripartite schemata because everything relates to everything else and cannot really be separated so neatly. Nevertheless, ·the diagram is useful as it fits pieces together to present the larger picture. The full identity of the performance paradigm is found in the interaction of all these parts; for example, how syntagmatic oral formulas, distinctive rhythmic patterns, cohesion in discourse, and receptive speech competency are all related.

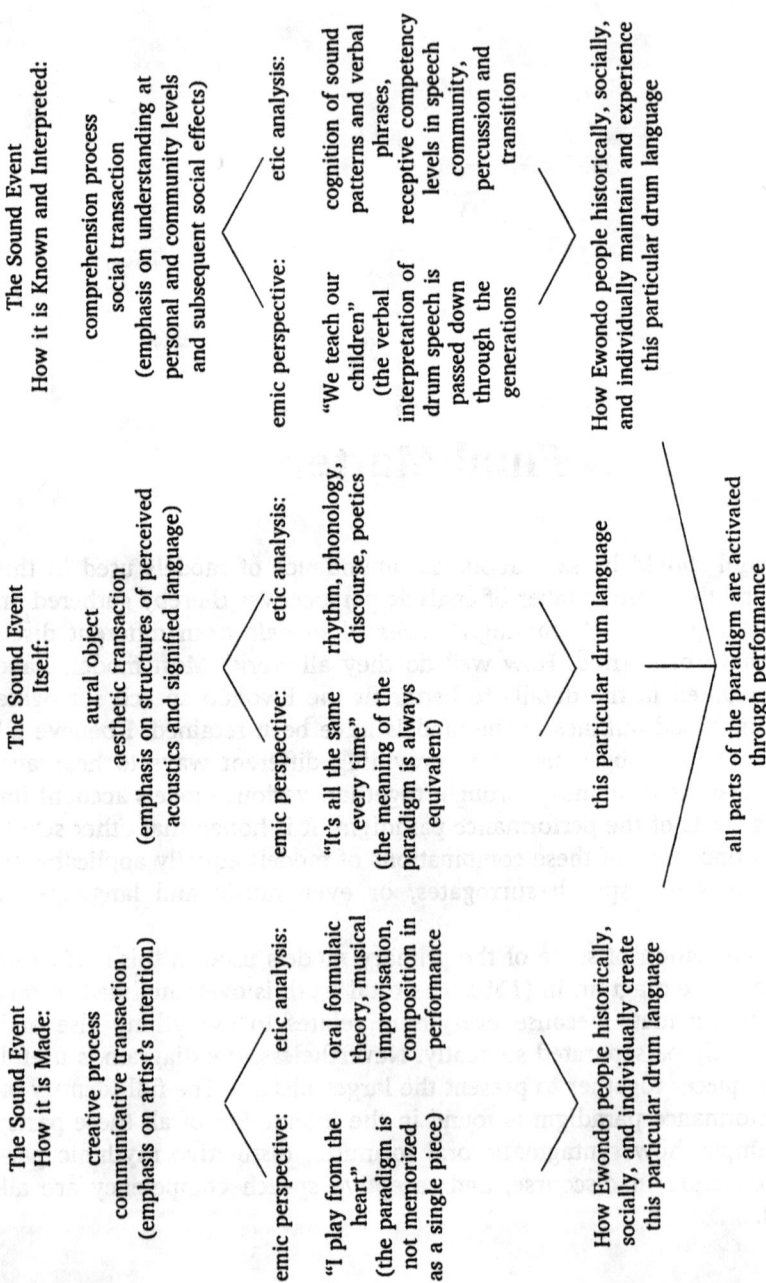

(115)

**The Sound Event
How it is Made:**

creative process
communicative transaction
(emphasis on artist's intention)

emic perspective:

"I play from the heart"
(the paradigm is not memorized as a single piece)

etic analysis:

oral formulaic theory, musical improvisation, composition in performance

How Ewondo people historically, socially, and individually create this particular drum language

**The Sound Event
Itself:**

aural object
aesthetic transaction
(emphasis on structures of perceived acoustics and signified language)

emic perspective:

"It's all the same every time"
(the meaning of the paradigm is always equivalent)

etic analysis:

rhythm, phonology, discourse, poetics

this particular drum language

all parts of the paradigm are activated through performance

**The Sound Event
How it is Known and Interpreted:**

comprehension process
social transaction
(emphasis on understanding at personal and community levels and subsequent social effects)

emic perspective:

"We teach our children"
(the verbal interpretation of drum speech is passed down through the generations

etic analysis:

cognition of sound patterns and verbal phrases, receptive competency levels in speech community, percussion and transition

How Ewondo people historically, socially, and individually maintain and experience this particular drum language

Separate parts of the performance paradigm have been examined. Now an attempt will be made to tie together some of the loose ends in an overview as well as to examine elements previously unconsidered.

Further performance perspectives of the sound event

An introduction to the sound event as performance was given in chapter 2. Now that the reader is well acquainted with the drumming, let us examine it again from this perspective.

A message drummed to gather a community together is unique in terms of performance studies and ethnographies of communication.[62] There is absolutely zero visual communication, such as facial expressions, gestures, costumes, masks, colors, movement, and regalia which are well known in many African performance situations (see Agovi 1988 for an overview). An unseen performance of a drummed summons is about as bare-boned as a performance can get.

Most physical framing devices (Goffman 1964) are absent. There are no preliminary indications to begin the encounter; human-made sound erupts abruptly from the sounds of dawn. There are no excluded participants; everyone is part of the passive audience. There is no special social arrangement; all people remain in their own bed and hear the sound. These performances have no spatial boundary (except that established by hearing range) and only a closing temporal boundary marker (the final rhythmic coda).

In the case of some community's performances, months of work and planning and hundreds of people are necessary to successfully create a performance or ceremony with songs, involving a great deal of collective action to manifest the art (Finnegan 1982:8–12). In contrast, Antoine wakes up, carries his drum and stool to his front yard, and drums.

The visual, aural, and temporal boundaries of the day begin simultaneously, marked by Antoine's drumming on Tuesdays and Fridays. The sunrise breaks from darkness to light as the drumming breaks from near-silence to sound that fills the air. Now the sounds of animals and people begin to be heard. The rhythms of drummed speech lead into the rhythms of daily life from the timelessness of night and sleep. The ordered sound reveals ordered time; the drum reveals the dawn.

---

[62]A message drummed when the community is already gathered, say at a dance, funeral, or wrestling match, is much more typical.

Metacommunicative devices in the performance paradigm

Verbal art may be marked on all levels of text, texture, and context, or only on one or two levels in some cases (Fine 1984:61). In the case of Ewondo speech surrogate all three levels are marked to indicate set-apart speech.

A number of metacommunicative devices may serve to frame or key a performance. Bauman (1977:16–22) has suggested that at least some of nine keys commonly mark set-apart speech in many performances around the world:

1. special codes
2. figurative language such as metaphors
3. parallelism of lines or meanings
4. special paralinguistic features of voice quality
5. special prosodic patterns of tempo and pitch
6. formal stylistic devices
7. special formulas
8. appeal to tradition
9. disclaimer of performance[63]

Bauman insists that the main task in every ethnography of performance is to determine *"the culture-specific constellations of communicative means that serve to key performance in particular communities"* (Bauman's italics, p. 22). I have tried to meet this goal in this study, narrowing the focus to determining what devices key one paradigm of performances in a single Ewondo community. This narrow focus brings up the matter of how much of this very specific ethnography of performance is applicable to the entire Ewondo speech surrogate system.

All nine of Bauman's suggested keys serve to mark performance in Antoine's drummed discourses. Some of them are also present in shorter drummed messages, although figurative language, appeal to tradition, and parallelism may be much less pronounced in a summons such as 'wife, bring food to the farm'. Does such a message, or others such as 'war, war, war', fit in the etic category of aesthetic folklore or performance?

Bauman defines performance as a mode of communication in which the performer assumes responsibility to an audience for a display of communicative skill, beyond the referential content of the communication. It is "the enactment of the poetic function" (1986:3). By this definition, short, drummed messages which are purely practical and utilitarian, without

---

[63]Most of these keys have already been referenced to the drumming in this study. The disclaimer of performance is found in Antoine's reference to himself in the phrase "A small, old, broken drum calls and calls a long time..."

aesthetic intent or display, may be less clearly categorized as performance in these etic terms.

"Performance may be dominant in the hierarchy of multiple functions served by speech" (Bauman 1986:3), or it may be subordinate to other functions such as referential or rhetorical. It seems that the function of performance as defined above is subordinate in short, drummed messages in Ewondo but increases to be the dominant function in some longer messages. With a thirty-second drum message Antoine could remind the residents of Mekomba of an impending church service; the fact that he drums for five or six times that long indicates that he has assumed responsibility for a display of communicative skill which is as important as the referential content.

In a performance in Bauman's terms, the beauty of the speech may be of equal importance to the meaning of the speech. This value holds true for the speech of many surrogate instruments. "Art of the use of [Ewondo] instruments is judged to the degree of its instrumental eloquence" (Ngumu 1975:35).

What initially keys or frames all Ewondo speech surrogate performances, whether short or long, is the sound of the drum (or the "paralinguistic feature of voice quality" in Bauman's list of keys). The drum beats alone create the performance context. There is no previously-marked social context into which this speech act is inserted, no visual indications that the performance is about to begin.

Drumming as enactment and pure performance

Abrahams has proposed the term ENACTMENT to include not only artistic performances, but also games, rituals, festivities, etc. An enactment is "any cultural event in which community members come together to participate, employ the deepest and most complex multivocal and polyvalent signs and symbols of their repertoire of expression, thus entering into a potentially significant experience" (1977). Each kind of a culture's enactment entails special vocabulary, artificial codes, ways of behaving, and physical and temporal frame markers. Enactments, compared to daily life, are more highly focused, redundant, and stylized.

The church service is a religious enactment by this definition. Antoine's drummed summons is also an enactment, aurally uniting the community with complex, redundant, stylized, and polysemous signs. It is doubtful, however, that each of the four thousand or so performances in Mekomba has always been a significant experience for most of the audience members. I suspect it is taken for granted for the most part, especially since only a minority understand the verbal meaning of the signs.

The scheduled performance of a speech surrogate can also be considered as what Bauman and Abrahams have termed pure performance: "restricted in setting, clearly bounded, widely public and involving the most highly formalized performance forms and accomplished performers of the community" (Bauman 1976:36). The church drumming in Mekomba is restricted to a few minutes two mornings a week, bounded by silence, as public as a loudspeaker, and involves formalized language performed by a recognized expert of the community.

Context and content in the performance paradigm

Scholars have rightly connected the "textual tradition and social interaction [which] become one in performance" (Briggs 1988:xvi). Content and context interact in unpredictable ways in many types of performances. Briggs suggests that folklore performances "provide common ground between a shared textual tradition and a host of unique human encounters" (p. xv). But in Antoine's anomaly of performance there are no unique human encounters; it is always the sound of the catechist's drum reaching the ears of whoever is in hearing range. Audience context is very important in the case of many membranophone speech surrogates; audience context is completely irrelevant to what and how Antoine speaks on his drum as long as the who, why, when, and where remain the same. In the case of the catechist's drumming in Mekomba, the performance context is completely fixed and the peculiar features of each drummed discourse are due entirely to the drummer's composition-in-performance choices.

It has been shown that Antoine's discourses use a paratactic structure, where he can mix and match about one hundred phrases with quite a bit of creative liberty. There is a high degree of variability from performance to performance, except for the final stanza.

In the introduction to this study, I posed the question, how many ways can a message be drummed and still be understood? When I first recorded Antoine, I naively thought he drummed the same words in every performance. After two recordings I realized that was not the case. When I returned from the field with transcriptions, I naively thought I could present a generative phrase grammar, assuming that each performance had a lot of structural similarities that could be easily formalized. After discourse-level analysis it is clear that Antoine does not break up his performances into equal, neat, consistent chunks. This study has shown to some extent the great flexibility that Antoine has in ordering his summons. Each performance is not an automatic replaying of a precomposed text learned by rote.

A performance as a finished product does not exist in anyone's memory, only parts awaiting potential use. The discourse pieces await assembly into the structure of a fleeting performance.

In Antoine's case, it is hard to see any external momentary exigencies in the context of the performance event. There are no contextual reasons for rearranging his discourse twice a week. He regularly awakens the village and has done so more than four thousand times. There is no audience present to directly interact with. The performance is one man's soliloquy that begins in the dark and ends in daylight. Antoine's audience is everybody (aural perspective) and nobody (visual perspective) at the same time, and the members' movements have no discernable effect on the length or form of the drummed speech act.

Concerning the paratactic structure of Antoine's drumming, he drums variable poetry for his own internal momentary exigencies. His senses of verbal and musical aesthetics interact with his knowledge of Ewondo tradition and the speech community, and this interaction produces his personalized art. "What's in the heart is what comes out in the hands," as Antoine said. Each performance "is more than the sum of its communicative codes" (Fine 1980:3). It is also an expression through drumming of how Antoine connects at that moment what he feels about God, church, himself, and his congregation.[64]

The performance of oral African narrative is a "confluence of four crucial elements of oral tradition": performer, images inherited from the past, contemporary world, and audience members (Scheub 1977a:346). For Mekomba, all four of these elements have remained the same to various extents for several decades. While the first three elements are of primary importance in making and defining a performance, the last element is not crucial for the church summons in Mekomba. As long as the village exists, any of the many Catholics in town will serve as the involuntary audience.

A few simple repetitions of the stall pattern *ku ku ku ku lu ku ku ku* would serve the basic purpose of a wake-up call. Without verbal-based drum phrases, the medium itself would be the message. Why does Antoine play an involved three-minute poetic discourse each time? Partly because the purpose is not only to serve as a wake-up call but also to be a lengthy persuasive reminder to be serious about church attendance. More than an alarm clock, the sound is a poetic, persuasive alarm clock. All three aspects of the communicative/aesthetic/social transaction

---

[64]"Whenever one speaks of performance, there are always two implications: that of the performance for self and that of the performance for other" (King 1980:171).

would be severely undermined if only the stall pattern were briefly drummed, though that would get the job done.

Performance paradigm as product, process, meanings, and relationships

In any creative tradition, both product and process are important topics for study. Rather than analyze only one transcribed performance text, attention must also be given to the manner of creating each performance. As Finnegan has pointed out,

> The text alone is an insufficient guide to the art form, and that to understand it fully one must go further and also study the processes of performance and audience reception as they actually take place in space and time. (1986:74)

Without the performance, there is no text. Even within the performances, the term text can be used only by stretching the definition. The aural tradition exists within the memory of the speech community and is realized only during actual performances. It is a fallacy to speak of the text, or to think that one performance contains all other performances. Aural tradition and performance are inextricably intertwined.

> But especially in an oral tradition, performance is a mode of existence and realization that is partly constitutive of what the tradition is. The tradition itself exists partly for the sake of performance; performance is itself partly an end....There is no more an "Ur-performance" than there is an "Ur-text." Only the systematic study of [plural] performances can disclose the true structure. (Hymes 1975:19–20)

Performance texts are born of a creativity that is governed by rules for bringing order, aesthetics, and comprehensibility to the performances. Guttgemanns (1977:77) has termed this theory "generative poetics." Understanding the processes of creation and comprehension will lead to understanding the aural product. Folklore is not only what is said but also "a way of speaking" (Bauman 1986:2).

This emphasis is in direct opposition to the view expressed by Jason, "For the purposes of understanding its properties as a literary genre, the origin and formation processes in time and space of a single piece, or even of a whole genre, are irrelevant (and are for the most part impossible to determine)" (1977:4–5). This view forcibly fits any oral poem into a literary straitjacket and cannot lead to any emic conception of the piece.

Oral criticism, much more than literary criticism, is concerned with the process of creating poetry (Okpewho 1979:33, Lord 1960:5). Literary critics are conditioned to the fixity of the written details, "more interested in the independent merits of the finished work of art than in the raw human and contextual resources out of which it has been put together" (Okpewho 1979:50). When it comes to oral/aural art, however, Okpewho goes so far as to assert "the means is more worthy of our attention than the end, for poetry here implies more the moment and process of creation than the finished product itself" (pp. 51–52).

A text once performed is a product only if recorded and available for study. In performance it is "a continuous process of semantic choice, a movement through the network of meaning potential with each set of choices constituting the environment for a further set" (Halliday and Hasan 1989:10). This is the true performance text: a set of verbal/musical choices leading to other choices.

Among Western scholars dealing with Western music, it has been argued that "a notational score rather than a performance defines the identity of a musical work" (Fine 1984:216), nor is this insistence on the written record uncommon in dealing with verbal art. The statement is obviously untrue in the case under study here, even though literate scholars tend to depend upon written transcriptions.

In Halliday and Hasan's (1989) terms, the identity of Antoine's performance paradigm is demarcated by the phrases he uses (mode/textual meaning), the context of the sound event (field/experiential meaning), and the leader-congregation social structure represented (tenor/interpersonal meaning). Far from being a score, the identity of the drumming is found in the meaning intended and performed, the meaning heard and comprehended, and the meaning of actions subsequent to the summons.

As stated in chapter 3, the identity of each performance may also be represented as relationships between drumstrokes, words, and people. The basic six relationships are between words (grammar), between words and drumstrokes (phonology), between drumstrokes (musical performance), between drumstrokes and people (aesthetic transaction), between words and people (communicative transaction), and between the people of Mekomba village (social transaction).

The interaction of these relationships can be said to create the fluid form of each performance while retaining the constants of the paradigm as a whole.

Cultural and personal decisions in the performance paradigm

Corporate culture is always being invented and shaped by the decisions made by individuals. Such decisions are often manifested in discourse as shared patterns of language interact with personal reasons for speaking and ways of speaking. The shared patterns, of which the speaker is often unconscious, arranges the personal speaking which may be made through conscious choice.

> [The study of language] shows that the forms of a person's thoughts are controlled by inexorable laws of pattern of which he is unconscious. These patterns are the unperceived intricate systematizations of his own language....And every language is a vast pattern-system, different from others, in which are culturally ordained the forms and categories by which the personality not only communicates, but also analyzes nature, notices or neglects types of relationship and phenomena, channels his reasoning, and builds the house of his consciousness. (Whorf in Carroll 1956:252)

The nature of the Ewondo speech surrogate system is that of a vast pattern-system containing unspoken verbal patterns, patterns of assembling sound, patterns of perceived sound, patterns of understanding sound, and patterns of people's behavior based on sound. All of these patterns seem taken for granted in Mekomba, for the most part functioning unconsciously within the lives of community members.

The community decided long ago that this genre should be performed on certain regular occasions. On Tuesdays and Fridays at dawn, Antoine decides that "it is time today to gather the congregation." This intent is then channelled in the form of drummed formulaic phrases stacked in paratactic fashion for a few minutes until he decides "it is time to stop," at which point the final stanza is tacked on. It "is possible to stop at some points, but not at others, and have the cumulative sequence count in a community as complete" (Lemke 1988:160).

Individual drum phrases are stored in the Ewondo performer's memory in an exact surface structure form. The text as a whole is not, but may be stored in memory as a structured series of choices or cues (Goody 1987:177). One phrase or set of phrases calls to mind another phrase or set of phrases, and so co-occurrent clusters are developed.

A Yoruba drummer's explanation of his art sheds light on how speech surrogate performances are conceived in that culture:

> "What we say with the drum is inside us, like a stack of gramaphone records. Once we pick up the drum, even things that were not previously thought-out begin to come out. After the performance, you cannot remember what it was you said."

The reference to gramaphone records implies a subconscious filing away of appropriate phrases, sentences, and passages of text in the drummer's memory, whose recall are then triggered off when the drummer picks up his drum. The drum acts as a "catalyst" to bring out previously heard texts which, perhaps unknown to the drummer, are lodged in his memory. (Euba 1988:480)

Creation in the performance paradigm is a set of real-time decisions, primarily by choosing which phrases to use and their discourse arrangement. Creation is largely a matter of ordering the formulaic phrases, arranging the stack of gramaphone records. Antoine does not have a text learned by verbatim memory. Rather, each performance is created by heart, by what he feels and believes and thinks to say today. There is no idea of simply reproducing verbatim one performance many times. What is regularly reproduced is personal communication filtered through cultural language patterns appropriate to the performance context. "The performer knows—though he may not be overtly aware of such knowledge—a set of rules, a system of communication, a grammar, in which the relationships between the attributes of verbal messages and the social-cultural reality are in constant interplay..." (Ben-Amos and Goldstein 1975:3).

The choices made in drumming are not fully predictable even by the drummer. This genre drummed by this performer in this one community has brought forth more than four thousand closely related performances. In the details of performances, however, each is probably a once-in-a-lifetime event. In life and performance, our options are not always predictable. "Real life and its texts are full of surprises" (Lemke 1988:161).

Comprehension in the performance paradigm is also a set of real-time choices, primarily in matching what patterns are heard with those stored in the audience's memory. What is already known is of primary importance.

Improvisation

There is no term in Ewonds that matches the Engllish term IMPROVISA-TION. The closest word to it perhaps is nkanese. This term has the meaning of "resting in the middle of a song and singing or playing something new" (Etua 1993, personal communication). nkanese can be applied to singing and instrumental music, including that produced on the mvet (chordophone) and mendzang (xylophone). This concept of pausing then resuming with something different is found in different musical settings, including bibom music, ozila music, ngos music, and others (Etua 1993, personal communication).

This term is not usually applied to speech surrogate drumming. In this case, the term *nkanese* can be applied only if the drummer says something markedly different from the previous context in which he has been communicating to the audience (Etua 1993, personal communication).

The phrases used by Antoione remain in one semantic domain. Therefore, there is no emic Ewondo concept of improvisation in Antoine's performance paradigm. However, several etic concepts of improvisation have a direct impact on our understanding of Antoione's performance.

The first concept is that improvisation and composition are not fixed opposites, but tendencies on a continuum. According to Waterhouse (1986), completely random improvisation and completely determined composition, at each end of the continuum, are only "logical fictions." After giving evidence, he writes: "In sum, we have to say that all improvisations contain an element of composition; and that all performances of a composition contain an element of improvisation" (Waterhouse 1986:374, also see Nettl 1974:4–6). As Canzio's definition phrases it, improvisation is "composition in real time" (Bensmore 1989:553). Compositional (structural) types of choices are made at the moment in performance. Nettl suggests, "Should we not then speak perhaps of rapid and slow composition rather than of composition juxtaposed to improvisation?" (1974:6).

A musical tradition can be distinguished by the type of decisions made before or during performance. Some macro-level decisions affect the sound's aural structure, other micro-level choices affect how that wouond is created. Music genres are weighted toward certain types of decisions made at certain times. In Persian classical music a mode is chosen before the "improvisation decisions" begin and fingering choices are made; in European classical music details of breath pauses and phrasing are made in performance, while the song's structural decisions were made previously by a composer. In jazz, structural restraints of a key and often a model are chosen beforehand, while what to do within those restraints is spontaneously decided. Structural choices made before performance suggest repeatable "composition," while structural decisions made in performance suggest nonrepeatable "improvisation" in common Western usage.

Whether structural choices are made before or during performance, other decisions are made in performance practice concerning the aural manifestation of the structural choices. Patterns of Antoine's sticking are probably habitual for each phrase, but adjusted as phrases are combined in new configurations. Note the two separate elements in Oh's definition: "Improvisation in perfromance is a process of decision-making and physical sound or movement realization..." (Oh 1985:23). In Antoine's case, *rapid composition* decisions that affect the discourse structure are made in performance and realized with physical hand movement which produces sound.

For example, his hands can drum the stall pattern while he thinks ahead and decides which compositional phrase to put next in the discourse structure. This process is evidenced by the stall pattern leading *directly* into the next textual section. If he waited until the last *ku* stroke to decide which verbal phrase would come next, there would be a pause of some sort. The fact that the final drumstroke of the stall pattern always flows smoothly and immediately into the textual phrase seems to indicate that his mind was made up before he reached that point in the performance.

A musical performance may or may not be planned out in detail to the end. What is in the performer's mind may be "the song" as a whole discrete unit, or it may be "some concatenation of principles of selection and order and actual melodic bits or formulas—call it an improvisatory system—that allow him to make it up as he sings" (Treitler 1991:78). What is in Antoine's mind seems to be this type of improvisatory system of formulaic phrases and principles of selection and combination. Lower-level choices such as drum phonology were decided long ago. Higher-level discourse decisions are made in performance; co-occurrent clusters are reinforced by "the familiarity of critical turning points" (Treitler 1991:78). The abstract "model" is quite general on how to get from the first direct address phrase to the closing stanza.[65]

Antoine's rapid composition is habitual with regard to the community soundscape, physical hand movements, and organization of material. He reorganizes previous patterns. As Antoine is habitual in his improvisation, the meaning is habitualized, taken for granted, by the speech community (see Stone 1982:25). This is an excellent example of Saville-Troike's observation, "Within a specific speech event some patterns are so regular, so predictable, that a very low information load is carried even by a long utterance or interchange, though the social meaning involved can be significant" (1987:662). The selection and arrangement of drum patterns within a performance are somewhat predictable; the meaning from context and social interaction is very predictable and carries much of the transaction's information.

Intention and meaning in the performance paradigm

Intentions and meanings are crucial in determining the difference between performing sounds and performing a speech act (Searle 1965). Sounds made "in the performance of a speech act are said to have meaning"; the performer intends to mean something by these sounds.

---

[65]For studies of variation in African song, both vocal and instrumentsl, see Agawu (1990:221). In each study a small number of models is "transformed in a wide variety of ways during performance."

The performer "intends to produce a certain effect by means of getting the hearer to recognize his intention to produce that effect" (Searle 1965). Antoine intends that his hearers should come to the church meeting; he must make his hearers recognize and understand his intention to move, their hearts to think of God, and their feet to bring mouths to talk of God. He does not intend to merely wake them, or entertain them, or remind them of the scheduled meeting (though all of these notions are present). He believes that as he drums his illocutionary act, people will understand his intention and meaning at some level, and the desired result will be produced: church attendance.

Exchange of meanings through symbols

Signs become meaningful when they are exchanged and shared through discourse in social interaction. As pointed out by Halliday,

> In order for the meanings which constitute the social system to be exchanged between members they must first be represented in some exchangeable symbolic form, and the most accessible of the available forms is language. So the meanings are encoded in (and through) the semantic system, and given the form of text. (1978:139–40)

In the case of speech surrogates, the exchangeable symbolic form of language is further encoded in rhythmic-tonal patterns. The catechist's intended meaning is exchanged with the community in aurally perceived performance, a communicative/aesthetic/social transaction. Though the actual interaction between performer and audience is very minimal, it is effective enough to convey the intended meaning and produce the desired result of church attendance in some congregants.

Besides being meaningful, signs are social. The drummed signs fall fleetingly in the air while shared strategies of creation and comprehension are used to aurally connect the community. In Stockmann's terms (1991:333), the drumming is a summons to reduce the aural "field of distance" to the physical "field of contact." It is used to condense a scattered community into the local representation of the Body of Christ. The scattered community is summoned to enter a "bounded sphere of interaction" (Stone 1982:2). The drumming is an unseen presentation by a skilled professional in the hearing of a passive audience. When the congregation gathers to sing and pray, interactive communication (music and speech) takes place within the social group (Stockmann 1991:331).

All poets "create and re-order the situation through their poetic expression" (Finnegan 1977:274). Antoine and other drumming catechists do this concretely as their poetry calls people to reorder their lives before God and create a church (living community) by coming together. Performance, "like any form of communication, carries the potential to rearrange the structure of social relations within the performance event and perhaps beyond it" (Bauman 1986:4). Relations between participants, words, and drumstrokes all emerge in the performance of signs in discourse.

It is possible to consider structural relations in a text as the relations between the actions of its participants. Drumming becomes discourse through the actions of community members in providing the context for the creation and comprehension of the performance and in assigning meaning to those actions. As well, the "structure of a text is the result of the structured social practices that create the text" (Lemke 1988:158). The momentary structure of each performance is developed through the longstanding communicative practices of the local community and the larger Ewondo group.

Communication objectives and intent are channelled into pre-established formulaic phrases which are transformed into aurally perceived patterns in performance. The acoustic signals are shaped by intentions and the identity of the performer, the sociolinguistic and performance situation, the size of the drum, and the structure of the Ewondo speech surrogate system from the level of phonology of drumstrokes to discourse.

The discourse of signs shared through social interaction does three things: it forms structures, conveys meaning, and accomplishes actions (Schiffrin 1987:6). All three of these results are based in performance within Antoine's drummed discourse paradigm. In each performance, aural structures of line, stanza, and performance levels are formed and used in the creation and comprehension of the drumming. When the signified linguistic structures are comprehended, shared meaning is given to the signs by the speech community. When meaning is recognized, the goals and intentions of the catechist are acted upon by a portion of the community. Discourse, even that of the drum, is thereby viewed "as the result of relationships between what is said, what is meant, and what is done" (Schiffrin 1985:281).

An ethnomusicology model and the performance paradigm

In the introduction to this study, I proposed to use Rice's (1987) model developed for ethnomusicology:

$$\text{"How do people} \begin{Bmatrix} \text{historically} \\ \text{socially} \\ \text{individually} \end{Bmatrix} \begin{Bmatrix} \text{create/construct} \\ \text{maintain} \\ \text{experience} \end{Bmatrix} \text{music?"}$$

With reference to this set of questions, one major focus of this study has been "How does one drummer individually create/construct a performance?" An answer to this question alone, however, does not mean that an understanding of the whole set of questions has been reached. The other combinations of questions fill out our understanding of Antoine's performances, as we consider, for example, individual's communicative competency and the use of historical common stock phrases.

Answers to these questions in the context of Antoine's drumming in Mekomba have been given throughout this study. They will be summarized in three units.

Creation/construction

A number of Antoine's phrases have been found in different contexts in previous Ewondo studies. In part, Antoine's discourses are constructed from historical phrases that have been part of the common stock of Ewondo speech surrogate drumming for many years. Though Antoine, as an individual, recreates his performances each time, they have truly been socially constructed and must be socially interpreted (someone must give a face-to-face oral interpretation for initial understanding).

Maintenance

The church members in the community historically had a need for this gathering and wake-up drum call and have maintained it for more than a generation. The current residents of Mekomba maintain the institution of this performance paradigm with their response to the communication event: their immediate church attendance. The younger people, however, show little interest in learning speech surrogate drumming. The next village catechist, who is not a drummer, has been chosen to replace Antoine upon his death. The institution and genre of drummed church summons in this village may cease in this decade, but the speech surrogate system as a whole will be maintained by other Mekomba drummers.

Antoine seems to maintain his interest in performance by making it a deep, personal expression and not a memorized exercise drummed by rote. By exercising the flexibility available in the speech surrogate system he avoids artistic dryness and is able to play from the heart as he creates each performance.

Experience

The fact that the church leader uses a pre-Christian form of communication helps the congregation feel historical ties with Ewondo ancestors. Drumming is a culture-sensitive mode of communication. In addition, Mekomba residents have experienced Antoine's performance paradigm for forty-odd years.

The village residents as a social unit experience Antoine's performances as an involuntary, visually absent audience. They know that the whole village is hearing the drum, though each resident may be alone in bed. Antoine addresses the church members as a group. If they understand the drum language, they know they are part of a group that is being exhorted by their leader. The community of believers should prepare to physically gather together.

As individuals, they experience and interpret the drumming according to their own receptive level of surrogate speech competency. Furthermore, the discourse's final stanza contains stringent warnings to each individual: "No one should do this..."

A musical approach to the performance paradigm

According to Béhague,

The study of music performance should concentrate on the actual musical and extra-musical behavior of participants (performers and audience), the consequent social interaction, the meaning of that interaction for the participants, and the rules or codes of performance defined by the community for a specific context or occasion. (1984:7)

This model has been followed and integrated with others throughout this study.

Four broad categories of focus have emerged in recent ethnomusicological theory. This study has attempted to integrate these four overlapping areas of focus as summarized and applied to the drummed church summons in Mekomba:

1. Music as communication: the interplay among communicative resources (drum language), individual competence (in drumming and comprehending), and participant's goals (church attendance motivated by a poetic, persuasive alarm clock).

2. Music as cultural performance: the sharing of experience through socially organized sound in a set-apart performance mode which reflects and establishes cultural values and community structure.
3. Music as an event: a unit of community-wide interaction distinct from everyday interaction, setting up a special social context for creation and interpretation of the drum's meaning.
4. Music as cognitive phenomenon: the way in which the sound is perceived, signified words are understood, and meaning is transacted and negotiated at different levels of receptive competency within the speech community.

A semiotic study applied to the performance paradigm

A semiotic study involves not only a system of signs, but a system of the use of signs by people in actual performance. Using a frame originally developed by Gerard (1957) for the study of biology, Sebeok suggests that a semiotic system be studied from three perspectives (1976:72). A comprehensive study of the entire Ewondo speech surrogate system is beyond the scope of this study, so these three perspectives will be specifically applied to Antoine's performance paradigm as part of a total semiotic system.

What is the sign system?

This question relates to structure. The signified verbal structure is organized through a paratactic arrangement of formulaic phrases into variable aural lines and stanzas. The perceived sound structure consists of stereotyped patterns composed of drumstrokes, which are of low or high pitch and short or long duration. The drumstrokes exhibit an abridgment of prosodic features available in oral speech. The drum pattern signs are in iconic relationship to the formulaic verbal phrases. Signs in isolation are meaningless, but must be combined into phrases and drummed in prescribed contexts for the signs' referents to be deduced. Also, the signifier (drum sound) means little unless the signified (words) are already known, i.e., have been verbalized at some point.

Referring to this study's tripartite analysis, we would say that the sign system resides not only in the audible drumstrokes and base words but also in the meanings intended by the drummer in creation and assigned by the community members in comprehension. The sign system of the paradigm is a set of stereotyped relationships between drumstrokes, words, and people in a communication setting with a well-defined context.

How does the sign system behave? How is it affected by environment?

These questions relate to function. The sign system is used to communicate a message at long distances to a few hundred people at the same
time. It functions twice a week and is taken for granted to a large extent
by many members of the community. The structural levels of line and
stanza change with each performance, though the details of formula
choice and arrangement are up to the drummer's discretion at the moment of performance in a basically unchanging environment.

How did the sign system come to its present state?

This question relates to history. The genre of drummed church summons came into being when the need arose through the introduction of
Christianity into Cameroon. A number of phrases were already in use in
other genres and were integrated into the new genre. Antoine knew
many phrases of various genres and developed his particular performance paradigm in this genre over a period of years through being a
catechist in several Ewondo villages. Cumulative changes in the wider
surrogate system and in his own performance paradigm have led to the
current identity of the paradigm, which is integrally tied up with the
identity of the drummer.

All three aspects of this sign system study point to creation and maintenance of the sign system by the community. The relationship between
signifier (sound) and signified (text) is rooted in relationships between
people. People create the signs, give them meaning, and teach them to
their grandchildren.

In the communicative/aesthetic/social transaction of performance,
each aspect builds on the others. A community develops a sign system
with communicative and aesthetic potential, while the sign system orders
and guides the community. The sign system is intimately connected with
the social system. Regarding this emphasis, Okpewho speaks of "representing social man in creative capacity within the context of a system of
signs recognized by his community" (1990a:3).

Future research on speech surrogates

Most of the following topics have been examined in this study and are
potentially of interest in future speech surrogate studies:

1. What is the precise relationship between the surrogate signs and
   spoken syllables?

2. Can metric phonology provide insight into the relationship of words and the duration of the signs?
3. What variations are acceptable at levels of phonology, formula, and discourse in a given speech surrogate system? Are they considered to be emically the same?
4. What differences are common between speech surrogate systems played on idiophones and those played on membranophones? How do they compare with nonpercussive speech surrogates such as horns and whistles?
5. What differences are inherent between speech surrogates used in metric and nonmetric situations?
6. How do strategies of creation and comprehension differ between speech surrogate systems?
7. How do communities, contexts, and text interact to create each unique performance? Can some performances be grouped together in a related paradigm?

The Ewondo drumming is related to many things but in other ways unlike anything else. From the origin myth of "sound struck first by forest chimpanzees" it has evolved into a complex, polysemous sign system useful for many purposes. In Antoine's hands in Mekomba, it is a set of dualities brought together in sound: high and low pitch, short and long duration, a rapid composition in real time, a process and a product, an individual and a community, music and words from a carrier of tradition and a creative artist, fleeting performance choices summoning people to make choices with eternal consequences. "All people of the drum of God, let us meet, let us unite."

Appendix 1

Performances by Antoine Owono

Performance 1

a bo- nə be fam a-la-dag a bo- nə be bi- nin- ga–
   bon   bon
To children-males in addition to children-females

ya en-go- ko-mo mvog o-wo-ndzu- li
of the tree of the lineage of Owono, the son of Ndzuli,

mi- ni wu- lu-gu˜a-vo- lo du-lu a me-kol e–
                       avol
you walk with quickness in the feet,

mi zu wo-go do-a-te- ne
      wog   doten
you come hear doctrine,

be-ke-ri- se-te- ne
bekristen
Christians,

a-ke di a- ke a n-da
now it goes in the house [church].

ku ku ku ku lu ku ku ku ku ku ku ku lu ku ku ku

♪   ♪
♩ ♪   ♩ ♩ ♩

mi- a ke mi- a wu- lu~
You go, you walk

♩   ♩
♩ ♪ ♩ ♩   ♩ ♪ ♪

e-wu-wu- lu~ e-wu-wu- lu
aimlessly,

♩ ♪   ♪ ♩ ♪ ♩ |
   ♩   ♩ ♩   ♪ ♩ |

mi ta- me zu- ə bo do- a-te- ne |
       zu   doten |
you should come do doctrine. |

♩   ♩   ♩   ♩   ♩   ♩ | ♩   ♩   ♩   ♩   ♩   ♩
          ♪   ♩ | ♪

ku ku ku ku lu ku ku ku| ku ku ku ku lu ku ku

♩ ♪ ♪ ♩ ♪   ♪ ♪ ♩   ♩   ♩
♩   ♩ ♪ ♪ ♩   ♪   ♪

a bo-nə be fam a-la- dag a bo-nə be bi-nin- ga—
   bon   bon
To children-males in addition to children-females

♪   ♩ ♪   ♪
  ♩   ♩   ♩ ♩ ♪ ♩

ya en-go-ko-mo mvog o-wo- ndzu-li
of the tree of the lineage of Owono, the son of Ndzuli,

    ♩
♪ ♩ ♩

mot a be fe
no one, he must no longer

to-bo˜a to-bo to-bo˜
sit and sit and sit [uselessly]

o-tu-tu-tu-tu-tu- dza
otutu
in his little old village.

ku ku ku ku lu ku ku ku ku ku ku ku lu ku ku

a mvo-go ta-ra ŋgo-go
   mvog
To descendants of my father,

mo-tə an- dzi-ki lo-mo mo-tə
mot   lom   mot
no one has sent me anyone.

ku ku ku ku lu ku ku ku ku ku ku ku lu ku ku

bo-te be-te be ŋga zu-ə ma bo dze ben
bot   zu
These people, they came [for baptism], to really do what [now]?

mot a-ko-do a-si˜a dzal die ŋye na |
Someone leaves the bed in his village, he says, |

ma tam ke a-ke a do- a-te-ne |
              doten |
"I must go for doctrine." |

a-bo-go a- ye wo- go do-a-te-ne |
abog   wog   doten |
When he will hear doctrine, |

a ŋga ke a wu- lu˜
[instead] he goes walking

e-wu-wu- lu˜e- wu-wu- lu
aimlessly

a mi-na- mə mi- nam|
  minam |
from place to place. |

a bo-nə be fam a-la-dag a bo-nə be bi- nin- ga-
  bon   bon
To children-males in addition to children-females

ya su-ga mvo-go m- ba le-nem-be
          mvog
of the end of the lineage of Mba Nnembe,

ko-do-gan a-si
[all of you] leave the bed,

mi zu wo-go do-a-te-ne
          wog   doten
you come hear doctrine;

a- ke di a- ke a n-da
now it goes in the house [church].

ku ku ku ku lu ku ku ku ku ku ku ku lu ku ku ku

a mvo-go ta- ra ngo-go
   mvog
To descendants of my father,

nge mi- na bom-bo a- si
if you lie in bed,

(musical notation)

ma-gə me- bom- bo a-si
ma
I will lie in bed.

(musical notation)

ma-gə me- ne a- zaˉe-bu-gu- e
ma   ebugu
For me it is what concern?

(musical notation)

ku ku ku ku lu ku ku ku | ku ku ku ku lu ku ku ku

(musical notation)

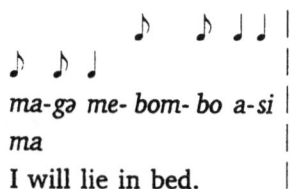

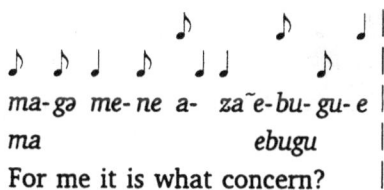

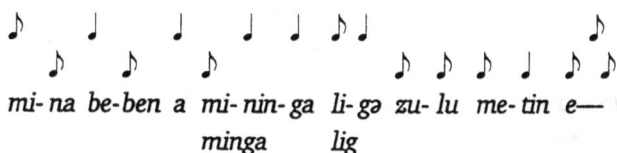

mi- na be-ben a mi- nin- ga li- gə zu- lu me- tin e—
                    minga   lig
You yourselves made promises [appointment]

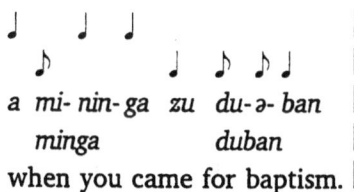

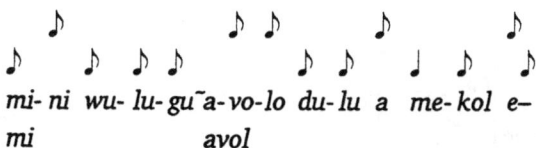

(musical notation)

a mi- nin- ga zu du- ə- ban
  minga   duban
when you came for baptism.

(musical notation)

ku ku ku ku lu ku ku ku

(musical notation)

mi- ni wu- lu- guˉa-vo-lo du- lu a me- kol e—
mi   avol
You walk with quickness in the feet,

mi zu kpa-a-nə zu-lu me-tin e—
     kpaan
you come fulfill your promises [appointment].

ku ku ku ku lu ku ku ku | ku ku ku ku lu ku ku ku

a mvo-go ta-ra ngo-go
   mvog
To descendants of my father,

mo-tə an-dzi-ki lo-mo mo-tə
mot   lom   mot
no one has sent me anyone.

bo-te be-te be nga zu-ə ma bo dze ben
bot   zu
These people, they came [for baptism], to really do what [now]?

mot a-ko-do a-sĩa-dzal die nye na
Someone leaves the bed in his village, he says,

ma tam ke a-ke a do-a-te-ne
             doten
"I must go for doctrine."

a-bo-go a- ye wo-go do-a-te-ne |
abog   wog   doten |
When he will hear doctrine, |

a nga ke a wu- lu~
[instead] he goes walking

e-wu-wu-lu~e-wu-wu-lu
aimlessly

a mi- na-mə mi- nam |
   minam |
from place to place. |

a bo-nə be fam a-la-dag a bo-nə be bi- nin-ga—
  bon   bon
To children-males in addition to children-females

ya en-go-ko-mo mvog o-wo-ndzu-li
of the tree of the lineage of Owono, the son of Ndzuli,

ko- do-gan a-si
[all of you] leave the bed,

mi zu wo-go do-a-te-ne
       wog   doten
you come hear doctrine;

a- ke di a- ke a n- da
now it goes in the house [church].

ku ku ku ku lu ku ku ku ku ku ku ku lu ku ku ku

a mvo-go ta- ra ngo-go
  mvog
To descendants of my father,

mo-tə te bo na
mot
no one should do this:

a- bo-go a- ye ke a-wu-lu a su-ga be-kon
abog
When he will go, he walks, to the end of the dead

a ŋga ka-tə-ka-tə n-ton-do-be o-fo-foe na— |
    kat   kat |
he tells God, whispering over and over, that |

bi- bu-gi bi do-a-te-ne bi-ne-ə ma ko-koa a mo |
bibug   doten   bine |
"words of doctrine, they are not in my hands." |

mvo-go ta-ra ŋgo-go |
mvog |
Descendants of my father, |

ko-do-gan a-si |
[all of you] leave the bed. |

e- ko-ko-do ͠e-ko-ko-do ͠e-ko-ko-do ͠e-ko-ko-do
Leave [forever, carelessly, all at once],

mi zu wo-go do-a-te-ne te— |
    wog   doten |
you come hear this doctrine. |

a-ke di a- ke a n-da
Now it goes in the house [church].

mi- nin-ga ba-re-ə fe-ge ma dzo˜a-ya
miŋga   bar   fe
You will say to me what else [excuses]?

END

Performance 2

♩ ♪ ♩ ♪ ♪

be- ke- ri- se- te- ne
bekristen
Christians,

♪ ♪ ♩ ♩ ♩ |

be- se ya me- kom- ba |
all in Mekomba, |

♩ ♪ ♪ ♪ ♩ ♩ |

nge mi- na o- yo- a— ve- be- gan |
if you are sleeping, [all of you] wake up! |

♩ ♩ ♪ ♩ ♩ |

a mvo- go ta- ra ŋgo- go |
mvog |
To descendants of my father, |

♩ ♪ ♪ ♪ ♩ ♩ |

nge mi- na o- yo- a— ve- be- gan |
if you are sleeping, [all of you] wake up! |

♪ ♪ ♩ ♪ ♩ |

bi- em bi ki- di |
Signs of morning |

♩ ♩ ♪ ♪ ♩ ♩ |

bi nga man- e- ya- ko- bo |
they are finishing to speak. |

bi-em bi ki-di |
Signs of morning |

bi ŋga man-e-ya-ko-bo
they are finishing to speak.

ki-di ndzõ̃e-len-de-ya- hm
Morning—the day has already dawned.

mot a-be fe
No one, he must no longer

ke o-yo-a—
sleep

o ma-nə so-ba-no kpe-kpa-a-ga
 man   soban   kpekpaa
You finish washing [teeth] with brush.

o ma-nə so-ba-no men-dim
 man   soban
You finish washing [face] with water.

♪ ♪ ♩ ♩ |
♩ |
o ko-do a-si |
You leave the bed. |

♩   ♪ ♩ ♪
♩ ♪   ♪   ♩ ♩ ♩
o no-n man n-tu e-yie–
You take your small old cloth,

♩ ___3___   ♩ |
♩ ♩ ♩ ♩ ♪ ♩ ♪   ♩ |
o nga zu wa wu-lu˜a zen e-se |
you start coming, you walk along the road. |

♩   ♪ ♩ ♪   ♩
   ♩   ♩ ♪
mi zu wo-go do-a-te-ne
       wog   doten
You come hear doctrine,

      ♪
♩ ♪ ♩ ♩ ♩
be-ke-ri-se-te-ne
bekristen
Christians,

   ♪ ♩ ♩ ♩ ♩ |
♩ ♩ ♪ ♪   ♪ |
a-ke di a- ke a n-da– |
now it goes in the house [church]. |

♩ ♩ ♩   ♩ ♩ ♩ | ♩ ♩ ♩   ♩ ♩ ♩ |
      ♪   ♩ | ♪   ♩ |
ku ku ku ku lu ku ku ku| ku ku ku ku lu ku ku ku |

ku ku ku ku lu ku ku ku

mi-a ke mi-a wu-lu˜
You go, you walk

e-wu- wu- lu˜e- wu-wu- lu
aimlessly,

mi ta-me zu-ə bo do-a-te-ne
     zu   doten
you should come do doctrine.

ku ku ku ku lu ku ku ku | ku ku ku ku lu ku ku ku

be-ke-ri- se-te- ne
bekristen
Christians,

be-se ya su-ga mvo-go m-ba le-nem-be
           mvog
all at the end of the descendents of Mba Nnembe,

♪   ♩
   ♩ ♪ ♩ ♩

mvo- go ta- ra ngo- go
mvog
descendants of my father

♪   ♪ ♪ |
   ♩ ♪ ♪ ♩|

nge mi na o-yo-a– |
if you are sleeping, |

♩
♩ ♩

ve- be-gan
[all of you] wake up!

♩ ♩ ♩   ♪   ♩♩
      ♩ ♪

ki- di ndzo˜e-len- de- ya- hm
Morning—the day has already dawned,

   ♩
♪ ♩ ♩

mot a-be fe
No one, he must no longer

  ♪ ♪
♪ ♪ ♪

ke o-yo-a–
sleep.

♩ ♪ ♩ ♪ ♩   ♩|
  ♩   ♪ ♪ |

mi zu wo-go do-a- te- ne–|
     wog   doten |
You come hear doctrine. |

ku ku ku ku lu ku ku ku | ku ku ku ku lu ku ku ku |

ku ku ku ku lu ku ku ku

a mvo-go ta-ra ngo-go
   mvog
To descendants of my father,

mo-tə an-dzi-ki lo-mo mo-tə |
mot   lom   mot |
no one has sent me anyone. |

ku ku ku ku lu ku ku ku

bo-te be-te be nga zu-ə ma bo dze ben
bot   zu
These people, they came [for baptism], to really do what [now]? |

mot a-ko-do a-sī͡a-dzal die nye na
Someone leaves the bed in his village, he says,

ma tam ke a-ke a do-a-te-ne
doten
"I must go for doctrine."

wo-
a-bo-go a- ye go do-a-te-ne
abog wog doten
When he will hear doctrine,

a ŋga ke a wu- lu˜
[instead] he goes walking

e-wu-wu-lu˜e-wu-wu-lu
aimlessly

a mi-na-mə mi- nam
minam
from place to place.

a bo-nə be fam a-la-dag a bo-nə be bi-nin- ga—
bon bon
To children-males in addition to children-females

ya en-go-ko-mo mvog o- wo-ndzu- li
of the tree of the lineage of Owono, the son of Ndzuli,

ko-do-gan a-si
[all of you] leave the bed.

mi zu wo- go do-a-te- ne
         wog   doten
You come hear doctrine;

a-ke di a- ke a n-da–
now it goes in the house [church].

ku ku ku ku lu ku ku ku| ku ku ku ku lu ku ku ku

a mvo- go ta- ra ngo-go
   mvog
To descendants of my father,

nge mi-ni bom- bo a-si
if you lie in bed,

ma- gə me-bom- bo a-si

ma

I will lie in bed.

ma- gə me-ne a- za˜e-bu- gu |

ma |

For me it is what concern? |

ku ku ku ku lu ku ku ku

5

mi- na be-ben a mi- nin- ga li- gə zu- lu me- tin e—

minga   lig

You yourselves made promises [appointment]

a mi-nin- ga zu du-ə-ban |

minga   duban |

when you came for baptism. |

ku ku ku ku lu ku ku ku

mi- ni wu- lu-gu˜a- vo-lo du-lu a me- kol e—

mi   avol

You walk with quickness in the feet,

mi zu kpa-a-nə me-tin e-
        kpaan
you come fulfill your promises [appointment].

ku ku ku ku lu ku ku ku | ku ku ku ku lu ku ku ku

a mvo-go ta-ra ngo-go
    mvog
To descendants of my father,

mot a ka-tə wo-a dzam
        kat   wo
someone tells you something,

wo o ka-tə man- yon
    kat
you in turn tell your brother.

m-bo: lo n-ne-mə 'wa ko-bo an-yu te fa-li bi-se
mbol   nnem
Everything the heart speaks, the mouth cannot say all.

mi- a ke mi-a wu- lu˜
You go, you walk

e-wu- wu- lu~e- wu- wu- lu
aimlessly,

mi ta- me zu-ə bo do- a- te- ne |
          zu   doten |
you should come do doctrine. |

ku ku ku ku lu ku ku ku| ku ku ku ku lu ku ku ku

a mvo- go ta- ra ngo- go |
   mvog |
To descendants of my father, |

mo-tə te bo- na
mot
no one should do this: |

mo-tə te dzo na—
mot
no one should say this: |

[mistake] a-ve-bə da-ka-rə ma bo an-yo-le
          aveb   dakar   anyo
          "coldness is in my body."

mi-ni wu-lu-gu˜a-vo-lo du-lu a me-kol e-
mi   avol
You walk with quickness in the feet,

mi zu wo-go do-a-te-ne-
        wog   doten
you come hear doctrine.

ku ku ku ku lu ku ku ku ku ku ku ku lu ku ku ku

ku ku ku ku lu ku ku ku

a mvo-go ta-ra ngo-go
  mvog
To descendants of my father,

mo-tə te bo-na
mot
no one should do this:

a-bo-go a- ye ke a-wu-lu a su- ga be- kon |
abog |
When he will go, he walks, to the end of the dead |

an- ga ka-tə- ka-tə n- ton-do-be o-fo-foe na— |
      kat   kat |
he tells God, whispering over and over, that |

bi-bu-gi bi do-a-te-ne bi- ne-ə ma ko-koa a mo |
bibug   doten   bine |
"words of the doctrine, they are not in my hands." |

mvo-go ta- ra ngo- go |
mvog |
Descendants of my father, |

ko-do-gan a- si |
[all of you] leave the bed. |

e-ko-ko-do˜e-ko- ko-do-e-ko-ko-do˜e-ko- ko-do
Leave [forever, carelessly, all at once],

mi zu wo-go do-a-te-ne–
      wog   doten
You come hear doctrine.

a-ke di a- ke a n-da–
now it goes in the house [church].

mi-nin-ga ba-re-ə fe-ge ma dzoˉa-ya
minga   bar   fe
You will say to me what else [excuses]?

END

Performance 5

Note: Performance 5 indicates drum stick patterns.
       R equals right hand.
       L equals left hand.
       D equals double stroke (both hands).

D R L R R   L R L   R R L R L R   R L

a bo-nə be fam a- la- dag a bo-nə be bi- nin- ga –
   bon   bon
To children-males in addition to children-females

R   L   R   R L R   L L   R   L

ya en- go- ko- mo mvog o- wo- ndzu- li
of the tree of the descendants of Owono, the son of Ndzuli,

L R L R L   R L R L R L L   RL

mi- ni wu- lu- guˆa- vo- lo du- lu a me- kol e–
mi   avol
You walk with quickness in the feet,

R   L   R L R L R L R |

mi zu wo-go do-a- te- ne-e |
        wog   doten |
you come hear doctrine. |

R   L   R   L   R   L   R   L | R   L   R   L   R   L   R   L

ku ku ku ku lu ku ku ku| ku ku ku ku lu ku ku ku

a mvo-go ta-ra ngo-go
mvog
To descendants of my father,

mot a-be fe
no one, he must no longer

to-bõa to-bo to-bõ
sit and sit and sit [uselessly]

o- tu- tu- tu- tu- tu dza
otutu
in his little old village.

ku ku ku ku lu ku ku ku ku ku ku ku lu ku ku ku

do-a-te-ne
doten
Doctrine,

L L R LRL R RL |

a- ke di a- ke a n-da |
now it goes in the house [church]. |

R   L   R   L   R   L   R   L | R   L   R   L   R   L   R   L

ku ku ku ku lu ku ku ku | ku ku ku ku lu ku ku ku

L R L   R L   R L R   L R L R L

mi-ni wu- lu-gu˜a- vo- lo mbi a- vo-lo du-lu
mi   avol   avol
You walk, running fast, walking fast,

R L R   L R R L R L LRL |

mi zu kpa- a-nə zu-lu me-tin e— |
      kpaan |
you come fulfill your promises [appointment]. |

R   L   R   L   R   L   R   L | R   L   R   L   R   L   R   L

ku ku ku ku lu ku ku ku | ku ku ku ku lu ku ku ku

D R   L L R L   L

a mvo-go ta-ra ngo-go
  mvog
To descendants of my father,

R   L L R   L R L

mot a ka-tə wo-a dzam
      kat   wo

someone tells you something,

R   L L   R   D   R

wo o ka-tə man-yon
     kat

you in turn tell your brother.

R L R L R L R L   R L R L R L R L

ku ku ku ku lu ku ku ku ku ku ku ku lu ku ku ku

R L R L R L R R L L R L R L R L

bi- bu- gi n-ne-mə wa-ko-bo an-yu te fa-li bi- se
bibug   nnem

Everything the heart speaks, the mouth cannot say all.

R L R L R L R L

ku ku ku ku lu ku ku ku

R L L R L R L R   L R L   R L

mi- a zu mi- a wu-lu nde-ne-le min-ku-mu

You come, you walk,   [nonchalantly] waving bodies [like tall trees],

R   L   R   L   R   L R·L |

mi zu wo-go do-a-te-ne-e |
        wog   doten |
you come hear doctrine. |

R   L   R   L   R   L   R   L | R   L   R   L   R   L   R   L

ku ku ku ku lu ku ku ku | ku ku ku ku lu ku ku ku

L   L   R L R L

be- ke- ri-se- te- ne
bekristen
Christians,

R   L   R   R L R   L R L   R R   L

be-se ya su-ga mvo-go m-ba le-nem-be
                       mvog
all at the end of the lineage of Mba Nnembe,

R   L   L   R L   R L|

nge mi-na o-yo-a- |
if you are sleeping, |

D   L |

ve- be- gan |
[all of you] wake up! |

nge mi-na o- yo-a— ve-be-gan |
If you are sleeping, [all of you] wake up! |

R L |
♪ ♪ |
      |
ki- di |
Morning, |

ndzo˜e-len-de-ya- hm
the day has already dawned.

mot a-be fe
No one, he must no longer

ke o-yo-a —
sleep,

mi zu wo-go do-a-te-ne-e |
      wog   doten |
you come hear doctrine. |

R   L   R   L   R   L   R   L │ R   L   R   L   R   L   R   L │

ku ku ku ku lu ku ku ku │ ku ku ku ku lu ku ku ku │

R   L   R   L   R   L   R   L

ku ku ku ku lu ku ku ku

D R   L   L   R   L   L

a mvo-go ta-ra ŋgo-go
   mvog
To descendants of my father,

R   L R L

mot a-be fe
No one, he must no longer

L R L R   L R L   R │

bo- bi- bu- gi be ko- ni │
   bibug   │
do things of tricks. │

R   L   R   L   R   L   R   L │ R   L   R   L   R   L   R   L

ku ku ku ku lu ku ku ku │ ku ku ku ku lu ku ku ku

L   RR L   RL RL RL RL RL RL

man e-tug nkul̃a lo-no lo-no lo-no lo-no lo-no lo-no
A small, old, broken drum calls and calls [a long time],

L R   RLRRLL R L

ve mi bo- a- si o-tu- tu dza
but you are on the bed in your little old village. |

D R L R R   LR L   RRLRLR RL

a bo-nə be fam a- la- dag a bo-nə be bi- nin- ga —
    bon   bon
To children-males in addition to children-females

R R L R   L RL   RR   L

ya su-ga mvo-go m- ba le-nem- be
         mvog
at the end of the descendants of Mba Nnembe,

R L R   L R

ko-do-gan a- si
[all of you] leave the bed. |

R L R L R LR L

mi zu wo-go do-a-te- ne-e
     wog   doten
you come hear doctrine. |

R L R LRL R R L

a-ke di a- ke a n-da
now it goes in the house [church].

R L R L R L R L | R L R L R L R L

ku ku ku ku lu ku ku ku| ku ku ku ku lu ku ku ku

D R L L R L   L

a mvo-go ta-ra ngo-go
   mvog
To descendants of my father,

R L R R   L RR |

nge mi-na bom-bo a-si |
if you lie in bed,

R L R R   L RR |

ma-gə me-bom-bo a-si |
ma
I will lie in bed.

R L R L RLD R L R|

ma-gə me-ne a- zaˉe-bu-gu-e |
ma   ebugu
For me it is what concern?

R L R L R L R L | R L R L R L R L

ku ku ku ku lu ku ku ku| ku ku ku ku lu ku ku ku

R L R L R L R L R L R L R L LRL |

mi-na be-ben a mi-nin- ga li-gə zu-lu me-tin e— |
        minga   lig |
You yourselves made promises [appointment]. |

R L R L R L R L

ku ku ku ku lu ku ku ku

L R L R L   R L R L R L L L RL

mi- ni wu-lu- gu˜a- vo-lo du-lu a me-kol e—
mi   avol
You walk with quickness in the feet,

R L R L R R L R L LRL |
                                                   |
mi zu kpa-a-nə zu-lu me-tin e— |
        kpaan |
you come fulfill your promises [appointment]. |

R L R L R L R L | R L R L R L R L

ku ku ku ku lu ku ku ku| ku ku ku ku lu ku ku ku

```
D R   L  L R  L   L
♩ ♪      ♩
♩    ♩ ♪   ♩ ♩
```
a mvo-go ta-ra ŋgo-go
  mvog
To descendants of my father,

```
        R    L R  L
              ♩
♩        ♪ ♩  ♩
```
        mot a be fe
[mistake] no one, he must no longer

```
R  L R  L R  L   R        |
  ♪  ♪ ♪ ♩     ♩          |
♪  ♪        ♩             |
```
bo- bi-bu- gi be fon-go |
   bibug |
do things too small [insignificant]. |

```
L   RR  L     R L  R L  R L  R L  R L  R L
  ♩♪  ♩   ♪   ♪   ♪   ♪   ♪   ♪
♩          ♩   ♩   ♩   ♩   ♩   ♩
```
man e-tug nkul̃a lo-no lo-no lo-no lo-no lo-no lo-no
A small, old, broken drum calls and calls [a long time],

```
L  R  RLRR LL R  L              |
  ♩  ♪ ♩♪     ♩                |
♪     ♪   ♩♩  ♩                |
```
ve mi bo- a-si o-tu-tu dza |
but you are on the bed in your little old village. |

```
D R L  R  R  L R L   R R L  R L  R  R L
♩ ♪ ♪ ♩ ♪       ♪ ♪ ♩  ♩ ♪
♩  .      ♩ ♪ ♪ ♩     ♪       ♪
```
a bo-nə be fam a-la-dag a bo-nə be bi-nin-ga—
  bon   bon
To children-males in addition to children-females

R   L   R   R   L   R   L L   R   L
♪   ♩ ♪   ♪
      ♩   ♩   ♩♩ ♪   ♩

ya en-go- ko-mo mvog o-wo-ndzu-li
of the tree of the descendants of Owono, the son of Ndzuli,

R L R   L R |
♪ ♪   ♩ ♩ |
      ♪ |

ko-do-gan a- si |
[all of you] leave the bed. |

R   L   R   L   R L R L
♩   ♪ ♩ ♪ ♩
      ♩   ♪ ♩

mi zu wo-go do-a- te- ne-
       wog   doten
you come hear doctrine.

L L   R   L R L   R R L |
    ♪   ♩   ♩ ♪ ♩ |
♩ ♩   ♪ ♪   ♪ |
a- ke di a- ke a n-da —— |
now it goes in the house [church]. |

R   L   R   L   R   L   R   L | R   L   R   L   R   L   R   L
♩   ♩   ♩   ♩   ♩   ♩ | ♩   ♩   ♩   ♩   ♩   ♩
               ♪   ♩ | ♪   ♩

ku ku ku ku lu ku ku ku| *ku ku ku ku lu ku ku ku*

R   L   R   L   R L   R L
♩   ♩   ♩   ♩ ♩   ♩
          ♪   ♩

ku ku ku ku lu ku ku ku

```
D  R    L   L   R   L    L
```

a *mvo-go ta- ra ngo- go*
   mvog

To descendants of my father,

```
R   L   L   D   L           |
```

mo-tə te bo na |
mot |

no one should do this: |

```
R L  R  LRLR  L R   L   R L R L   R        |
```

a- bo-go a-ye ke a- wu-lu a su-ga be- kon |
abog |

When he will go, he walks, to the end of the dead |

```
D   L  D   L  L   R L L   R  L   L R L   R LR |
```

an- ga ka- tə-ka-tə n-ton-do-be o-fo-foe na— |
        kat   kat |

he tells God, whispering over and over, that |

```
L  R   L  R  R   L R L  R R L R   D  D   R L  |
```

bi-bu- gi bi do- a-te-ne bi-ne-ə ma ko-koa a mo |
bibug   doten   bine |

"words of doctrine, they are not in my hands." |

mvo-go ta- ra ngo- go
mvog
Descendants of my father,

ko-do-gan a- si
[all of you] leave the bed.

e-ko- ko-do˜e-ko- ko-do- e-ko-ko-do˜e-ko-ko-do
Leave [forever, carelessly, all at once],

mi zu wo- go do-a- te-ne te —
        wog   doten
you come hear this doctrine.

a-ke di a- ke a n-da
now it goes in the house [church].

mi-nin- ga ba- re-ə fe-ge ma dzo˜a-ya
minga   bar   fe
You will say to me what else [excuses]?

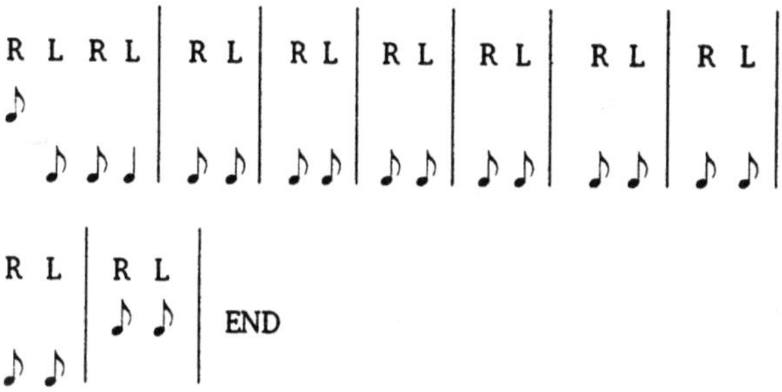
R L R L
R L
R L
R L
R L
R L
R L
R L
R L
END

Appendix 2

Performance by Atemengue Marcus

Performance 1

a bo-nə be o-ken o-dzo-go a-ba-də fe-ge
To children of "sword-hanging" surpassing wisdom
   [the most wise authority],

a- ka-rə yi ? ? ? a-fu-lan
he always has need of a mixture

a bo-nə be fam a bo-nə be bi-nin-ga
of children-males and children-females,

be-ke-ri- se-te-ne
Christians,

be zu wo-go do-a- te-ne
they [should] come hear doctrine.

a do-a- ten a do-a-ten | a do-a-ten a do-a-ten
to doctrine to doctrine | to doctrine to doctrine

a do-a-ten   a do-a-ten
to doctrine to doctrine

n-sol e- sie o-yan-ga mo-tə e-men
The share of the work awaits the man himself.

a do-a- ten a do-a-ten | a do-a-ten a do-a- ten
to doctrine to doctrine | to doctrine to doctrine

mi be fe ke mia wu-lu e-wu- wu- lu
You must no longer go walking aimlessly

ke-ri- se-te-ne
Christians,

mi zu bo do-a- te- ne
you come do doctrine,

ke-ri- se-te-ne |
Christians. |

a do-a- ten a do-a-ten | a do-a-ten a do-a- ten
to doctrine to doctrine | to doctrine to doctrine

ko-do ko- do a so a me-se

Leaving, leaving, it brings many things.

a do-a- ten a do-a-ten | a do-a-ten a do-a- ten

to doctrine to doctrine | to doctrine to doctrine

a bi- a ye ke son a be-kon

We will go into the grave of the dead.

bi-bu-gi bi do-a-te-ne

Words of doctrine,

bi-a ka-rə lo-no be-ke-ri-se-te-ne

they always call Christians.

a-bo-go w'a-ye ke do-a-te-ne

When you will go to doctrine,

o nga ke wa wu-lu~e- tam e-tam

You will go walking alone, alone,

a-ne ku- mu- du ŋgoe
like a solitary bush pig.

[slower speed]

do-a- te-ne do-a- te- ne | do-a- te- ne do-a- te- ne |
doctrine   doctrine | doctrine   doctrine |

do-a- te- ne do-a- te- ne | do-a- te- ne do-a- te- ne |
doctrine   doctrine | doctrine   doctrine |

[regular speed]

ke-ri- se- te- ne
Christians,

ri- se- te- ne an-to- ya- zu- lu me-tin
we are at promises [appointment].

do-a- te- ne do-a- te- ne | do-a- te- ne do-a- te- ne
doctrine   doctrine | doctrine   doctrine

a- bo- go mi-a zu bo do-a- te- ne
When you come to do doctrine,

min-toa a-ko-koe da-ka-lan min-tud a-ya-
[instead] you become little monkeys who play on some bushes—why?

do-a-te-ne do-a-te-ne | do-a-te-ne do-a-te-ne
doctrine   doctrine | doctrine   doctrine

bi-bu-gi bi do-a-te-ne bi-a kar yi ve be-ke-ri-se-te-ne
Words of doctrine, they always have need of Christians.

[no words—phrase marker "for repose"—"shows the drum is thinking
  of the end"—points to finish]

be dzo˜a nya te wog e-
It has been said but nobody listens.

[end marker—"used only when calling Christians"]

a mvog a-la-nan nna-ma˜
To descendants staying eternally in the countryside,

a-ke di a ma ke˜a n-da
now I go in the house [church].

Appendix 3

List of Tape Contents

Tape 1, Side A

1. Performance 1 by Antoine Owono, Mekomba
2. Innocent reading text of Performance 1
3. Performance 2 by Antoine
4. Phrase-by-phrase match of Performance 2
5. Performance 3 by Antoine
6. Performance 4 by Antoine
7. Innocent reading text of Performance 4
8. Performance 5 by Antoine

Tape 1, Side B

9. Performance 6 by Antoine
10. Performance 7 by Antoine
11. Phrase-by-phrase match of Performance 7
12. Performance 8 by Antoine
13. Performance 9 by Antoine
14. Performance 9 at slow speed[66]
15. Performance 10 by Antoine

Tape 2, Side A

16. Marijean reading Antoine's dictated text
17. Antoine playing dictated text phrase by phrase
18. Antoine leading doctrine class in church
19. Performance 1 by Atemengue Marcus, Mfou-villáge
20. Innocent reading text of Performance 1
21. Performance 2 by Atemengue
22. Performance 3 by Atemengue
23. Atemengue's drum appellation, Mfou-villáge
24. Manga Luc's drum appellation, Yaoundé
25. Paul's drum appellation drummed and spoken by Antoine
26. Rene's drum appellation, Mekomba
27. Two catechists' phrases read by Innocent, Mekomba
28. Phrases drummed and spoken by Atemengue, Mfou-villáge
29. Drum phrase and performance by Benoit Embang, 4 kilometers from Mekomba

---

[66]This performance is recorded at roughly 40 percent normal speed, the tapes speed used in transcribing all performances, and is included here so the hearer can more easily follow along with a transcription.

Tape 2, Side B

30. Phrases drummed and spoken by Owoudou Marcus, Mekomba
31. Performance 1 by Manga Luc, Yaoundé
32. Six excerpts of dance drum patterns by Manga
33. Funeral drum by Manga
34. Three excerpts of funeral dance drum ensemble at Mekomba
35. Seven excerpts of dance drum duets by Manga and Paul
36. Drum ensemble in Presbyterian church service at Mfou
37. Three excerpts of drum ensemble in traditional religion healing service at Yaoundé

Examples From 1913 Recording, Germany[67]

38. Drum name for an authority figure (common stock formula)
39. *Come, run, quickly, quickly* (common stock formula)
40. *A man walks alone, he was born alone* (common stock formula)
41. *Three by three, two by two* (common stock formula)
42. Complete drum message announcing death: nkul awu
43. Two drum patterns for a dance

These tapes and other transcribed performances are available from the author. Send inquiries to:

Paul Neeley
c/o Ethnomusicology
7500 W. Camp Wisdom Rd.
Dallas TX 75236

---

[67]Recorded at the *Seminar für Africanische und Sudseesprachen* of the University of Hamburg. They are part of about 100 selections in which the words were transcribed and translated in an article by Heep (1920). Note that this earlier drumming is played at a faster speed than that used by drummers in my later recordings.

References

Abbs, James H. 1986. Invariance and variability in speech production: A distinction between linguistic intent and its neuromotor implementation. In Parkell and Klatt, 202–25.

Abega, Prosper. 1969. La grammaire de l'Ewondo. Yaoundé: Université Fedérale du Cameroun, Section de Linguistique Appliquée.

Abega, Séverin Cécile. 1987. L'Esana chez les Beti. Yaoundé: Editions CLE.

Abrahams, Roger D. 1970. Creativity, individuality, and the traditional singer. Studies in the Literary Imagination 3:5–34.

———. 1977. Toward an enactment-centered theory of folklore. In Bascom, 79–120.

Agawu, V. Kofi. 1987. The rhythmic structure of West African music. Journal of Musicology 5(3):400–18.

———. 1990. Variation procedures in Northern Ewe song. Ethnomusicology 34:221–43.

Agovi, Kofi. 1988. The aesthetics of creative communication in African performance situations. Research Review (Legon) NS 4(1):1–9.

Aka, Emmanuel A. 1988. How Catholicism came: A rejoinder. Yaoundé: Cameroon Tribune, August 23, p. 16

Akoa-Mongo, François. 1993. personal correspondence.

Allen, George D. 1975. Speech rhythm: Its relation to performance universals and articulatory timing. Journal of Phonetics 3:75–86.

Ames, David W., Edgar A. Gregersen, and Thomas Neugebauer. 1971. Taaken Samaarii: A drum language of Hausa youth. Africa 41:12–31.

Angenot, Jean-Pierre. 1971. Aspects de la phonétique et de la morphologie de l'Ewondo. Ph.D. dissertation. University of Leiden.

Anonymous. 1911. The call-drum. Atlantic Monthly 107:140–42.

Anyidoho, Kofi. 1983. Oral poetics and traditions of verbal art in Africa. Ph.D. dissertation. University of Texas at Austin.

———. 1986. Musical patterns and verbal structures: Aspects of prosody in an African oral art. Black Orpheus 6:27–43.

Apter, Andrew. 1992. Black critics and kings: The hermeneutics of power in Yoruba society. Chicago: University of Chicago Press.

Arewa, Ojo and Niyi Adekola. 1980. Redundancy principles of statistical communications as applied to Yoruba talking-drum. Anthropos 75:185–202.

Armstrong, R. G. 1955. Talking instruments in West Africa. Explorations 4:140–53. Reprinted in Sebeok and Umiker-Sebeok 1976:865–77.

Arom, Simha. 1976. Le langage tambouriné des Banda-Linda (R.C.A.). In Luc Bouquiaux (ed.), Théories et méthods en linguistique africaine. Paris: Centre National de la Recherche Scientifique and L'Office de la Recherche Scientifique et Technique Outre-Mer. Société d'Etudes Linguistiques et Anthropologiques de France 54–55:113–69.

Atangana, Karl and Paul Messi. 1919. Jaunde-texte. Hamburg: L. Friederichsen.

Austerlitz, R. 1983. Meaning in music: Is music like language and if so, how? American Journal of Semiotics 2(3):1–12.

Avorgbedor, Daniel. 1986. The interaction of music and spoken texts in the context of Anlo-Ewe music. Black Orpheus 6:17–26.

Baines, Anthony and Klaus P. Wachsmann. 1961. Classification of musical instruments. Galpin Society Journal 14:4–29.

Barber, Karin. 1984. Yoruba oríkì and deconstructive criticism. Research in African Literatures 15:497–518.

——— and P. F. de Moraes Farias, eds. 1989. Discourse and its disguises: The interpretation of African oral texts. Birmingham University African Studies Series 1. Birmingham: Centre of West African Studies.

Bascom, William R., ed. 1977. Frontiers of folklore. AAAS Selected Symposium 5. Washington, D.C.: American Association for the Advancement of Science.

Bauman, Richard. 1976. The theoretical boundaries of performance. In Herndon and Brunyate.

———. 1977. Verbal art as performance. Rowley, Mass.: Newbury House.

———. 1986. Story, performance and event: Contextual studies of oral narrative. Cambridge Studies in Oral and Literate Culture 10. Cambridge: Cambridge University Press.

Beaugrande, Robert de and Wolfgang Dressler. 1981. Introduction to text linguistics. London and New York: Longman.

Béhague, Gerard, ed. 1984. Performance practice: Ethnomusicological perspectives. Westport, Conn.: Greenwood Press.

Belinga, Eno. 1965. Littérature et musique populaire en Afrique Noire. Paris: Cujas.

Ben-Amos, Daniel and Kenneth S. Goldstein, eds. 1975. Folklore: Performance and communication. The Hague: Mouton.

Berleant, Arnold. 1970. The aesthetic field: A phenomonology of aesthetic experience. Springfield: Charles C. Thomas.

Betz, R. 1976. Die Trommelsprache der Duala. Mitteilungen von Forschungreisenden und Gelehrten aus den deutschen Schutzgebieten 11:1–86. Reprinted in Sebeok and Umiker-Sebeok 1976:158–258.

Bex, A. R. 1992. Genre as context. Journal of Literary Semantics 21(5):1–16.

Biber, Douglas. 1988. Variation across speech and writing. Cambridge: Cambridge University Press.

Blacking, John. 1981a. The ethnography of musical performance. In Heartz and Wade, 383–85.

———. 1981b. The problem of 'ethnic' perceptions in the semiotics of music. In Wendy Steiner (ed.). The sign in music and literature, 184–94. Austin: UTA Press.

Boadi, L. A. 1989. Praise poetry in Akan. Research in African Literatures 20(2):181–93.

Bower, Gordon H. and Randolph K. Cirilo. 1985. Cognitive psychology and text processing. In Teun A. van Dijk (ed.), Handbook of discourse analysis 1:71–105.

Briggs, Charles L. 1988. Competence in performance: The creativity of tradition in Mexicano verbal art. Philadelphia: University of Pennsylvania Press.

Bright, William, ed. 1992. International encyclopedia of linguistics. New York and Oxford: Oxford University Press.

Brown, Calvin S. 1948. Music and literature: A comparison of the arts. Athens: University of Georgia Press.

Busnel, Rene Guy and Andre Classe. 1976. Whistled languages. Berlin and New York: Springer-Verlag.

Cable, Thomas. 1975. Parallels to the melodic formulas of 'Beowulf'. Modern Philology 73:1–14.

Canale, Michael. 1983. From communicative competence to communicative language pedagogy. In Jack C. Richards and Richard W. Schmidt (eds.), Language and communication, 2–27. London and New York: Longman.

Carrington, John F. 1949a. A comparative study of some central African gong-languages. Brussels: Institut Royal Colonial Belge.

————. 1949b. The talking drums of Africa. London: Harry Kingsgate Press.

————. 1971. The talking drums of Africa. Scientific American 225(6):90–94.

Carroll, John B., ed. 1956. Language, thought, and reality: Selected writings of Benjamin Lee Whorf. Cambridge: MIT Press.

Chafe, Wallace L. 1977. Creativity in verbalization and its implications for the nature of stored knowledge. In Freedle (ed.), 41–55.

————. 1982. Integration and involvement in speaking, writing, and oral literature. In Deborah Tannen (ed.), Spoken and written language: Exploring orality and literacy, 35–53. Norwood, N.J.: Ablex.

———— and Jane Danielewicz. 1987. Properties of spoken and written language. In Horowitz and Samuels (eds.), 83–113.

Chase, Gilbert. 1972. Structuralism, linguistics and musicology. Yearbook of Inter-American Musical Research 8:121–31.

Chenoweth, Vida. 1972. Melodic perception and analysis. Ukarumpa, Papua New Guinea: Summer Institute of Linguistics.

Clark, Sherri Rae. 1984. Speech vs. writing. Notes on Literacy 43:1–15.

Clynes, Manfred, ed. 1982. Music, mind, and brain. New York: Plenum Press.

Cohen, Antonie. 1986. Invariance and variability of words in the speech chain. In Parkell and Klatt, 524–39.

Cole, Hugo. 1974. Sounds and signs. London: Oxford University Press.

Coplan, David B. 1987. The power of oral poetry: Narrative songs of the Basotho migrants. Research in African Literatures 18:1–35.

Cowan, George M. 1948. Mazateco whistle speech. Language 24:280–86.

Crozier, W. Ray and Antony J. Chapman, eds. 1984. Cognitive processes in the perception of art. Advances in Psychology 19. North Holland: Elsevier Science Publishers.

Cushing, Steven. 1984. Dynamic model selection in the interpretation of discourse. In Lucia Vaina and Jaakko Hintikka (eds.), Cognitive constraints on communication, 351–61. Dordrecht: D. Reidel.

Cutting, James E., Burton S. Rosner, and Christopher F. Foard. 1976. Perceptual categories for musiclike sounds: Implications for theories of speech perception. Quarterly Journal of Experimental Psychology 28:361–78.

Danks, Joseph H. and Laurel J. End. 1987. Processing strategies for reading and listening. In Horowitz and Samuels, 271–94.

Du Bois, John W. 1992. Ritual language. In Bright, 3:335–37.

Dugast, Idelette. 1955. Monographie de la tribu des ndiki (Banen du Cameroun). Travaux et mémoires de l'Institut d'Ethnologie 50:567–602. Excerpted and reprinted in Sebeok and Umiker-Sebeok, 1976:708–41.

Dundes, Alan, ed. 1965. The study of folklore. Engelwood Cliffs, N.J.: Prentice-Hall.

———. 1989. Folklore matters. Knoxville: The University of Tennessee Press.

Eskelin, Gerald Ray. 1971. The cognitive aspect of musical rhythm, and a method for its application to teaching. Ph.D. dissertation. Indiana University.

Essono, Jean-Marie. n.d. Le système vocalique Ewondo. ms.

Etua, Joseph. 1993. personal communication.

Euba, Akin. 1974. Ìlù Èsù [drumming for Èsù]: Analysis of a dùndún performance. Essays for a Humanist. New York: The Town House Press.

———. 1988. Essays in music in Africa, vol. 1. Bayreuth, Germany: Bayreuth University.

———. 1991. Yoruba drumming: The dùndún tradition. Bayreuth, Germany: Bayreuth University.

Feld, Steven. 1984. Communication, music and speech about music. Yearbook for Traditional Music 16:1–18.

———. 1986. Orality and consciousness. In Tokumaru and Yamaguti, 18–28.

———. 1990. Sound and sentiment. 2nd ed. Philadelphia: University of Pennsylvania Press.

Fine, Elizabeth C. 1980. Aesthetic patterning of verbal art and the performance-centered text. In Richard Bauman and Joel Sherzer (eds.), Sociolinguistic working paper 74:1–39. Austin: Southwest Educational Development Laboratory.

———. 1984. The folklore text: From performance to print. Bloomington: Indiana University Press.

Fine, Jonathan. 1988. Cognitive processes in context: A systemic approach to problems in oral language use. In Steiner and Veltman, 171–82.

Finnegan, Ruth. 1977. Oral poetry. Cambridge: Cambridge University Press.

———. 1982. Short time to stay. Bloomington: Indiana University, African Studies Program.

———. 1986. The relation between composition and performance: Three alternative modes. In Tokumaru and Yamaguti, 73–87.

———. 1988. Literacy and orality: Studies in the technology of communication. Oxford and New York: Basil Blackwell.

Fleming, Ilah. 1988. Communication analysis: A stratificational approach, 2. Dallas: Summer Institute of Linguistics.

Foley, John Miles. 1978. A computer analysis of metrical patterns in Beowulf. Computers and the Humanities 12:71–80.

————, ed. 1981a. Tradition-dependent and -independent features in oral literature: A comparative view of the formula, 262–81. Oral traditional literature. Columbus: Slavica Publishing.

————. 1981b. Oral texts, traditional texts: Poetics and critical methods. Canadian-American Slavic Studies 15:122–45.

————. 1985. Oral-formulaic theory and research. New York: Garland Publishing.

————. 1988. The theory of oral composition. Bloomington: Indiana University Press.

————, ed. 1990. Oral-formulaic theory: A folklore casebook. New York and London: Garland Publishing.

Frederiksen, Carl H. 1977. Semantic processing units in understanding text. In Freedle, 57–87.

Freedle, Roy O., ed. 1977. Discourse production and comprehension. Norwood, N.J.: Ablex Publishing.

Friedman, Robert A. 1982. Making an abstract world complete: Knowledge, competence, and structural dimensions of performance among Bata drummers in Santeria. Unpublished dissertation. Indian University. Ann Arbor: University Microfilm International.

Friedrich, Paul. 1986. The language parallax: Linguistic relativism and poetic indeterminacy. Austin: University of Texas Press.

Fry, D. B. 1970. Speech reception and perception. In Lyons, 29–52.

Fry, Donald K. 1981. Formulaic theory and Old English poetry. In Heartz and Wade, 169–73.

Geary, Christraud. 1989. Slit gongs in the Cameroon grassfields: Sights and sounds of beauty and power. In Marie-Thérèse Brincard (ed.), Sounding forms, 63–71. New York: The American Federation of Arts.

Geertz, Clifford. 1973. The interpretation of cultures. New York: Basic Books.

————. 1983. Art as a cultural system. In Clifford Geertz (ed.), Local knowledge: Further essays in interpretive anthropology, 94–120. New York: Basic Books.

George, Kenneth M. 1990. Felling a song with a new ax: Writing and the reshaping of ritual song performance in Upland Sulawesi. Journal of American Folklore 103(407):3–23.

Gerard, Ralph. 1957. Units and concepts of biology. Science 125:429–33.

Gerbner, George. 1985. Mass media discourse: Message system analysis as a component of cultural indicators. In Teun A. van Dijk (ed.), Discourse and communication, 13–25.

Goffman, E. 1964. The neglected situation. American Anthropologist 66(6):133–36.

Good, A. I. 1942. Drum talk is the African's wireless. Natural History 50(2):69–74.

Goody, Jack. 1987. The interface between the written and the oral. Cambridge: Cambridge University Press.

Gray, Bennison. 1971. Repetition in oral literature. Journal of American Folklore 84:289–303.

Guillemin, R. P. 1948. Le tambour d'appel les Ewondo. Etudes Camerounaises 21–22:69–84.

Gumperz, John J. 1972. Introduction. In John and Dell Hymes (eds.), Directions in sociolinguistics: Ethnography of communications, 1–25, New York: Holt, Rinehart and Winston.

——, Hannah Kaltman, and Mary Catherine O'Connor. 1984. Cohesion in spoken and written discourse: Ethnic style and the transition to literacy. In Tannen, 4–17.

Guttgemanns, Erhardt. 1977. Fundamentals of a grammar of oral literature. In Heda Jason and Dimitri Segal (eds.), Patterns in oral literature, 77–97. The Hague: Mouton.

Hall, Edward T. 1992. Improvisation as an acquired, multilevel process. Ethnomusicology 36:223–35.

Halliday, M. A. K. 1978. Language as social semiotic. Baltimore: University Park Press.

—— and Ruqaiya Hasan. 1989. Language, context, and text: Aspects of language in a social-semiotic perspective. 2nd ed. Oxford: Oxford University Press.

Handel, Stephen. 1973. Temporal segmentation of repeating auditory patterns. Journal of Experimental Psychology 101:46–54.

Harries, Jeanette. 1973. Pattern and choice in Berber weaving and poetry. Research in African Literatures 4:141–53.

Headland, Thomas N., Kenneth L. Pike, and Marvin Harris, eds. 1990. Emics and etics: The insider/outsider debate. Frontiers of Anthropology 7. Newbury Park: Sage Publications.

Heartz, Daniel and Bonnie Wade, eds. 1981. Report of the twelfth congress Berkeley 1977. Basel: Bärenreiten Kassel and the American Musicological Society.

Heepe, Martin. 1920. Die trommelsprache der Jaunde in Kamerun. Zeitschrift fur kolonialsprachen 10:43–600. Reprinted in Sebeok and Umiker-Sebeok, 316–33.

Heinitz, Wilhelm. 1940–41. Zum problem der Afrikanischen Trommelsprache. Afrika Rundschau 6(10):142–43. Reprinted in Sebeok and Umiker-Sebeok, 1976:481–531.

Hermann, E. 1976. Schallsignal sprachen in Melanesian und Afrika. Nachrichten der Akademie der Wissenschaften zu Göttingen; Philologisch-Historische Klass, May 26, 1943: 127–86. Reprinted in Sebeok and Umiker-Sebeok 62–118.

Herndon, Marcia and Roger Brunyate, eds. 1976. Proceedings of a symposium on form in performance, hard-core ethnology. Austin: College of Fine Arts.

————— and Norma McLeod. 1980. Music as culture. Darby, Penn.: Norwood Editions.

Hood, Mantle. 1971. The ethnomusicologist. 2nd ed. Kent, Ohio: Kent State University Press.

Horowitz, Rosalind and S. Jay Samuels. 1987. Comprehending oral and written language: Critical contrasts for literacy and schooling. Comprehending oral and written language. San Diego: Academic Press, Inc.

Humphreys, Paul. 1991. Time, rhythm, and silence: A phenomonology of the Buddhist accelerating roll. In Yosihiko Tokumaru et al. (eds.), Tradition and its future in music, 287–93. Tokyo: Mita Press Swita.

Hymes, Dell. 1964. Language in culture and society. New York: Harper and Row.

—————. 1972. Discovering oral performance and measured verse in American Indian narrative. New Literary History 8:431–57.

—————. 1975. Breakthrough into performance. In Ben-Amos and Goldstein, 11–74.

Jackendoff, Ray and Fred Lerdahl. 1982. A grammatical parallel between music and language. In Clynes, 83–117.

Jairazbhoy, Nazir Ali. 1991. The first restudy of Arnold Blake's fieldwork in India. In Nettl and Bohlman, 210–27.

Jarrett, Dennis. 1985. Pragmatic coherence in an oral formulaic tradition: I can read your letters/sure can't read your mind. In Deborah Tannen (ed.), Coherence and written discourse, 155–71. Advances in Discourse Processes 12. Norwood, N.J.: Ablex.

Jason, Heda. 1977. Ethnopoetry: Form, content, function. Forum Theologiae Linguisticae 11. Bonn, Germany: Linguistica Biblica.

Jones, A.M. 1964. African metrical lyrics. African Music Society Journal 3(3):6–14.

Kartomi, Margaret J. 1990. On concepts and classifications of musical instruments. Chicago: University of Chicago Press.

Kawada, Junzô. 1986. Verbal and non-verbal sounds: Some considerations of the basis of oral transmission of music. In Tokumaru and Yamaguti, 158–72.

King, Arden R. 1980. Innovation, creativity, and performance. In Herndon and McLeod, 167–75.

King, Roberta R. 1989. Pathways in Christian music communication: The case of the Senufo of Côte d'Ivoire. Ph.D. dissertation. Fuller Theological Seminary, School of World Mission.

Kippen, James. 1987. An ethnomusicological approach to the analysis of musical cognition. Music Perception 5(2):173–96.

———. 1989.

Knauft, Bruce M. 1979. On percussion and metaphor. Current Anthropology 20:189–90.

Kramer, Jonathan D. 1986. Temporal linearity and nonlinearity in music. In J. T. Fraser (ed.), Time, science, and society in China and the West. The study of time 5. Amherst: University of Massachusetts Press.

———. 1988. The time of music. New York: Schirmer Books.

Kropp Dakubu, Mary Esther. 1971. The language and structure of an Accra horn and drum text. Research Review (Legon) 7(2):28–45.

——— and Cathleen Read. 1985. Language and music in the luŋa drumming of Dagbon: A preliminary study. Papers in Ghanaian Linguistics 5. Legon: Institute of African Studies.

Kubik, Gerhard. 1977. Pattern perception and recognition in African music. In John Blacking and Joann W. Kealiinohomoku (eds.), The performing arts, 221–49. The Hague: Mouton.

———. 1984. Pattern perception and recognition in African music. In Folklore in Africa today: Proceeding of the 1982 Budapest workshop. Arte Populares, vols. 10–11, 1:323–35. Budapest: African Research Project.

Laver, John. 1970. The production of speech. In Lyons, 53–75.

Lehiste, Ilse. 1972. Units of speech perception. Working Papers in Linguistics 12:1–32. Ohio State University, Computer and Information Science Research Center.

Lemke, Jay L. 1988. Text structure and text semantics. In Steiner and Veltman, 158–70.

Lessa, William A. and Evon Z. Vogt, eds. 1972. Reader in comparative religion: An anthropological approach. 3rd ed. New York: Harper.

Locke, David. 1990. Drum Damba: Talking drum lessons. Crown Point, Ind.: White Cliffs Media Company.

———. 1992. Kpegisu: A war drum of the Ewe. Tempe, Ariz.: White Cliffs Media Company.

Longacre, Robert E. 1983. The grammar of discourse. New York: Plenum Press.

Longuet-Higgins, H. Christopher and Christopher S. Lee. 1982. The perception of musical rhythms. Perception 11:115–28.

Lord, Albert B. 1960. The singer of tales. Harvard: Harvard University Press. New York: Atheneum.

Luetkemeyer, Jean, Caroline Van Antwerp, and Gloria Kindell. 1984. An annotated bibliography of spoken and written language. In Deborah Tannen (ed.), Coherence in spoken and written discourse. Advances in Discourse Processes 12:265–81. Norwood, N.J.: Ablex.

Lyons, John, ed. 1970. New horizons in linguistics. Middlesex: Pelican Books.

Marfurt, Luitfrid. 1957. Musik in Afrika. Munchen: Nymphenburger Verhagshandlung.

Martin, J. G. 1972. Rhythmical (hierarchical) versus serial structure in speech and other behavior. Psychological Review 79:487–509.

Maxwell, Kevin B. 1983. Bemba myth and ritual: The impact of literacy on an oral culture. New York: Peter Lang.

Meinhof, Carl. 1894. Die geheimsprachen Afrikas. Globus 66:117–19. Reprinted in Sebeok and Umiker-Sebeok 1976:151–57.

Meyer, Hans. 1909. Das deutsche kolonialreich. Leipzig: Verlag der Bibliograpische Institut.

Meyer, Leonard B. 1989. Style and music: Theory, history, and ideology. Philadelphia: University of Pennsylvania Press.

Monts, Lester P. 1980. Music in Vai society. Ph.D. dissertation. University of Minnesota.

Munby, John. 1977. Applying sociocultural variables in the specification of communicative competence. In Muriel Saville-Troike (ed.), Linguistics and anthropologys 231–47. Georgetown University Round Table on Languages and Linguistic. Washington, D.C.: Georgetown University Press.

Nattiez, Jean-Jaques. 1990. Music and discourse: Toward a semiology of music. Translated by Carolyn Abbate. Princeton, N.J.: Princeton University Press.

Needham, Rodney. 1967. Percussion and transition. Man 2(2):606–14.

Nekes, P. Hermann. 1912. Trommelsprache und Fernruf bei den Jaunde und Duala in Sudkamerun. Mittelilungen des Seminars fur orientalische Sprache 15(3):69–83. Reprinted in Sebeok and Umiker-Sebeok, 289–306.

Nettl, Bruno. 1981. Some notes on the state of knowledge about oral transmission in music. In Heartz and Wade, 139–44.

———. 1983. The study of ethnomusicology: Twenty-nine issues and concepts. Urbana: University of Illinois Press.

——— and Philip V. Bohlman, eds. 1991. Comparative musicology and anthropology of music. Chicago: University of Chicago Press.

Ngumu, Pie-Claude. 1975/76. Les mendzaŋ des Ewondo du Cameroun. African Music Society Journal 5(4):6–26.

———. 1975. Musique et langue Ewondo. Camellang 4:29–42. Section de Linguistique Appliquée. Yaoundé.

———. 1985. Cameroonian cultural identity and musical art. The Cultural Identity of Cameroon. Yaoundé: Ministry of Information and Culture, Department of Cultural Affairs.

Niangoran-Bouah, George. 1981. Introduction à la drummologie. Abidjan, Cote d'Ivoire: Université Nationale de Côte d'Ivoire, Institut d'Ethnologie.

Nida, Eugene A. 1964. Towards a science of translating. Evanston: Adlers Foreign Books.

Nketia, J. H. Kwabena. 1958. Akan poetry. Black Orpheus 3:5–27.

———. 1963. Drumming in Akan communities. London: University of Ghana and Thomas Nelson and Sons.

———. 1971a. Surrogate languages of Africa. In Thomas A. Sebeok (ed.), Current trends in linguistics 7:699–732. The Hague: Mouton.

———. 1971b. The linguistic aspect of style in African languages. In Thomas A. Sebeok (ed.), Current trends in linguistics 7:733–57. The Hague: Mouton.

———. 1984. The aesthetic dimension in ethnomusicological studies. The World of Music 26:3–28.

Nkili, Agnes-Marie. 1975/76. Le nkul des Mvele: Essai d'analyse semiotique. Yaoundé: Université de Yaoundé.

O'Connell, S. J. and Daniel C. O'Connell. 1991. The spoken flies away; the written stays put. Georgetown Journal of Languages and Linguistics 2:274–83.

Okpewho, Isidore. 1977. Does the epic exist in Africa? Research in African Literatures 8:171–200.

———. 1979. The epic in Africa. New York: Columbia University Press.

———. 1990a. The oral performance in Africa. Ibadan, Nigeria: Spectrum Books.

———. 1990b. The primacy of performance in oral discourse. Research in African Literatures 21(4):121–28.

Ong, Walter. 1977. African talking drums and oral noetics. Interfaces of the word, 92–120. Cornell, N.Y.: Cornell University Press.

Opland, Jeff. 1983. Xhosa oral poetry: Aspects of a black South African tradition. Cambridge: Cambridge University Press.

Parkell, Joseph S. and Dennis H. Klatt, eds. 1986. Invariance and variability in speech processes. Hillsdale, N.J.: Lawrence Erlbaum Associates.

Parry, Milman. 1930. Studies in the epic technique of oral verse-making. I. Homer and Homeric style. Harvard Studies in Classical Philology 41.

Pawley, Andrew. 1992. Formulaic speech. In Bright, 2:22–25.

Peacock, James L. 1971. Class, clown, and cosmology in Javanese drama: An analysis of symbolic and social action. In Pierre Maranda and Elli Köngäs Maranda (eds.), Structural analysis of oral tradition, 139–68. Philadelphia: University of Pennsylvania Press.

Perlman, Marc. 1991. The spirits speak through the flute: Recent Indonesian history and Toba Batak spirit mediumship. Paper presented at Society of Ethnomusicology 1991 Annual Meeting, Chicago.

Phillipson, John. 1964. Recording collector, 'Psalms of the Cameroons'. Smithsonian Folkways cassette 08910.

Pike, Kenneth L. 1971. Language in relation to a unified theory of the structure of human behavior. 2nd rev. ed. The Hague: Mouton.

Polanyi, Livia. 1992. Text understanding. In Bright, 4:147–49.

Porter, Lewis. 1985. John Coltrane's "A Love Supreme." Journal of the American Musicological Society 38(3):593–621.

Povel, Dirk-Jan and Peter Essens. 1985. Perception of temporal patterns. Music Perception 2:411–40.

Poyatos, Fernando. 1983. New perspectives in nonverbal communication. Oxford: Pergamon Press.

Pressing, Jeff. 1984. Cognitive processes in improvisation. In Crozier and Chapman, 345–63.

Preusser, David, Wendell R. Garner, and Richard L. Gottwald. 1970. Perceptual organization of two-element temporal patterns as a function of their component one-element patterns. American Journal of Psychology 83:151–70.

Pribram, Karl H. 1982. Brain mechanism in music. In Clynes, 21–35.

Rakowski, Andrzej. 1985. On the formation of auditory codes for music and language. Trends and Perspectives in Musicology 48. Stockholm: Royal Swedish Academy of Music.

Rattray, R. S. 1923. Ashanti. Oxford: Oxford University Press.

Redden, James E. 1979. A descriptive grammar of Ewondo. Occasional Papers on Linguistics 4. Carbondale, Ill.: Southern Illinois University.

Rice, Timothy. 1987. Toward the remodeling of ethnomusicology. Ethnomusicology 31:469–88.

Rosenberg, Bruce A. 1975. Oral sermons and oral narrative. In Ben-Amos and Goldstein, 75–101.

———. 1978. The formula: New directions? Indiana University Folklore Institute: Preprint Series P6:4.

———. 1986. The message of the American folk sermon. Oral Tradition 1:695–727. Reprinted in Foley (1990) (ed.), 137–168.

Rouget, Gilbert. 1964. Tons de la langue, en Gun (Dahomey), et tons du tambour. Le revue de musicologie 50(128):3–29.

Rubin, David C. 1981. Cognitive processes and oral traditions. In Heartz and Wade, 173–80.

Samuels, S. Jay. 1987. Factors that influence listening and reading comprehension. In Horowitz and Samuels, 295–325.

Saville-Troike, Muriel. 1987. The ethnography of speaking. In Ulrich Ammon, Norbert Dittmar, and Klaus J. Matteier (eds.), Sociolinguistics: An international handbook of the science of language and society, 660–71. New York: Walter de Gruyter.

————. 1989. The ethnography of communication. 2nd ed. New York and Oxford: Basil Blackwell.

————. 1992. Communicative competence. In Bright, 1:273.

Scheub, Harold. 1977a. Body and image in oral narrative performance. New Literary History 8:345–67.

————. 1977b. Performance of oral narrative. In Bascom, 54–78.

Schieffelin, Edward. 1985. Performance and the cultural construction of reality. American Ethnologist 12:707–24.

Schiffrin, Deborah. 1985. Multiple constraints on discourse options: A quantitative analysis of causal sequences. Discourse Processes 8:281–303.

————. 1987. Discourse markers. Studies in interactional sociolinguistics 5. Cambridge: Cambridge University Press.

————. 1992. Discourse markers. In Bright, 1:361–64.

Schneider, Marius. 1952. Zur trommelsprache der Duala. Anthropos 47:235–43. Reprinted in Sebeok and Umiker-Sebeok, 669–78.

————. 1967. Le langage tambouriné des Doula. Musique de tous les temps 44 (45).

Scollon, Ron. 1981. The rhythmic integration of ordinary talk. In Deborah Tannen (ed.), Analyzing discourse: Text and talk. 335–49. Washington, D.C.: Georgetown University Press.

Searle, J. 1965. What is a speech act? In Max Black (ed.), Philosophy in America, 221–39. Allen and Unwin and Cornell University Press.

Sebeok, Thomas A. 1976. Contributions to the doctrine of signs. Studies in Semiotics 5. Bloomington: Indiana University Research Center.

———— and Donna Jean Umiker-Sebeok, eds. 1976. Speech surrogates: Drum and whistle systems. Approaches to Semiotics 23:1–2. The Hague: Mouton.

Seeger, Anthony. 1987. Why Suyá sing. Cambridge: Cambridge University Press.

————. 1991. Styles of musical ethnography. In Nettl and Bohlman, 342–55.

Seeger, Charles. 1969. On the formational apparatus of the music compositional process. Ethnomusicology 13:213–47.

————, ed. 1977. Studies in musicology (1935–1975). Berkeley, Los Angeles, and London: University of California Press.

Serafine, Mary Louise. 1981. Cognitive processes in music: Discoveries vs. definitions. Bulletin of the Council for Research in Music Education 73:1–14.

Shelemay, Kay Kaufman. 1991. Recording technology, the record industry and ethnomusicology scholarship. In Nettl and Bohlman, 277–92.

Shepherd, John, P. Viden, Graham Vulliamy, and Trevor Wishart. 1977. Whose music? A sociology of musical language. London: Latimer.

Sherzer, Joel. 1987. Poetic structuring of Kuna discourse: The line. In Sherzer and Woodbury, 103–39.

———. 1992. Ethnography of speaking. In Bright, 1:419–21.

Silva, Moises. 1983. Biblical words and their meaning. Grand Rapids: Zondervan.

Sherzer, Joel and Anthony C. Woodbury, eds. 1987. Native American discourse: Poetics and rhetoric. Cambridge: Cambridge University Press.

Simmons, Donald. 1955. Efik iron gongs and gong signals. Man 55:107–8.

———. 1960. Tonality in Efik signal communication and folklore. In Anthony C. F. Wallace (ed.), Men and cultures, 803–8. Philadelphia: University of Pennsylvania Press.

Sloboda, John A. 1977. Phrase units as determinants of visual processing in music reading. British Journal of Psychology 68:117–24.

———. 1985. The musical mind: The cognitive psychology of music. Oxford Psychology Series 5. Oxford: Clarendon Press.

Smith, Barbara. 1968. Poetic closure: A study of how poems end. Chicago: Chicago University Press.

Smith, Donald K. 1992. Creating understanding. A handbook for Christian communication across cultural landscapes. Grand Rapids: Zondervan.

Steiner, Erich H. and Robert Veltman, eds. 1988. Pragmatics, discourse and text: Some systemically-inspired approaches. Norwood, N.J.: Ablex.

Stern, Theodore. 1957. Drum and whistle 'languages': An analysis of speech surrogates. American Anthropologist 59:487–506. Reprinted in Sebeok and Umiker-Sebeok, 124–48.

Stockmann, Doris. 1991. Interdisciplinary approaches to musical communication structures. In Nettl and Bohlman, 318–41.

Stoll, R. P. Antoine. 1955. La tonètique des langues bantu et semi-santu du Cameroun. Douala, Cameroon: Institut Français d'Afrique Noire (Memorandum IV).

Stone, Ruth M. 1982. Let the inside be sweet. Bloomington: Indiana University Press.

———. 1988. Dried millet breaking. Bloomington: Indiana University Press.

Tanehaus, Michael K. 1992. Comprehension. In Bright, 1:288–91.

——— and Mark S. Seidenberg. 1981. Discourse context and sentence perception. Discourse Processes 4:197–220.

Tannen, Deborah, ed. 1984. Coherence in spoken and written discourse. Norwood, N.J.: Ablex.

———. 1992. Interactional linguistics. In Bright, 4:9–12.

Tarasti, Eero. 1985. Music as sign and process. In Anders Lönn and Erik Kjellberg (eds.), Analytica: Studies in the description and analysis of music. Uppsala, Sweden: Institute of Musicology, Uppsala University.

Tedlock, Dennis. 1977. Toward an oral poetics. New Literary History 8:507-19.

―――. 1983. The spoken word and the work of interpretation. Philadelphia: University of Pennsylvania Press.

Thieme, Darius. 1969. A descriptive catalog of Yoruba musical instruments. Ph.D. dissertation. Catholic University of America. Ann Arbor: University Microfilms.

Tokumaru, Yosihiko and Osamu Yamaguti, eds. 1986. The oral and the literate in music. Tokyo: Academia Music Ltd.

Treitler, Leo. 1974. Homer and Gregory: The transmissions of epic poetry and plain chant. The Musical Quarterly 60(3):333-72.

Trimillos, Ricardo and William Feltz, eds. 1985. Improvisation in the performing arts. Honolulu: East-West Center.

Tsala, Theodore. 1955. Nkul ou le tam-tam. Presses Missionaires 22(3).

Turner, Victor. 1986. The anthropology of performance. New York: Practical Anthropology Journal Publications.

Umiker, Donna Jean. 1974. Speech surrogates: Drum and whistle systems. In Thomas A. Sebeok (ed.), Current trends in linguistics 12:497-536. The Hague: Mouton.

van Dijk, Teun A., ed. 1985a. Handbook of discourse analysis, 4 vols. London: Academic Press.

―――, ed. 1985b. Discourse and communication: New approaches to the analysis of mass media discourse and communications. Berlin and New York: Walter A. Gruyter.

―――. 1987. Episodic models in discourse processing. In Horowitz and Samuels, 161-96.

Vansina, Jan. 1985. Oral tradition as history. Madison: University of Wisconsin Press.

Vīķis-Freibergs, Vaira. 1984. Creativity and tradition in oral folklore, or the balance of innovation and repetition in the oral poet's art. In Crozier and Chapman, 325-43.

Vygotsky, Lev Semenovich. 1978. Mind in society: The development of higher psychological processes. Cambridge: Harvard University Press.

Waterhouse, David. 1986. The logical priority of performance for the analysis of music. In Tokumaru and Yamaguti, 371-77.

Watson, Rita and David R. Olson. 1987. From meaning to definition: A literate bias on the structure of word meaning. In Horowitz and Samuels, 329-53.

Wegner, Ulrich. 1989. A project on pattern perception in Buganda xylophone music. The World of Music 31:160-61.

White, Landeg. 1989. Poetic license: Oral poetry and history. In Barber and Moraes Farias, 34–38.

Wollheim, Richard. 1978. Aesthetics, anthropology and style: Some programmatic remarks. In Michael Greehalgh and Vincent Megaw (eds.), Art in society, 3–14. New York: St. Martin's Press.

Wood, Charles C. 1974. Parallel processing of auditory and phonetic information in speech discrimination. Perceptions and Psychophysics 15:501–8.

Woodbury, Anthony C. 1987. Rhetorical structure in a Central Alaskan Yupik Eskimo traditional narrative. In Sherzer and Woodbury, 176–239.

Woodson, Craig DeVere. 1983. The atumpan drum in Asante. Ph.D. dissertation. UCLA. Ann Arbor: University Microfilms.

Yankah, Kwesi. 1985. Voicing and drumming the poetry of praise: The case for aural literature. In Kofi Anyidoho, Abioseh M. Porter, Daniel Racine, and Janice Spleth (eds.), Interdisciplinary dimensions of African literature, 137–53. Washington, D.C.: Three Continents Press.

Yeston, Maury. 1976. The stratification of musical rhythm. New Haven and London: Yale University Press.

www.ingramcontent.com/pod-product-compliance
Lightning Source LLC
Chambersburg PA
CBHW060148280326
41932CB00012B/1683